Upstream Petroleum Concessions

Upstream Petroleum Concessions

Evolution For the Energy Transition

PETER ROBERTS

OXFORD
UNIVERSITY PRESS

OXFORD
UNIVERSITY PRESS

Great Clarendon Street, Oxford, OX2 6DP,
United Kingdom

Oxford University Press is a department of the University of Oxford.
It furthers the University's objective of excellence in research, scholarship,
and education by publishing worldwide. Oxford is a registered trade mark of
Oxford University Press in the UK and in certain other countries.

Published in the United States of America by Oxford University Press
198 Madison Avenue, New York, NY 10016, United States of America

British Library Cataloguing in Publication Data
Data available

Library of Congress Control Number: 2025942158

ISBN 978-0-19-895143-8

DOI: 10.1093/law/9780198951438.001.0001

Printed and bound by
CPI Group (UK) Ltd., Croydon, CR0 4YY

FSC www.fsc.org MIX Paper | Supporting responsible forestry FSC® C013604

The manufacturer's authorised representative in the EU for product safety is
Oxford University Press España S.A., Parque Empresarial San Fernando de Henares,
Avenida de Castilla, 2 - 28830 Madrid (www.oup.es/en or product.safety@oup.com).
OUP España S.A. also acts as importer into Spain of products made by the manufacturer.

Contents

Table of Cases

GHANA

UNITED KINGDOM

COURT OF JUSTICE OF THE EUROPEAN UNION (CJEU)

ARBITRATION

Table of Legislation

ACTUAL CONCESSIONS

NATIONAL LEGISLATION

Angola

Belize

Brazil

France

Ghana

Guyana

Indonesia

Ireland

New Zealand

Nigeria

Spain

Trinidad and Tobago

United Kingdom

INTERNATIONAL INSTRUMENTS

United Nations Convention on the Recognition and Enforcement of Arbitral Awards (New York, 1958) 141
United Nations Framework Convention on Climate Change 1992 (UNFCCC) 26, 28
Art 2 26
Art 4.8(h) 28
Art 10 28
Kyoto Protocol 1997 .... 26, 170

Introduction

This book examines the interface of three issues: the meaning, use and content of concessions for petroleum exploration and production; the meaning of the energy transition; and how concessions could evolve to reflect the energy transition. The book is in three parts.

Part A considers the key elements of concession usage and the energy transition by reference to: the logic for and the use of a concession; the forms of concession which are most widely used and how concessions are awarded; the meaning of the energy transition and the risks to a state which the energy transition can present; and examples of state-sponsored withdrawals from future petroleum exploration and production to meet the needs of the energy transition.

Part B reviews the typical content of a concession, which will be relevant to understanding potential future changes. This review relates to: the parties to a concession (and the management of their relationships) and how their concession interests can be transferred; the scope of a concession and a concession's duration (including the circumstances in which a concession can be terminated); the concession's area (and how that area can be modified over time) and the scope for collaborative development activities; the investor's petroleum operations obligations and the investor's required performance standards; the fiscal terms of a concession (for the grantor and the investor) and the role of taxation; other non-fiscal benefits which could accrue to the grantor under a concession; and the constitutional provisions which make up a concession.

Part C suggests several initiatives which could be undertaken by a state in order to promote its energy transition ambitions (in each case assuming that the state has elected to continue with the business of petroleum production as part of those ambitions). These initiatives relate to: how the terms of concessions could be modified to reflect the energy transition and enhance the state's role, and how the award of concessions could be better managed; understanding the attraction of gas, and how concessions could be modified to promote gas project developments; and promoting the state's national oil company in the continuing management of the state's concessions and in addressing the energy transition.

Discussions about the energy transition can be contentious. This book identifies the energy transition and reflects on what its requirements could entail for petroleum-producing states, but it does not offer a wider commentary on the rights or wrongs of the definition or the ambitions of the energy transition. Nor does this book suggest how or when (or even whether) a state could choose to make increased investments in non-petroleum-based energy generation activities, and/or reduce its focus on petroleum exploration and/or production, as part of a commitment to implementing the energy transition. Such decisions are strategic and socioeconomic matters for each state to consider. This book assumes that a state has decided to continue its involvement with upstream petroleum sector activities (including the continuing award of concessions) as part of the state's response to the energy transition.

The observations made in this book regarding the terms of a concession are based on two elements:

(1) *The apparent wording of the concession*—observations made are based on the language of the concession taken at face value, and do not equate to interpreting the meaning of a concession. This is because the chosen governing law of the concession could modify the apparent meaning of the concession's words. Where the actual interpretation of a concession is required it is necessary to examine the words of the concession and the impact of the concession's governing law in equal measure.
(2) *The English language version of the concession*—English could be the determinative language of the concession, but where this is not so, an English translation of the concession (which could be official or unofficial) could have been prepared. The wording used in an English translation of the concession should be considered accordingly.[1]

This book considers a wide geographical spread of publicly available concessions to indicate the various positions which can be taken, referencing model form concessions and actual (but sometimes redacted) concessions.

Model Form Concessions

Angola Production-sharing agreement between Sociedade Nacional de Combustíveis de Angola—Empresa Pública (Sonangol, E.P.) and the Contractor Group (2008).

Bangladesh Offshore model production-sharing contract between the Government of the People's Republic of Bangladesh and Bangladesh Oil, Gas and Mineral Corporation and the Contractor (2023).

Brazil Production-sharing agreement for exploration and production of oil and gas between the federal government, the National Agency of Petroleum, Natural Gas and Biofuels, Empresa Brasileira de Administração de Petróleo e Gás Natural S.A.—Pré-sal Petróleo S.A. and Petróleo Brasileiro S.A.- Petrobras (2017).

[1] The Azerbaijan 1996 production sharing agreement (PSA) provides (at 30.1) that: 'This Agreement is executed in the English, Azeri and Russian languages and ... all three languages shall have equal force.' The Suriname 2015 production sharing contract (PSC) provides (at 41.2) that: 'This Contract will be executed in the English and Dutch languages, and both will have equal force and effect. In case of a dispute and arbitration between the Parties, except for a manifest error or misprint, the Dutch version shall prevail.' The Afghanistan 2013 exploration and production sharing contract (EPSC) provides (at 31.4) that: 'This Contract shall be executed in English and in Dari ... In the event that a dispute arises under this Contract between the English and Dari versions, the English version shall be definitive as to the terms and conditions of this Contract and the rights and obligations of the Parties.'

Cameroon Model production-sharing contract between the Republic of Cameroon and the Contractor (2007).

Cyprus Model production-sharing contract between the Republic of Cyprus and the Contractor (2007).

Egypt Concession agreement for gas and crude oil exploration and exploitation between the Arab Republic of Egypt and the Egyptian Natural Gas Holding Company and the Contractor (2021).

Equatorial Guinea Production-sharing contract between the Republic of Equatorial Guinea and Guinea Ecuatorial de Petróleos and the Contractor (2007).

Ethiopia Model production-sharing agreement between the Government of the Federal Democratic Republic of Ethiopia and the Contractor (2011).

Gambia Model petroleum, exploration, development and production licence (Block A1) between the Republic of The Gambia and the Licensee (2022).

Ghana Model petroleum agreement between the Government of the Republic of Ghana, Ghana National Petroleum Corporation, and the Contractor (2000).

Guyana Model production-sharing agreement for petroleum exploration, development, and production (deepwater areas) between the Government of the Cooperative Republic of Guyana and the Contractor (2023).

India Model production-sharing contract for offshore areas between the President of India and the Contractor (2010).

Iraq Exploration, development and production contract between the Regional Oil Company of the Iraqi Ministry of Oil and the Contractor (2018).

Kenya Model production-sharing contract between the Government of the Republic of Kenya and the Contractor (2014).

Kurdistan Iraq Production-sharing contract between the Kurdistan Regional Government of Iraq and the Contractor (2007).

Liberia Model production-sharing contract between the Republic of Liberia, the National Oil Company of Liberia (NOCAL), and the Contractor (2013).

Mexico Contract for the extraction of hydrocarbons under production-sharing modality between the National Hydrocarbons Commission and the Contractor (2015).

Mozambique Exploration and production concession contract between the Government of the Republic of Mozambique and the Concessionaire (2006).

Pakistan Offshore production-sharing contract between the President of the Islamic Republic of Pakistan and Government Holdings (PVT) Limited and the Contractor (2000).

Qatar Model development and production-sharing agreement between the Government of Qatar and Contractor (North Field) (2002).

Somalia Model offshore production-sharing agreement between the Federal Government of the Federal Republic of Somalia and the Contractor (2019); model production-sharing agreement between the Federal Government of the Federal Republic of Somalia and the Contractor (2023).

Suriname Production-sharing contract for petroleum exploration, development, and production between Staatsolie Maatschappij Suriname NV and the Contractor (2015).

Tanzania Model production-sharing contract between the Government of the United Republic of Tanzania and the Tanzania Petroleum Development Corporation and the Contractor (2013).

Trinidad and Tobago Model production-sharing contract between the President of the Republic of Trinidad and Tobago and the Minister of Energy and Energy Affairs and the Contractor (2012); model production-sharing contract between the President of the Republic of Trinidad and Tobago and the Minister of Energy and Energy Industries and the Contractor (2023).

Turkmenistan Model production-sharing agreement for petroleum exploration and production between the Competent Body of Turkmenistan and/or State Concern and the Contractor (1997).

Uganda Model production-sharing contract for petroleum exploration, production, and development between the Government of the Republic of Uganda and the Licensee (1999); model production-sharing contract for petroleum exploration, production, and development between the Government of the Republic of Uganda and the Licensee (2015).

Zanzibar Model production-sharing agreement between the Revolutionary Government of Zanzibar and Zanzibar Petroleum Development Company and the Contractor (2024).

Actual Concessions

Afghanistan Exploration and production-sharing contract for hydrocarbons exploration, development, and production in Sanduqli Block between the Ministry of Mines & Petroleum of the Government of the Islamic Republic of Afghanistan and the Contractor (2013).

Azerbaijan Agreement on the exploration, development, and production-sharing for the Shah Deniz prospective area in the Azerbaijan area of the Caspian Sea (1996).

Gabon Exploration and production-sharing contract between the Republic of Gabon and Vaalco Gabon (Etame), Inc (1995).

Guyana Petroleum agreement between the Government of the Cooperative Republic of Guyana, Esso Exploration and Production Guyana Limited, CNOOC Nexen Petroleum Guyana Limited, and Hess Guyana Exploration Guyana Limited (2016).

Indonesia Production-sharing contract between SKK Migas, PT Cogen Nusantara Energi, and PT Hutama Wiranusa for contract area Citarum (2018).

Kenya Production-sharing contract between the Government of the Republic of Kenya and Camac Energy Kenya Limited for Block L1B (2012).

Mauritania Exploration-production contract between the Islamic Republic of Mauritania and Tullow Mauritania Limited for Bloc C18 (2012).

Nigeria Production-sharing contract renewal agreement for OML118 between Nigerian National Petroleum Corporation and Shell Nigeria Exploration and Production Company Limited and Esso Exploration and Production Nigeria (Deepwater) Limited and Nigerian Agip Exploration Limited and Total E&P Nigeria Limited (2021).

Sao Tome and Principe Production-sharing contract between the Democratic Republic of Sao Tome and Principe and BP Exploration (STP) Limited and Kosmos Energy Sao Tome and Principe for Block 10 (2018).

Senegal Hydrocarbon exploration and production-sharing contract between the Republic of Senegal and Petro-Tim Limited and Société des Pétroles du Sénégal for Saint Louis Offshore Profond (2012).

Tajikistan Production-sharing contract between the Ministry of Energy and Industry of the Republic of Tajikistan and Kulob Petroleum Limited (2008).

The concessions referenced in this book are freely obtainable from the internet (see various government websites and petroleum company websites, and see also <www.resourcecontracts.org>; <www.eiti.org/>; and <www.sec.gov>).

The views expressed in this book are my own and are not attributable to, nor are they representative of the views of, any states, companies, or clients with which I am associated.

Peter Roberts
Cape Town
July 2025

PART A

CONCESSIONS AND THE ENERGY TRANSITION

1
The Logic for a Concession

1.1 Introduction

A state could award a concession to a private sector investor to regulate the exploitation of its indigenous petroleum reserves, in preference to undertaking such exploitation at its own risk and expense. An investor which could be awarded a concession has a number of criteria which it will assess as part of doing so.

The award of a concession to an investor will create, and will oblige the state to manage, a number of competing interests. The principal competition is between the state and the investor (where the concession is the forum for the resolution of their competing interests), but competitive tension could also arise between the state and the state's population, and between the state and other states awarding concessions.

1.2 The State's Perspective

In most jurisdictions, in-ground petroleum reserves, both onshore and offshore, belong to the state, and the state will have the exclusive exploitation right in respect of those reserves (which right the state could elect to exercise through another person).[1] In-ground petroleum reserves are the state's patrimony, the importance of which will be enhanced by the amount of wealth which the exploitation of that patrimony could deliver to the state (and to the state's population). The United States is the most-cited exception to this principle, where private ownership of in-ground petroleum reserves is a possibility (although even in the United States federal land ownership, and ownership of the associated mineral rights, applies in respect of the continental shelf and certain onshore land areas).

Each state has unique physical, social, political, and economic characteristics, and will develop its own strategy for realizing its petroleum sector ambitions.

A state which possesses petroleum reserves could choose to develop those reserves itself, assuming the associated economic and operational risks and being entitled to enjoy the economic benefits of any resultant petroleum production for its own account.

[1] The first two recitals of the Somalia 2023 production sharing agreement (PSA) illustrate this principle: 'A. The title to all Petroleum existing in its natural condition in the territory of the Federal Republic of Somalia is the common good of the people of Somalia, owned by the Federal Republic of Somalia and vested in the Federal Government B. In accordance with the Act, the Federal Government has the authority to grant an authorisation for the Petroleum Operations and to enter into production sharing agreements.'

This approach represents the ultimate embodiment of a state's management of its patrimony. A state could however lack the economic and/or technical capacity to undertake such development, and could also be reluctant to accept the risks (both economic and reputational) of mis-performance or failure which could be associated with such development.

As a partial departure from a state's exclusive sovereignty over its own patrimony a state could choose to award a concession (in some form) to an investor (5.2) for the exploitation of the state's petroleum reserves. Where this is so, the form of the concession which is used will be as much about a reflection of the political philosophy of the state as it will be about managing the operational and economic aspects of the investor's efforts.

A concession is awarded by a grantor (acting on behalf of a state) to an investor to facilitate the undertaking by the investor of certain petroleum exploration and/or production activities within a defined part of the state's territory, and represents the award by a grantor of a right and an obligation to an investor to undertake activities (typically at the sole risk and expense of the investor) which the state is unable or unwilling to undertake itself. This is done with the prospect of various returns (both fiscal and non-fiscal) accruing to the grantor. The essence of a concession is a long-term, collaborative arrangement for the provision of specialized goods, services, and know-how by the investor, in exchange for the sharing of costs and profits between the investor and the grantor, according to agreed levels.

In designing the terms of a concession, a grantor has to balance the state's desire to retain a fair measure of return from an investor's exploitation of the state's patrimony with presenting an investment opportunity which an investor will find sufficiently attractive to want to pursue. Into this equation can be added the petroleum prospectivity of the intended concession area (7.2), which will influence the model for state take (9.2) and the appetite of a prospective investor to become involved.

Historically the assessment by an investor of the terms for the award of a concession has required the reconciliation of three features: the fiscal (and other) terms which a grantor is offering; the quality of the petroleum geology which underlies an intended concession area; and the track record of the state in respect of honouring investments which have been made into the state by investors. To this trinity can be added a fourth element, which relates to the likely carbon intensity of the prospective investment (3.3). Investors will be interested to predict, quantify, and account for the likely ecological impact of their intended petroleum exploration and/or production activities as a part of a growing recognition of the requirements of the energy transition.

The petroleum geology which underlies a concession area is an accident of nature. The form of a concession which is used by a state, and the level of state take which the concession effects, are both man-made constructions. The essential rendition to note from this is that a higher level of state take (and generally less attractive concession terms) could be acceptable to an investor where the geology of the concession suggests a higher chance of exploration success, of cost-effective production, and of significant quantities of petroleum which can be recovered over the long term. Correspondingly, if the geology of the concession indicates lower degrees of petroleum prospectivity, cost-effective production, or petroleum recoveries, then an investor could require to be compensated for accepting that risk through a lower level of state take and more attractive concession terms. Investors have long since become accustomed to dealing with an inversion of the relationship between concession terms and geology.[2]

There is also a relationship to note between the fiscal terms of a concession (9.1) and the likely levels of petroleum production which could be achieved under the concession. A petroleum discovery which has (from an investor's perspective) relatively poor fiscal terms but high production levels could give a better net return than a low-producing petroleum discovery with relatively better fiscal terms. But at the time when an investor negotiates and accepts the fiscal terms in a concession the investor could have relatively little insight into the petroleum prospectivity of a concession area, or into how a prospective petroleum discovery might perform over time.

A particular paradox to which a grantor is subject in a nascent grantor/investor relationship is that offering better terms to prospective investors to make a concession more attractive could come at the expense of reducing the level of state take (9.2) from the concession. The parameters for the design of a successful concession could pull in opposite directions for a grantor. And despite the efforts which a grantor makes in its concession design to attract investors, sometimes the terms (both fiscal and non-fiscal) of the grantor's concession may be comparatively less attractive to a prospective investor than those which might be on offer in another state.

There may be arrangements within a state for the sharing of petroleum entitlements between a federal government and the federated regions. In 1975 the 13 states which together made up Malaysia entered into accords with the state petroleum company Petronas and the federal government which entitled each state to a 5 per cent cash-paid royalty on revenue from domestic petroleum production (notwithstanding that petroleum production took place in only five states). Since then the royalty percentage has been the subject of frequent dispute and occasional modification.

Petroleum revenue-sharing arrangements (based on the sharing of revenues according to agreed ratios or according to needs) have also been applied in Nigeria (where a petroleum-producing state receives a fixed percentage of the petroleum revenues generated locally, and all states receive a share of total net petroleum revenues allocated according to agreed percentages), and the Federal Republic of Somalia, where a petroleum revenue-sharing agreement has been entered into between the federal government and Somalia's member states.[3]

[2] 'The oil industry is comfortable with tough terms if they are justified by sufficient geological potential. This is the birthplace of dynamic negotiations.' Daniel Johnston, *International Petroleum Fiscal Systems and Production Sharing Contracts* (PennWell Books 1994).

[3] Available at <www.hbs.gov.so/somali-resource-sharing-agreement-file/> accessed 3 April 2025.

1.3 Managing Competing Interests

The design and implementation of a concession cannot be realized in a vacuum. In awarding a concession, a state will need to manage a number of competing interests. The most notable of these are the differing perspectives of a grantor and an investor. These persons will share one common objective under a concession, which is to find petroleum in commercially producible quantities at the earliest opportunity. Beyond that, however, the expectations of a grantor and an investor could diverge in a number of ways:

(1) *Exploration*—an investor wants to achieve exploration success at the lowest possible cost and with the greatest possible amount of flexibility being reserved in a concession to defer or to disapply its agreed exploration period obligations (8.2), since the investor will be funding the exploration works and will have to bear the lost costs if the exploration effort is unsuccessful. Data generated during the performance of the exploration period obligations will be concession area-specific and will be of limited usefulness to an investor.

    A grantor wants full performance of the exploration period obligations and for that to be done as expeditiously as possible, since a grantor can use the data which is generated to build a wider picture of geological and geophysical conditions within its resource base, and also because the relinquishment process in respect of explored or unexplored parts of the concession area (7.6) could be accelerated to benefit the grantor.

(2) *Production*—an investor may want to deplete a petroleum discovery which has been made by production at the greatest possible rate so that the investor can achieve an economic breakeven on its investment as soon as possible, whereas a grantor may want more careful management of the exploitation of the discovery so that the discovery's productive lifetime can be extended (which could even reach beyond the scheduled duration of the concession). With that in mind, an investor could require priority rights to extend or renew the concession at the end of its scheduled lifetime, whereas a grantor may have other ideas (6.3).

(3) *Fiscal terms*—'economic rent' is a term sometimes used to describe the surplus of revenues which accrue to an investor from petroleum production over the costs which have been incurred by the investor in realizing that production. The difference between the two measures is essentially the investor's profit, and the investor's interest is in maximizing the economic rent through increasing revenues and reducing costs. Correspondingly, a grantor's interest is in capturing for itself the economic value which is associated with the production of petroleum. As part of this balancing act, an investor wants to secure the best possible fiscal terms, whereas a grantor's objective is to maximize the level of state take.

(4) *Alienability*—an investor (or, more likely, one of the investor parties (5.2)) will want its interests in a concession to be readily capable of being transferred to a

proposed transferee of its choosing, at any time and with a minimum of administrative interference from a grantor. This would enable an investor party to exit a concession if it felt its ambitions were not being realized, and to allow a gain to be realized from the value of any improvements which the investor party has made to the concession during its tenure.

A grantor may wish to control such a process, through any of having an approval right (whether absolute or conditional) in respect of the proposed transferee, a pre-emptive right to acquire the interest which is proposed to be transferred, or the ability to tax the outgoing investor party on the improvement value of the concession (5.6). Any of these devices could operate to inhibit the free alienability of the concession interest by an investor party. The existence of a state participation right in respect of a concession (10.8), whether it has been or is yet to be exercised by a state, could also reduce the extent to which a transferable interest is created.

(5) *Legal governance*—an investor may accept that the law of the state will be selected to govern the concession (11.2) but, in exchange for accepting the risk of a change in that law over time which could adversely affect the value of the concession, an investor may require the inclusion in the concession of the protections afforded by a stabilization provision (11.6), and by a provision that disputes between a grantor and an investor concerning the concession would be resolved through an independent medium such as international arbitration (11.4).

A grantor may regard a stabilization provision as being unduly restrictive of its sovereign rights, and may also be reluctant to accept a dispute resolution mechanism in a concession which is not domestically focused.

(6) *Other commitments*—to benefit the wider interests of the state a grantor could require an investor to fund various capacity-building initiatives (10.2), and to commit to certain domestic market obligation (10.6) and local content (10.3) initiatives. In contrast, an investor may wish to minimize its exposure to these commitments, which could have the combined effect of lowering the overall level of investor take.

A concession represents a balancing of the competing interests of a grantor and an investor. Each party wants to recover what it regards as its fair share of the produced petroleum, but a grantor may also have other strategic imperatives which it wants to realize from the award of a concession, namely:

(1) reducing the state's dependency on imported energy, and establishing a new form of domestic economic activity;
(2) developing as much geological and geophysical data as possible (and as quickly as possible) relating to the state's patrimony. Consequently, a grantor will not be interested in any other commitments or opportunities which an investor might have which could delay the performance of the concession's obligations;

(3) maximizing the state's ambitions in relation to matters such as exploiting local content, the localization of employment opportunities, technology transfer, and capacity building generally.

Other competing interests which may need to be managed as a consequence of the award of a concession are those which might exist between a state and its population, and between a state and other states.

The elected government of a state is usually expected to be accountable to the state's population for the effective management of the state's patrimony (to be reflected through the ways in which a grantor awards concessions, maintains an adequate level of state take, and applies options for state participation). A state's population, which may expect the prompt advent of national and personal wealth from the exploitation of the state's patrimony by investors, is likely to be more focused on seeing immediate financial improvement, and less interested to understand issues (relating, eg, to mitigating exploration risk, determining viable project timetables, securing satisfactory returns, and ensuring the sanctity of contract) which could be vital to investors.

A state's population might also be keen to see a grantor exercising a very visible measure of control over the exploitation of the state's patrimony by investors. This could be evidenced by any of the creation of a prominent national oil company (14) and the securing of participation rights for that national oil company (or for another state entity) in a concession (10.8), the creation of local content (10.3) and localization provisions (10.2) in a concession, or by a requirement for concessions to be held through local companies (10.3).

A state should also appreciate that its concession terms have to address the possibility of competition to secure investment from prospective investors from other states which are offering concessions of their own. Other states may conduct licensing rounds or may have open door offers for their acreage (2.5), and may also conduct periodic reviews of their concession terms, against which the terms of the state's concession could be measured. The prospect of withdrawals by investors from specific petroleum projects (and possibly also from participation in certain states generally) as part of attempts by investors to realize the energy transition may lead to increased competition between states to attract the remaining levels of investment.

2

Concession Forms and Mechanics

2.1 Introduction

There is no standard form of a concession, but distinct concession forms have emerged over time. Some states have awarded different forms of concession to investors over the years (sometimes simultaneously) in the search for a concession which best suits the state's political and commercial requirements.

The form of a concession may also be informed in part by the manner in which a concession creates a proprietary interest in petroleum quantities for an investor, and the consequent ability of an investor to record those petroleum quantities as assets within its business.

Different methodologies have been developed for the award of a concession to an investor (and the manner in which a state chooses to award a concession may influence the degree of success which the state might enjoy in attracting investors to participate in the exploitation of the state's patrimony).

2.2 Concession Forms

There is no standard form of a concession. The term 'concession' is used in this book generically to encompass all the different forms of arrangement which are considered below.

A distinction is sometimes made between 'concession-based arrangements' (which includes concession agreements and licences) and 'contractual-based arrangements' (which includes productionsharing contracts (PSCs) and service contracts), where these arrangements are distinguishable by reference to an investor's entitlements and the extent of the operational autonomy which the investor enjoys in the performance of the petroleum operations.

At one end of the scale a concession could be a relatively thin document, referring to further primary and secondary legislation (sometimes described collectively as a 'petroleum law') to fill out the arrangements between a grantor and an investor.[1] Moving further along the scale, a concession could be relatively detailed, but could also import

[1] Licensing arrangements in the United Kingdom take this approach. The basic content of a licence for petroleum exploration and production is supplemented by: 'model clauses which shall be incorporated in any such licence' (Petroleum Act 1998, s 4(1)).

further detail through references to a petroleum law.[2] In this instance care needs to be taken to manage the risk of inconsistencies between the concession document and the petroleum law.

At the other end of the scale, there may be limited legislation to which a concession might refer to complete its terms (which could be the case in a nascent petroleum economy), and a comprehensive concession document becomes almost the exclusive embodiment of the relationship between a grantor and an investor.

There is no industry-wide organization or international body which designs or mandates the form of a concession. A concession which applies in a state will be very much the product of the requirements of that state (1.2). And yet, whilst recognizing the fact of that idiosyncrasy and that there are inevitable variations in the content of different concessions, concession terms also tend to be relatively formulaic. The basic architecture (and content) of a concession which applies in one state may be readily recognizable to the users of a concession in another state. Why might there be such homogeneity? The common denominator may be investors (and their lenders), because investors (and lenders) operate across a multitude of jurisdictions, and their expectations may be a guiding force which has shaped concession terms over time.

A grantor may issue what it describes as a 'model form' concession for use within its jurisdiction (with the intention that all investors who agree to enter into a concession with the grantor will do so on the basis of the model form). Such a model form will illustrate the positions which could be taken by a grantor and an investor at a particular point in time, although the key commercial terms remain to be completed and so a model form paints an imperfect (albeit a relatively comprehensive) picture.

A model form concession which is issued by a grantor can be updated and reissued by the grantor over time, reflective of ongoing evolution in the grantor's thinking about what the terms of the concession should say (and possibly also reflective of the evolving expectations of investors). This process may result in the creation of a series of successive, specifically dated model form concessions.[3] The issue of a later model form does not automatically modify the terms of an actual concession which has previously been entered into between a grantor and an investor based on a previous model form, nor does it displace or diminish the value of an earlier model form. The earlier model form will remain in existence, as a testament to the thinking of a grantor as to what terms were appropriate to apply in its concession as at the date of its issue. Some of the terms from an earlier model form may also be reapplied in later iterations of a concession, if a grantor and an investor so require.

The descriptions of the various forms of concession arrangements which are set out below should not be taken as rigid demarcations. A particular concession may be

[2] The Ghana 2000 petroleum agreement is a lengthy agreement but much of the relationship between the grantor and the investor is also governed by legislative provision. See note 2, Chapter 11.

[3] Successive iterations of a model form PSC have been issued in Bangladesh in 1997, 2008, 2012, 2019, and 2023, and in Tanzania in 1995, 2004, 2008, 2010, and 2013. In the United Kingdom there have been multiple iterations of model clauses (see note 1 above) to supplement licence terms—see the Petroleum (Current Model Clauses) Order 1994, SI 1999/160.

described as one thing but may, in substance, present itself as something else, and some concessions appear as hybrids of the various forms which are described below.[4]

(1) *The absolute concession*—in this arrangement a grantor gives an investor an exploration entitlement over a defined area and a right to take any petroleum which is found in that area, with little or no control by the grantor over the timing, the extent, or the content of the investor's activities. In exchange for these entitlements the investor may pay the grantor a defined royalty on the produced petroleum.

The absolute concession, as described above, is a historical throwback[5] and in its original form proved to be untenable as states began to recognize the economic value and the geopolitical influence of petroleum and to better assert their rights because of the abrogation of state rights which such a concession applied in exchange for relatively modest returns. Nevertheless, the notion of a grant of wide freedom to an investor to explore for and to exploit petroleum, largely free from state control over the conduct of the petroleum operations, remained evident within certain concession arrangements which were further created between the 1950s and the 1970s.[6]

The key evolutions which were apparent in these later forms of concession agreement were that they tended to be awarded for shorter periods of time, and in respect of smaller geographical areas, and that the state would retain title to the underlying petroleum in-ground, with an investor assuming a proprietary interest only after the petroleum had been produced and delivered at the wellhead (although at that point the entirety of the produced petroleum would become the property of the investor, for the investor to dispose of as it wished). Those later agreements also reflected the trend towards greater involvement by the state in the management of the petroleum operations and over the investor's activities, which is more characteristic of the other concession arrangements which are described below.

(2) *The licence*—in this arrangement an investor (called the 'licensee') is created as the beneficiary of a regulatory permit which has been granted by a duly authorized representative of the state to allow the licensee an exclusive right to explore for and to produce petroleum from a defined area, subject to making rental

[4] Other forms of concession-type arrangements which are not dealt with in detail here include reconnaissance permits, technical assistance agreements, and contracts of work.

[5] What is widely regarded as the first recognized example of such a concession is the 1901 D'Arcy Concession in the former Persia. A summary of the key terms of this concession is instructive: the investor was given exclusive rights of exploration, production, and sales (including the freedom to shut in production during low price periods) over an area which covered approximately 75 per cent of the land mass of Persia. The concession was intended to subsist for 60 years, imposed no minimum work obligations or timing commitments on the investor, and gave the state £40,000 in cash and shares and a 16 per cent net profits royalty payable on the profits of the investor (but not its affiliates). Between 1932 and 1933, the concession was variously cancelled and renegotiated, and in 1951 the concession was cancelled completely when the Iranian oil industry was nationalized.

[6] A form of concession agreement entered into by the Tanzanian government with Shell and BP, from 1952 and well into the 1960s, regulated the first phase of the country's exploration history, and such arrangements were also used in the early days of petroleum exploration and production in Abu Dhabi, Brazil, Libya, and Oman.

payments to the state. The licensee is usually also taxed by the state on any profits which it makes from its petroleum operations. In consequence of these fiscal terms a licence-based concession is often described as a 'tax and royalty' arrangement. Title to in-ground petroleum remains with the state.[7] A licensee only acquires title to petroleum when it is produced at the wellhead, but at that point the entirety of the produced petroleum becomes the property of the licensee, for the licensee to dispose of as it sees fit (subject only to any royalty in kind rights to which a grantor is entitled under the terms of the licence).

Licences tend to be found in industrialized countries with well-developed systems of general law, taxation, and petroleum law and regulation (such as Australia, Canada, Denmark, Norway, and the United Kingdom). A licence, despite its terms often being derived from published legislation and despite also sometimes being described as a form of regulatory instrument or administrative authorization which could be unilaterally amended or withdrawn by the state, is generally regarded as being contractual in nature between a grantor and a licensee.[8]

(3) *The production-sharing contract (and the revenue sharing model)*—in certain states in the 1950s and the 1960s tensions had built up with investors over the adequacy of the sharing of petroleum production revenues and operational control which applied under certain arrangements which had at least some of the characteristics of a concession agreement. This tension was exacerbated by external factors such as growing nationalistic sentiments, the passing of certain United Nations (UN) resolutions in respect of the state ownership of natural resources,[9] a period of steadily rising oil prices which gave investors greater economic returns, and the foundation of the Organization of the Petroleum Exporting Counties (OPEC) in 1960 as a pan-national agency which was intended to consolidate and promote state interests in respect of oil production. A partial reaction to the belief of some states that they were losing out in the exploitation of their patrimonies was the introduction of what became known as the production-sharing contract (PSC). A form of PSC was introduced in Bolivia in the 1950s, but what would more easily be recognized today as a PSC first emerged in Indonesia in the 1960s.

[7] In the United Kingdom the Petroleum Act 1998 provides (at s 2) that: '(1) Her Majesty has the exclusive right of searching and boring for and getting petroleum to which this section applies. (2) This section applies to petroleum (including petroleum in Crown land) which for the time being exists in its natural condition in strata in Great Britain or beneath the territorial sea adjacent to the United Kingdom.'

[8] The decision of the English courts in *Dean v Secretary of State for Business, Energy and Industrial Strategy* [2017] EWHC 1998 (Admin) offered some useful clarifications as to the contractual and regulatory considerations applicable to UK petroleum production licences. At the heart of the case was the question of whether a licence granted under the Petroleum Act 1998 was a contractual relationship involving the grant of property rights, capable of being varied by agreement between the parties according to standard principles of the law of contract, or whether it was a regulatory instrument which was capable of being amended unilaterally. The Court decided that the licence was contractual in character and was: 'essentially a property transaction, akin to a mining licence or a mining lease'.

[9] Such as Permanent Sovereignty over Natural Resources, UNGA Res 1803 (XVII) (December 1962) <www.ohchr.org/en/instruments-mechanisms/instruments/general-assembly-resolution-1803-xvii-14-december-1962-permanent> accessed 3 April 2025.

The PSC is the most widely used concession model worldwide today (forms of PSC are found in south America, Africa, eastern Europe, central Asia, and Asia). Under its terms, an investor (called 'the contractor'—reflective of the service-provider mentality of this form of concession, and making it clear that a PSC really is contractual in nature between a grantor and a contractor) has an exclusive right to explore for and to produce petroleum from a defined area. The contractor recovers its sunk costs from the revenues accruing from the sale of produced petroleum if the exploration activity has been successful (a process known as 'cost recovery'), and thereafter each of the grantor and the contractor receives a defined share of the produced petroleum (known as 'profit sharing') (9.3). A contractor may also pay also various bonuses, rental payments, royalties, and taxes under the PSC, depending on what has been negotiated.

A PSC typically sets out a relatively detailed framework between a grantor and a contractor and for this reason the PSC may be attractive for use in jurisdictions which have relatively less developed legal and commercial systems. This self-sufficiency means that the terms of the PSC can constitute the principal statement of the relationship between the parties.

A PSC's ambit ordinarily includes the exploration function (where the agreement is an 'exploration and production sharing agreement' (EPSA)), although in some jurisdictions the PSC's ambit is limited to regulating the development and production function after the award of a separate exploration permit (where the agreement is a 'development and production sharing agreement' (DPSA)).

Under a PSC, title to in-ground petroleum is held by the state. The contractor acquires title to its agreed share of the petroleum when it is produced at a defined point.

Some commentators had suggested that provisions in a PSC which allowed a contractor to recover its sunk costs on a priority basis before profit sharing was applied between a grantor and a contractor could give a contractor an incentive to inflate its costs (through any combination of the contractor making false claims for costs which it did not actually incur (sometimes called 'phantom costs'), deliberately over-engineering its project to inflate its costs (sometimes called 'goldplating'), or engaging in transfer pricing with affiliates for the provision of goods and services at artificially high prices).[10] A consequence of these risks was that a grantor had to maintain a comprehensive audit capability for the administration of a PSC, to confirm the veracity of the costs which were claimed as recoverable by a contractor.

As a reaction to these concerns, some states have sought to re-engineer the fiscal terms of a PSC to give what is called the 'revenue-sharing' model (sometimes also called the 'gross split' model). Under the revenue-sharing model the gross quantities of produced petroleum are divided between the grantor and the contractor, and the contractor recovers its costs from its share. This approach, it

[10] Daniel Johnston, 'Changing Fiscal Landscape 2008–2017' [2017] JWELB 415.

was suggested, moved the incentive to reduce costs directly onto the contractor as the person which was best placed to do so. Sometimes called the 'Peruvian model', reflective of certain fiscal terms which were used in Peru in the 1970s which made no allowance for the recovery of costs before implementing a division of the associated profits, the revenue-sharing model in its full form first emerged in India.

PSCs had been used in India to govern the participation of foreign and domestic investors since 1997, but a change of direction came following a dispute concerning the terms of a particular PSC. In 2000 Reliance Industries was awarded a PSC to develop the KG-D6 offshore block. Commercial gas production commenced in April 2009. In 2011, the Indian government sought to disallow certain cost recoveries under the PSC on the grounds that Reliance had been incurring excessive levels of costs.

In 2012 the Indian government constituted what became known as the Rangarajan Committee to look into how cost recovery and profit-share mechanisms worked in India's PSCs. At the end of that year, the Rangarajan Committee recommended shifting to a revenue-sharing model, with the revenue-sharing ratios to be a contestable item and subject to competitive bidding by prospective investors in a licensing round.

The Rangarajan Committee's recommendations were the subject of some criticism, including from the subsequent Kelkar Committee which was constituted in 2014. Suggestions were made that the revenue-sharing model was not entirely suitable to petroleum exploration and production in India as many of the country's sedimentary basins were poorly explored and their prospects were uncertain (such that, because of uncertainty over the possible geology which was on offer, a party seeking to participate would likely only put in a bid which offered a low level of state take). Nevertheless, in 2016 the Hydrocarbon Exploration and Licensing Policy (HELP) was introduced, a key feature of which was the introduction of a revenue-sharing model as the basis for petroleum operations, in the interests of reducing the need for state oversight of the day-to-day operations and the scrutiny of costs which would be needed under a conventional PSC. The first HELP licensing round was launched in 2017, and a model form revenue-sharing contract was introduced.

The revenue-sharing model has also appeared in Indonesia. Concerned by suggestions that PSC contractors could be exaggerating project costs to the detriment of the state for cost recovery purposes, Regulation 8/2017 was issued and it set out a new economic structure for future concessions, based on dividing gross production between a grantor and a contractor but without a mechanism for the contractor to recover its sunk costs as a priority (although operating costs which were incurred by the contractor could be taken into account as a deduction against the contractor's income tax liability).[11]

[11] Brad Roach and Alistair Dunstan, 'The Indonesian PSC: The End of an Era' [2018] JWELB 116.

The new revenue-sharing structure became mandatory for all new PSCs awarded after January 2017, additionally with provision for its application to PSCs which were being extended. PSCs signed before these regulations came into force could also be converted to reflect the revenue-sharing mechanism at any time, on application by a contractor. In 2021 a licensing round offered investors the choice between the revenue-sharing mechanism and the traditional cost recovery mechanism, reflective of the perceived unpopularity of the revenue-sharing mechanism. Since then Regulation 8/2017 has been supplemented by Regulation 13/2024, which revised the terms of the revenue-sharing mechanism to offer better terms for investors.

(4) *The service contract (and the buyback contract)*—in this arrangement an investor (called 'the contractor'—again reflective of the service-provider mentality of this arrangement) provides certain technical services to a grantor (and procures any necessary equipment and infrastructure) in connection with the exploration for and the production and processing of petroleum within a defined area, in exchange for the payment by the grantor of a defined fee (which could be paid to the contractor in cash or in kind).

Service contracts are found variously in south America, north Africa, and the Middle East, and could be used where the prevailing regulatory regime does not permit private sector participation in a state's petroleum sector on a more conventional concession basis. Similar to a PSC, a service contract could set out a relatively detailed, legally binding framework between the parties, as a statement of their relationship.

The fee which is payable to a contractor under a service contract creates a stable income stream which can be relied upon as a hedge against the risk of low petroleum price environments and other forms of concession where an investor is entitled to recover petroleum in kind. Service contracts, because they vest the entirety of the produced petroleum in a grantor, are also arguably better suited to states which are (or which could become) overall net importers of petroleum and which need to retain the produced petroleum to meet their domestic needs.

Under a service contract, title to in-ground petroleum is held by the state and the grantor takes the produced petroleum for its own account. A contractor does not take title to any part of the produced petroleum. A service contract is more akin to a contract for services than it is to a concession in the true sense of the word.

In what is sometimes called a 'pure service contract' a contractor incurs the costs associated with petroleum exploration and production and is reimbursed for its effort through the payment of an agreed fee, regardless of whether the exploration and/or production activity is successful.

In contrast, in what is sometimes called a 'risk service contract', a contractor incurs the costs associated with petroleum exploration and/or production and is reimbursed for its efforts through the payment of an agreed fee—but only if the contractor's activity is successful.

Because of the greater level of risk to the contractor under a risk service contract the fee payable may be higher than under a pure service contract (and the fee may also be variable, compared to a flat fee payable under a pure service contract).

A risk service contract might only be attractive to a contractor where there is a high level of pre-existing knowledge about the underlying geological and geophysical conditions, such that the risk of unsuccessful performance is abated. A risk service contract may also be used to govern development and production activities in particular.

It is also relevant in this context to consider an arrangement sometimes described as a 'buyback contract'. This is a relatively short-term service contract which requires the provision of defined petroleum project services (and the procurement of any necessary equipment and infrastructure) by a contractor, in exchange for a grantor's commitment (which may be payable in cash or in kind) to reimburse the contractor's expenses and also to remunerate the contractor for the services which it has provided. The contractor may also have an option to buy back certain quantities of the produced petroleum from the grantor at an agreed price.

Buyback contracts were first formulated in Iran, where the 1979 Revolution sparked a wave of resource nationalism resulting in the emergence of autarkic policies. Lacking the necessary capital and technological skills, Iranian petroleum production levels dropped and it was suggested that a new approach was needed—one which applied a form of concession which drew in foreign capital and knowhow but which did not give a proprietary interest in produced petroleum quantities to a foreign investor.

In the first iteration of the Iranian buyback model the recoverable costs were fixed according to an agreed development plan and budget and an agreed element of profit was determined at a fixed rate, but a contractor's recovery was subject to the realization of a defined minimum level of international petroleum prices (where the contractor's recovery would be suspended for as long as international petroleum prices remained below that minimum level) and the continued production of petroleum from the contract area at agreed production levels. The contractor was also obliged to transfer operatorship of a project to the state once production had commenced.

The imposition on the contractor of the incidence of development cost overruns, and the absence of compensation to the contractor when payments were suspended, could combine to adversely impact the contractor's rate of return on a project. The term of the buyback contract (typically between seven and ten years) was also regarded as being too short to permit the full recovery by a contractor of its costs and remuneration expectations. And contractors were concerned about recovering their returns from a project which they were no longer operating. Despite some later modifications to their terms, buyback contracts were not successful in attracting and retaining inward investment.

In 2015, the Iranian government announced the introduction of a new form of service contract—the Iran Petroleum Contract (IPC)—which was intended to stimulate new levels of external investment. The IPC is essentially a long-term service contract but also contains several features more commonly found in a PSC (notably, cost recovery and profit petroleum mechanisms), which are intended to improve the overall economic picture for a contractor. The contractor is paid a fee per barrel of produced petroleum, with amounts due being payable in cash or in kind.

(5) *The co-operative joint venture*—a grantor could enter into an incorporated contractual joint venture with an investor to undertake petroleum exploration and production activities through a company which they both own. That company would then be the holder of a particular form of concession (such as a PSC or a service contract). The benefits which result from the activities conducted under the concession pass to the joint venture company and back through to its shareholders.

In the 1970s the Indonesian government introduced a particular form of concession, known as the 'joint operating body/joint operating agreement', wherein a grantor and an investor would participate on a 50/50 joint venture basis to develop a particular petroleum deposit, with fiscal terms similar to those of a PSC to apply between the parties.

A version of the co-operative joint venture model is used today for example in Qatar, where state participation in a particular petroleum project is a requirement.[12] To facilitate field development, the state's representative awards a long-term development and fiscal agreement to a joint venture company (to be incorporated between the state's representative and a foreign investor, with equity held typically in the ratio of 70:30), giving that company the right to develop and operate a defined project.

2.3 Evolution in Concessions

The form of concession which is chosen by a state will be a product of two (sometimes conflicting) ambitions: what form of concession the state feels best suits its constitutional requirements regarding managing sovereignty over its own resources, and the political and socio-economic expectations of the state's population; and what form of concession is necessary to attract and retain the necessary external investment for the exploitation of those resources.

[12] Talal Abdulla Al-Emadi, *Joint Venture Agreements in the Qatari Gas Industry, A Theoretical and an Empirical Analysis* (Springer 2020).

At one end of the concessions spectrum a state may prefer to award service contracts, thereby maintaining ownership of its petroleum at all times and relegating an investor to the status of hired help. At the other end, an investor may prefer a form of absolute concession which gives the investor extensive rights of petroleum ownership and a high degree of operational independence. In practice, the form of concession which is settled on between a state and its investors will lie somewhere between these extremes.

The form of concession which is used by a grantor, and the fiscal and non-fiscal terms which that concession contains, will reflect what the grantor perceives is best suited to enable the effective development of the state's petroleum interests with the assistance of an investor at the point in time when the concession is entered into.

It is possible that a state's perceptions of what it wants from its concessions will change over time. Growing dissatisfaction with the economic balance of the grantor/investor relationship, or the increased confidence which results from increasing levels of technical and financial capability within the state as a consequence of successful petroleum exploration and/or production experiences, could cause a grantor to seek to change the chosen concession basis going forward. Such a change could see a revision to the fiscal and non-fiscal terms of future concessions, or even a wholesale move away from one particular form of concession to another. This evolution was considered above in relation to Iran, and it can be seen in a number of other states.

In Guyana, offshore petroleum exploration first started in the 1950s and a form of tax and royalty arrangement was used to manage private sector participation. The original Stabroek discovery is governed by a form of concession which is described as a petroleum agreement (but which contains certain mechanisms for cost recovery and profit sharing similar to those found in a PSC).[13] In 2023, a form of PSC (with variations for shallow water and deep water operations) was introduced, to be applied to future licensing rounds.

In Russia, a need for foreign investment in the early 1990s to revitalize the country's petroleum sector (particularly for geographically isolated, technologically complex projects), to stimulate domestic petroleum production levels and to generate foreign currency earnings from exports, led to the Federal Law on Production Sharing Agreements (1995), which promoted the use of PSCs. In 2003, the 1995 Law was amended substantially, increasing the difficulty of securing a new PSC, and adjustments were also made to the federal tax code to make future PSCs less attractive to foreign investors. Since then no new PSCs have been awarded. Only three PSCs are still active in Russia today, and a return to a system of licensing has remained the principal option for the award of concessions.

In Brazil, the state oil and gas company Petrobras had a monopoly on petroleum exploration and production activities until the mid-1990s. In 1997 petroleum exploration and production by foreign and domestic private sector participants became possible through the award of a federally regulated form of concession agreement. Following

[13] Available at <www.s1.stabroeknews.com/images/2017/12/Petroleum-Agreement.pdf> accessed 3 April 2025. Other Guyana petroleum agreements are available at <www.eiti.gy/contracts-licenses/> accessed 3 April 2025.

significant offshore pre-salt discoveries made in 2007, the Brazilian government made a case for moving to the award of PSCs, where there was perceived to be lower exploration risk and greater production potential. In 2010 a PSC regime was introduced for pre-salt coastal shelf and other designated strategic areas. Consequently, two concession regimes now operate side-by-side in Brazil, with the geographic location of the petroleum discovery being the determining factor for which concession form will apply.

2.4 Title to Petroleum and Reserves Booking

A concession (or a petroleum law which underpins a concession) may declare that title to in-ground petroleum is held by the state,[14] although (depending on the form of the concession) an investor could become entitled to some or all of the produced petroleum at a defined point.

For some investors a critical commercial issue is the ability to record (or to 'book', to use the customary phrase) the petroleum reserves which are associated with the concession as an asset in the investor's accounts. Because the form of concession has a major bearing on whether reserves can be booked, for some investors a concession which allows an investor to book reserves extent may be more attractive than one which does not.

The rules around the booking of petroleum reserves depend on which accounting conventions the investor is subject to, and where the investor is listed on a public stock exchange, the listing rules of that exchange will impact the investor's ability to book the reserves.[15]

Certain industry protocols also offer guidance on reserves booking. In 2018 the Society of Petroleum Engineers (SPE) published the Petroleum Resource Management System (PRMS), as a methodology for the consistent definition and estimation of petroleum quantities.[16]

A PSC can be tricky to analyse from a reserves booking perspective because an investor (as the contractor) is contractually entitled to a variable share of the produced petroleum, effectively as a fee for its services. Under a PSC, certain petroleum quantities could be booked by an investor, through reliance on what is called the 'entitlement method'. This approach considers the investor's percentage entitlements to quantities of produced petroleum (based on cost recovery and profit shares) and translates those quantities to a certain number of barrels of oil equivalent at prevailing petroleum prices which then become bookable by the investor. The SPE PRMS provides that, in respect of a PSC, the contractor will have an entitlement to a portion of the produced petroleum, to be estimated based on the PSC's terms relating to the allocation of costs and profits.

[14] See note 1, Chapter 1 and note 7 above.

[15] In the United States the SEC oil and gas reserves definitions are found in Regulations S-X and S-K: <www.sec.gov/rules-regulations/staff-guidance/compliance-disclosure-interpretations/oil-gas-rules> accessed 3 April 2025.

[16] The SPE PRMS is available at <www.spe.org/en/industry/reserves/> accessed 3 April 2025.

The underlying petroleum reserves associated with a service contract, which gives an investor (as the contractor) an entitlement to a monetary fee for the services that it provides and gives the investor no direct petroleum entitlements, would ordinarily not be bookable, but this can be a grey area. The SPE PRMS recognizes the distinction between a risk service contract and a pure service contract, and suggests that an investor can book reserves in respect of a risk service contract, but cannot do so in respect of a pure service contract because there is insufficient exposure to petroleum exploration, development, and market risks by the investor.

A monetary fee which is payable to an investor under a service contract may be paid in kind (or, if it is due to be paid in cash, may be converted to in-kind equivalents by an exchange mechanism) to give physical quantities of petroleum available for lifting by the investor at a defined point.[17] This is something which an investor might seek to record. Sometimes the phrase 'working interest barrels' is used by an investor in its public statements to indicate an equivalence of petroleum quantities which the investor is entitled to recover under its arrangements with the grantor but which might not actually constitute reserves which are capable of being booked, in the interests of giving a fair value measure of the investor's entitlements.

In some forms of concession an investor's reserves position may also be affected by volatility in market prices for petroleum. Under a PSC, an investor's share of the produced petroleum (and so the investor's reserves) may be reduced during periods of high petroleum prices (since fewer barrels at the higher prices will be needed to cover the investor's cash entitlement for cost recovery), and correspondingly the investor's share (and its reserves) may be increased with lower petroleum prices (since more barrels at the lower prices will be needed to cover the cash entitlement for cost recovery).[18]

This is not the case under a tax and royalty arrangement, where higher petroleum prices may translate to greater reserves for an investor (because of the requirement for the certification of proved reserves that they are both technically and economically recoverable, meaning that higher petroleum prices may enhance the prospects of economic recoverability). Correspondingly, under a tax and royalty arrangement, lower petroleum prices could impact the economic recoverability of bookable reserves.

Also relevant to the issue of reserves booking is an investment metric known as 'the reserves replacement ratio'. This is a measure of the extent to which an investor has been able to add new reserves of petroleum (whether by exploration discovery and development, or by the purchase of proven reserves) to its portfolio to offset continued

[17] <www.bhp.com/-/media/bhp/documents/investors/news/ohanetdevelopment.pdf?la=en> accessed 3 April 2025 where, in respect of a risk service contract in Algeria, the contractor's monetary entitlements were translated into volumes of condensate, butane, and propane to be lifted from export ports on the Algerian coast.

[18] BP's 2023 annual report and accounts observes that: 'Our proved reserves are associated with both concessions (tax and royalty arrangements) and agreements where the group is exposed to the upstream risks and rewards of ownership, but where our entitlement to the hydrocarbons is calculated using a more complex formula, such as with PSAs ... In a PSA, we are entitled to recover volumes that equate to costs incurred to develop and produce the proved reserves and an agreed share of the remaining volumes or the economic equivalent. As part of our entitlement is driven by the monetary amount of costs to be recovered, price fluctuations will have an impact on both production volumes and reserves.' <www.bp.com/content/dam/bp/business-sites/en/global/corporate/pdfs/investors/bp-annual-report-and-form-20f-2023.pdf> accessed 3 April 2025.

depletion by production from its portfolio (and so booked reserves will contribute to the maintenance of that ratio). A high ratio number indicates (and gives comfort to actual and prospective shareholders in the investor) that the investor will be able to sustain its current levels of petroleum production into the future (and a ratio figure which exceeds 100 per cent indicates that the investor has room for production growth). This can be an important metric for some investors, shareholders, and the wider market.

Some investors have moved away from a focus on the reserves replacement ratio as a measure of investment health however, preferring instead to focus on high-grading portfolios with more emphasis on advantaged petroleum and 'value over volume' when it comes to making new reserves additions.[19]

2.5 Concession Award Mechanics

A licensing round (sometimes called a 'bid round') is a mechanism by which the award of a concession by a grantor to an investor can be realized. There are several options for how a licensing round can be conducted, and a grantor selects whichever model it feels best reflects the state's regulatory and commercial requirements from time to time. The principal distinction to note is between competitive bidding and direct negotiation.

In competitive bidding (sometimes called 'the fixed content system') a grantor will conduct a public licensing round, in which the key commercial terms of a prospective concession are made transparent by the grantor and prospective investors will submit their bids to be awarded that concession (with only a limited number of contestable items for a prospective investor to address). Within this model, there are two further options for how the terms of a concession can be arrived at:

(1) *Mandated terms, no negotiation*—the key commercial terms of the concession are mandated in detail by a grantor within the terms of the licensing round and there is little or no room for negotiation by a prospective investor of the terms of the concession (other than the completion of concession-specific outstanding issues such as the definition of the concession area (7.2) and the provision of collateral support in respect of the investor's obligations (5.4)).
(2) *Contestable terms, limited negotiation*—the key commercial terms of the concession are outlined by a grantor within the terms of the licensing round but there is some room for negotiation by a prospective investor of the final terms of the concession. This may relate to the finalization of issues such as the extent of the exploration period obligations which the prospective investor is willing to

[19] BP's 2020 annual report and accounts observed that: 'We have removed proved reserves replacement ratio from our [key performance indicators], as it no longer serves as a useful measure of our strategic performance.' <www.bp.com/content/dam/bp/business-sites/en/global/corporate/pdfs/investors/bp-annual-report-and-form-20f-2020.pdf> accessed 3 April 2025. In 2025 BP reaffirmed its commitment to maintaining a 100 per cent reserves replacement ratio.

undertake (8.2), the size of the signature bonus payable (9.4) if applicable, and the key fiscal terms of the concession (9.1). These items may be stated to be contestable matters, to be taken into account by the grantor when considering and ranking the competing bids of different prospective investors.

In direct negotiation (sometimes called 'the agreement system') the terms of a concession are arrived at by bilateral negotiation and agreement between a grantor and a prospective investor. This may take place on an ad hoc basis in respect of a potential concession area, outside the framework of a wider public licensing round (and for this reason direct negotiation is at odds with the notion of a licensing round). In the direct negotiation model there may be extensive dialogue between a grantor and a prospective investor before the terms of the concession are finalized.

Direct negotiation may be less attractive because of demands for states, grantors, and investors to embrace greater transparency in the process of how concessions are awarded and managed. The desire for transparency could, therefore, increase reliance on competitive bidding. On the other hand, competitive bidding relies for its effectiveness on the expectations that there is less acreage on offer by the grantor than there is appetite amongst prospective investors to secure it and that competition between those investors in respect of contestable items may be the deciding factor for the award of a concession. The failure of a licensing round which is conducted through competitive bidding to attract credible offers in respect of the acreage which is on offer could become public, and could create unease for a state and amongst prospective investors. Direct negotiation would at least avoid the stigma of a perceived failure of a licensing round to attract investment.

Licensing rounds may be conducted by a state within a defined time window (which the state itself may define). Alternatively, licensing may be effected through an 'open door' policy, where a prospective investor can contact the state at any time to investigate the possibility of the award of a concession in respect of concession areas (and on concession terms) which are permanently on offer.

The various requirements of a licensing round are typically recited in a set of guidelines which are published for the benefit of prospective investors. Such guidelines set out the mechanics for how a licensing round will be managed and the bid award criteria which will be applied, and they may also reference a model form of the concession which will be entered into between a grantor and an investor.[20]

In any of the above models for the award of a concession, a prospective investor will at a minimum be required to confirm and to prove its identity, constitution, and existence, its previous relevant experience, its current and future capability to perform the requirements of the prospective concession, and its current and future solvency and

[20] The licensing round guidelines issued by the Nigerian Upstream Petroleum Regulatory Commission (NUPRC) in respect of the 2024 Nigeria licensing round offer a useful example <www.br2024.nuprc.gov.ng/> accessed 3 April 2025.

financial worth. Beyond that, a prospective investor could also be required to confirm and to prove to a grantor certain characteristics which are relevant to the state's realization of the energy transition, if this is expressed to be a requirement of the state. From an investor's perspective a commitment to engage in such activities may be the price it has to pay for being awarded a concession which has high petroleum prospectivity.

3

The Energy Transition

3.1 Introduction

This chapter considers what the energy transition means, how and why that term has come into existence, and the various measurement units and terminology which are associated with the energy transition.

Interpreting the perceived requirements of the energy transition will be critical for states who wish to recognize its ambitions but who also wish to remain involved in petroleum exploration and/or production, to determine how their aspirations to do so could be achieved.

The energy transition also creates a number of potential risks for a state which is involved in petroleum exploration and/or production, which will need to be addressed if a successful transition is to be realized.

3.2 Defining the Energy Transition

There is no universally agreed definition of what constitutes the energy transition.[1] Understanding what this term means relies on certain beliefs, which are derived from multiple sources:

(1) That (over the course of relatively recent history) the earth's temperature has risen, that it is continuing to rise, and that it is now at a point which causes perceptible changes to the earth's climate and adverse impacts to mankind.
(2) That the rise in the earth's temperature can (at least to some extent) be attributed to anthropogenic activity—notably, including the production and consumption of fossil fuels (which cause the emission of greenhouse gases).[2]

[1] Previous energy transitions in mankind's history (from wood and organic waste to coal; from coal to oil; the growth of gas) were self-selecting economic evolutions which exploited progressively more efficient energy sources, and which took place over long timeframes of their own making. In contrast, the current anticipated transition from petroleum to renewable energies represents a move towards less efficient energy sources, and one which is intended to take place within defined and self-imposed timeframes.

[2] 'Fossil fuels' are carbon-based compounds (such as coal, peat, oil, and gas) which have been formed in the geological past from the decomposition of plant and animal life, and the term also includes products which result from the industrial processing of those compounds. 'Greenhouse gases' are gases resident in the earth's upper atmosphere which trap heat emissions and contribute to a rise in the earth's temperature. The most notable of these gases are carbon dioxide, methane, and nitrous oxide. The definition of greenhouse gases in the Kyoto Protocol (see below) includes those three gases and also hydrofluorocarbons, perfluorocarbons, sulphur hexafluoride, and nitrogen trifluoride. Naturally occurring water vapour also acts as a greenhouse gas.

(3) That mankind needs to move away from continued reliance on the production and consumption of fossil fuels (and instead needs to embrace greater reliance on renewable energy sources) if a continued rise in the earth's temperature (with all which that could entail for the earth's climate) is to be arrested.

A number of transnational regulatory declarations (which between them take different approaches to creating obligations which are intended to be legally binding) can be considered in order illustrate the foundations of the energy transition:

(1) *The United Nations Framework Convention on Climate Change of 9 May 1992 (UNFCCC)*—the UNFCCC is an international treaty which was originally signed in 1992 by 154 states (since then the number of state signatories has increased to 198). The UNFCCC's main objective is set out in Article 2, as the 'stabilization of greenhouse gas concentrations in the atmosphere at a level that would prevent dangerous anthropogenic interference with the climate system'. The UNFCCC's decision-making body, the Conference of the Parties (COP), meets annually to effect, and report on, the implementation of the UNFCCC.
(2) *The Kyoto Protocol of 10 December 1997*—now widely criticized and somewhat discredited as a tool for addressing climate change, the intentions of the Kyoto Protocol to operationalize the UNFCCC were focused on a top-down series of requirements which were asked mainly of developed nations, with the promulgation of market-based initiatives such as tradable emissions credits and a methodology for carbon pricing.
(3) *The Paris Agreement of 12 December 2015*—the Paris Agreement stressed the importance of a wider and more flexible approach to combat climate change, with differing approaches being taken (including by developing nations) to achieve a common objective. Signatories to the Paris Agreement present their own Nationally Developed Contributions (NDCs), as statements of their intentions to reduce greenhouse gas emissions. These NDCs do not have legal force in their own right, but may be implemented by domestic legislation, and on the back of its NDCs a state could design and implement a more detailed energy transition policy. The Paris Agreement set a target to limit global temperature growth to 2°C from pre-industrial levels (with a further target limit of 1.5°C to be achieved if possible). The United States withdrew from the Paris Agreement in 2017, rejoined in 2021, and withdrew again in 2025.
(4) *The 2030 Agenda for Sustainable Development*—this agenda, which was adopted by all United Nations (UN) members in 2015, created 17 integrated Sustainable Development Goals (SDGs); SDG 13 requires the taking of urgent action to combat climate change and its impacts.
(5) *The European Union's Carbon Border Adjustment Mechanism (CBAM)*—this mechanism seeks to place a price on greenhouse gases which are embedded in the production of certain goods being imported into the European Union (EU). The CBAM's carbon price is intended to be equivalent to the comparable price of EU-sourced production, thereby levelling the playing field on the costs

of greenhouse gas abatement between EU producers and importers into the EU. This is intended to encourage lower carbon intensity production processes in those importer states, so that the EU's carbon abatement and climate change targets are not undermined. The CBAM applies to goods with high carbon intensity during the production process (namely cement, iron and steel, aluminium, fertilizers, hydrogen, and electricity), with the possibility of later extension to other goods. Some commentators have questioned whether the CBAM could be extended to apply to petroleum imports into the EU.[3]

(6) *Methane Guiding Principles*—these are principles developed by the international petroleum industry (with the UN and the World Bank) for reducing methane emissions from gas activities.[4]

(7) *The European Green Deal*—this is a collection of proposals intended to reduce greenhouse gas emissions in the EU by at least 55 per cent (compared to 1990 levels) by 2030.[5]

For some observers the intentions of the energy transition were particularly indicated by a report issued by the International Energy Agency (IEA)[6] in May 2021,[7] which declared that no new fossil fuel exploration would be required because of an impending reduction in petroleum demand and the ongoing transition to renewable energy.[8]

Some states have declared an intention to withdraw from future petroleum exploration and/or production activities (4.1), some commercial lenders have declared their intention to scale back funding for petroleum project developments, and a number of major petroleum exploration and production companies have rebranded themselves as international energy companies, with a declared intention increasingly to develop renewable energy projects and to reduce petroleum project developments within their portfolios. In 2020 BP announced an ambitious plan to cut petroleum production levels by 40 per cent by 2030 whilst simultaneously growing its renewable energy portfolio, as part of a plan to decarbonize its business.[9]

[3] Chris Hilson, 'Emissions Intensity: Do We Need a CBAM for Oil and Gas Imports?' [2024] JWELB 136.

[4] <www.methaneguidingprinciples.org/> accessed 3 April 2025. See also the Global Methane Pledge (<www.globalmethanepledge.org/news/factsheet-2024-global-methane-pledge-ministerial> accessed 3 April 2025) wherein approximately 160 states and the European Commission declared an ambition to reduce methane emissions to 30 per cent below 2020 levels by 2030.

[5] <www.commission.europa.eu/strategy-and-policy/priorities-2019-2024/european-green-deal_en> accessed 3 April 2025.

[6] The IEA was established in 1974, in the aftermath of the 1973 oil crisis, to coordinate global oil supplies amongst its members (consisting of 32 member countries and 13 associated countries which together represent around 65 per cent of global energy consumption <www.iea.org> accessed 3 April 2025).

[7] International Energy Agency, *Net Zero by 2050—A Roadmap for the Global Energy Sector*, available at <www.iea.org/reports/net-zero-by-2050> accessed 3 April 2025.

[8] This approach was objected to by the American Petroleum Institute (API) at the time: 'IEA itself regularly acknowledges that half the technology to reach net zero has not yet been invented. Any pathway to net zero must include continued innovation and use of natural gas and oil, which remains crucial to displacing coal in developing nations and enabling renewable energy.' <www.api.org/news-policy-and-issues/news/2021/05/18/api-statement-on-iea-report-on-pathway-to-net-zero-by-2050> accessed 3 April 2025.

[9] Since then BP has pivoted back towards petroleum projects. In 2023 the 40 per cent figure was revised to 25 per cent, and in 2024 the 25 per cent figure was abandoned. In 2025 BP announced a plan to increase petroleum production and to scale back investments in renewable energy projects. BP still claims an ambition to realize net zero emissions by 2050 (for Scope 1 and Scope 2 emissions within BP's operational control).

In one incarnation the energy transition has the objective of achieving a complete exit from petroleum production and consumption, moving instead towards reliance on energy generated from renewable sources. A moderating requirement could be applied to this ambition, to ensure that implementation of the energy transition is balanced with ensuring continuing access to adequate and affordable energy such that the health and wellbeing of society is not adversely affected.

Against a state's desire to comply with the various declarations which define the energy transition must be weighed the state's current and prospective socio-economic position, and its relationship with the petroleum sector. However compelling the case might be for these declarations, they cannot be imposed, or implemented in the abstract. Further definition of the energy transition should recognize the reality that, for many states, petroleum exploration and/or production and consumption will not cease overnight, and those activities will continue to play a major role.[10] Following on from that, concessions will continue to be essential, and part of the energy transition should be reflected in the evolution of concession terms.

The UNFCCC observed that petroleum activities are major sources of greenhouse gas emissions, that a key ambition of the energy transition should be to create a pathway for the reduction of the emissions associated with those activities, and that, as part of this pathway, states should do more to diversify their economies away from a reliance on petroleum. The UNFCCC also took a pragmatic view, through recognition that the ability to effect diversification would vary between states, where such variation would be reflected in part by the extent to which petroleum activities contribute to a state's economy and the extent to which viable economic alternatives exist for a state, and also by recognizing that significant practical difficulties in achieving the suggested diversification may be faced by some states.[11]

Also relevant to the implementation of the energy transition is what one commentator has described as 'the green paradox'.[12] In this hypothesis the announcement of policies which have an increased focus on non-petroleum sector activities may be equated to the effective end of petroleum production. This could cause certain states (and investors) to accelerate the pace of petroleum project development and production, in order to capture the remaining market demand for their petroleum at the best possible prices whilst there is still an opportunity to do so.[13] The paradox lies in the fact

[10] Alex Epstein, *Fossil Future: Why Global Human Flourishing Requires More Oil, Coal, and Natural Gas—Not Less* (Portfolio 2022).

[11] UNFCCC, Art 4.8 (h) recognized the 'specific needs and concerns of developing country Parties arising from the adverse effects of climate change and/or the impact of the implementation of response measures', and especially 'countries whose economies are highly dependent on income generated from the production, processing and export, and/or on consumption of fossil fuels and associated energy-intensive products'. Article 10 also recognized the need to take into consideration in the implementation of the commitments of the UNFCCC the situation of states with economies that are highly dependent on 'the use of fossil fuels for which such Parties have serious difficulties in switching to alternatives'.

[12] Hans-Werner Sinn, *The Green Paradox: A Supply-Side Approach to Global Warming* (MIT Press 2012).

[13] Guyana is an instructive example. Commercial oil production began at the end of 2019 and has grown steadily since then, with some commentators foreseeing daily oil production levels in excess of one million barrels by 2030. Neighbouring Suriname could be on a similar trajectory.

that an announcement of increased non-petroleum sector activities could lead to increased petroleum production and greater environmental impacts as a result.

3.3 Measurement Units and Terminology

Understanding the energy transition requires an appreciation of certain measurement units and terminology which are frequently used.

'Carbon intensity' describes the quantity of greenhouse gases (commonly reduced to an equivalent basis of the largest of those gases by volume, carbon dioxide—referenced as CO^2e) which are associated with a particular industrial activity. In the context of petroleum production the most commonly used reference point, which allows for straight line comparison between different petroleum projects, is $kgCO^2e$/boe—this measures the quantity (in kilogrammes) of greenhouse gases (reduced to an equivalent basis of carbon dioxide) associated with the production of petroleum on a barrel of oil equivalent (boe) basis. The ability to make such comparisons assumes that carbon intensity is consistently measured, verified, and reported.

As a practical example of this, the UK government reports that gas which is extracted from the UK continental shelf has an average carbon intensity of 21 $kgCO^2e$/boe[14] (although the carbon intensity of individual gas production projects which together make up that average will vary).

Carbon intensity could be applied in respect of an individual petroleum project and a petroleum producing company,[15] and in respect of a petroleum-producing state which has a number of projects underway (which could lead to a comparative ranking of states according to their respective carbon intensities).[16]

Also relevant is an understanding of what are referred to as Scope 1, Scope 2, and Scope 3 emissions. Petroleum companies can record their associated carbon intensity by reference to these definitions, which are found in the Greenhouse Gas Protocol.[17] In summary:

(1) *Scope 1 emissions*—these are emissions which result from assets which a company directly owns or controls—in the context of a petroleum project, this would include emissions caused by the activities of petroleum exploration and/or production which a company undertakes.

14 <www.nstauthority.co.uk/the-move-to-net-zero/net-zero-benchmarking-and-analysis/natural-gas-carbon-footprint-analysis/> accessed 3 April 2025.

15 See the IPIECA petroleum industry guidelines for reporting greenhouse gas emissions which can be used by production companies <www.ipieca.org/resources/petroleum-industry-guidelines-for-reporting-greenhouse-gas-emissions-2nd-edition>accessed 3 April 2025.

16 <www.statista.com/statistics/1454500/average-co2-emissions-from-oil-production-by-country/> accessed 3 April 2025, which was published in respect of 2022 and which at one end of the scale attributed a figure of 36 $kgCO^2$/boe to Norway, and at the other end a figure of 397 $kgCO^2$/boe to Venezuela.

17 The Greenhouse Gas Protocol is a widely used standard which seeks to account for greenhouse gas emissions <www.ghgprotocol.org> accessed 3 April 2025. Also relevant to measuring and reporting emissions is the UN's Oil & Gas Methane Partnership 2.0 <www.ogmpartnership.com> accessed 3 April 2025.

(2) *Scope 2 emissions*—these are emissions which a company is indirectly responsible for, which result from the production of energy which the company uses coming from where energy which the company uses is produced—in the context of a petroleum project, this would include emissions caused by the generation of energy which the company uses for the operation of its project.
(3) *Scope 3 emissions*—these are emissions neither produced by a company nor which result from the company's ownership or control of assets, but which the company is indirectly responsible for because of their generation further down the value chain (and which are not otherwise accounted for as Scope 2 emissions). In the context of a petroleum project, this would include emissions caused by the combustion of petroleum which the company has produced by persons to whom the company has sold that petroleum.

The inclusion of Scope 3 emissions in the quantification of the carbon intensity of a petroleum project typically represents the largest proportion of the total emissions associated with the project, and Scope 3 emissions are also the most difficult for a company to control. In the United Kingdom, Scope 1 and Scope 2 emission reporting has become mandatory for publicly quoted companies and large companies, whereas Scope 3 emissions reporting is voluntary but is strongly recommended for material emissions sources.

3.4 Energy Transition Risks to a State

For rentier states with a high dependency on petroleum production to generate national income, the risks caused by a shortfall in income from a reduction in petroleum production could be overwhelming.[18] The decision of a state to reduce petroleum production as part of its commitment to realizing the energy transition could also expose the state to several other risks:

(1) *The fossil fuel debt trap*—this term describes the situation where a state relies on the generation of revenues from domestic petroleum production projects to pay down the debt which the state has incurred to finance the development of those projects in the first place, and reduced revenues from such projects (caused by reduced petroleum production) inhibits the state's ability to meet the remaining debt service requirements, and which could in due course lead to an irredeemable debt position. The state's position is made worse by the loss of associated local direct and indirect employment. An attempt by the state to overcome the problem by increasing state take (9.2) from its remaining concessions could

[18] According to one estimate, oil-producing states stand to lose US$13 trillion in projected income by 2040 <carbontracker.org/petrostates-13-trillion-gap-energy-transition-pr/> accessed 3 April 2025.

make things worse in the long run. Certain finance initiatives (14.4) may be applied to mitigate the risks to the state.

(2) *Stranded asset risk*—a retreat by private sector investors from petroleum production (which is not made good by a corresponding increase in the level of state involvement) could create stranded assets. These assets represent the sunk costs of investment which have been ploughed into a petroleum project which could be rendered valueless by the application of a regulatory factor. Stranded assets include discovered but undeveloped in-ground petroleum reserves, and physical infrastructure which has been developed for petroleum operations which is no longer required.

The risk to a state of the emergence of stranded assets needs to be viewed in perspective. An undeveloped petroleum resource represents a loss of prospective income but it does not represent an actual liability of the state, and is essentially a loss of psychic wealth for the state.[19] In the case of petroleum project infrastructure the liability for the costs of decommissioning should be borne by an investor under the terms of a concession, even though a grantor might become the owner of that infrastructure in some circumstances (10.4). An analysis of the risk of creating stranded assets on this basis is viewed from the perspective of a single petroleum project however; when the risk is multiplied across the entirety of a state's actual and prospective petroleum production profile the risk assumes a different magnitude.

The risk of the creation of stranded assets is not solely a consequence of the energy transition. Such a risk has always existed where there was a possibility that an investor would exercise a right to surrender a concession (6.6—which an investor might choose to do even before the scheduled end of the productive life of an active concession, where the continued production of petroleum no longer generated an acceptable level of economic return or had become inconsistent with strategic parameters or regulatory considerations).

(3) *Domino decommissioning*—infrastructure used for petroleum operations could be developed on a project-specific basis, such that ceasing to operate that infrastructure might impact only the investor which the infrastructure serves.

A common petroleum project development route is that an investor could utilize incremental capacity in infrastructure which is owned by another person (in exchange for the payment of an agreed tariff to that infrastructure owner), rather than asking the investor to develop its own infrastructure. Such a collaborative approach lowers the overall development costs for a new petroleum production project and prevents the proliferation of potentially duplicative infrastructure items. This right of an investor to access incremental capacity in

[19] Albeit that the amount of such foregone wealth could be significant (see note 18 above), and its loss might not be replaced by alternative sources of national income. The policy decision of states like Greenland and Ireland, which are possessed of abundant resource wealth, to withdraw from the further development of their indigenous petroleum reserves is notable (4.3).

another person's infrastructure may also follow on from the application of third-party access rights (7.7).

Where a right of access to infrastructure applies or can be agreed, the infrastructure owner and the investor enter into what is sometimes called a 'hosting agreement' (or a 'production handling agreement') to set out their commercial relationship. Repeated application of this approach could lead to the generation of a hub and spoke model for petroleum operations, where multiple satellite projects are tied in to a single set of central facilities which multiple investors rely on for the continued operability of their projects.

The decision of an infrastructure owner to cease the operation of certain infrastructure may be made for economic reasons (ie the revenues which the owner earns from its own petroleum project or from operating the infrastructure no longer provide a satisfactory return) or for operational reasons (ie the infrastructure has reached the end of its design life and is now uneconomical to repair or replace). Such a decision may also be made by an infrastructure owner for strategic reasons—such as where the owner wishes to withdraw from the petroleum business (whether in a particular state or more generally) and it has not been possible for the owner to sell the infrastructure to another person as a going concern.

In any of these instances the risk to an investor is that the cessation of operation of the relevant infrastructure could oblige the investor to make a premature decision to cease its own petroleum production, or to decommission its own infrastructure (hence the term which is sometimes applied to define this risk as 'domino decommissioning').

Some hosting agreements provide that where an infrastructure owner plans to cease operating its infrastructure, an investor which is using that infrastructure has a right to buy out and take over the owner's interests, thereby making the investor the infrastructure owner and allowing for continued petroleum production. The issue to consider is where an investor decides not to take on that additional burden. This could trigger domino decommissioning and result in reduced quantities of petroleum being produced from within a state.

To counter the risk to the state of uncontrolled domino decommissioning a national oil company (14.1) may reserve rights (or the national oil company may be obliged) to step in and take over the ownership and operation of infrastructure from the outgoing owner. Provision for meeting the costs of decommissioning which has been made by the outgoing owner (8.5) may be applied by the national oil company towards the costs of repairing, replacing, operating, and maintaining the infrastructure to prolong its useful life. Such prolongation is also consistent with principles of maximized economic recovery which are intended to apply in respect of a state's patrimony (8.4).

4
State-Sponsored Withdrawals

4.1 Introduction

For reasons principally attributed to meeting the requirements of the energy transition, a number of states have made public declarations of an intention to prohibit future petroleum exploration and/or production (but not necessarily petroleum consumption) within their territories, as part of a recognition of what is in their national interests.

The manner in which these state-sponsored withdrawals from future involvement with certain aspects of the petroleum sector are effected could set a precedent for other states to follow. The examples of state-sponsored withdrawals which have taken place are also interesting because they vary between states where petroleum production has not yet had a chance to form part of the state's economy, and states where petroleum production has previously been a significant economic feature.

4.2 Defining the National Interest

From a state's perspective, defining what might be in a state's national interest in managing the energy transition is not straightforward. A state's national interest might be primarily an economic ambition but it could also include achieving wider societal changes (which might also go beyond the boundaries of the state). The national interest of a state which has historically applied in respect of the petroleum sector could evolve to reflect the implementation of the energy transition in that state.

In broad terms it could be said that the national interest of a state which has petroleum reserves is best served by exploiting those reserves to generate the maximum revenues for the state, or by exploiting those reserves for the maximum benefit of the state.[1] This might be true for many states but it is not a universal truth, since some states have taken the view that their national interests could be better served by not facilitating such exploitation.

In the United Kingdom (which has a liberalized upstream petroleum sector, with relatively little state interference) legislation defines the overriding objective of the upstream sector as maximizing the economic recovery of UK petroleum reserves.[2] This

[1] Realizing maximum revenues and realizing maximum benefits might seem synonymous but they are not. Revenue maximization could be a shorter-term goal, to be achieved at the expense of wider societal ambitions which could be part of generating maximum benefits for the state.

[2] Petroleum Act 1998, s 9A(1).

objective is supported by implementation strategies which are required to be developed and reviewed periodically to ensure their continuing suitability, and in 2021 a net zero target was incorporated into those strategies.[3] Another example of a petroleum sector in evolution comes from Oman, where a state-mandated policy[4] seeks to promote economic diversification away from the state's historically significant reliance on the petroleum sector, whilst at the same time recognizing the importance of the sector through expanding certain gas projects and facilitating enhanced oil recovery projects.

4.3 State-Sponsored Withdrawals

Several states have declared an intention to prohibit future petroleum exploration and/or production within their territories, often citing environmental reasons for doing so. In some cases such a declaration has been made by a state which has a history of petroleum production and/or which has significant quantities of undeveloped in-ground petroleum reserves, which lends some substance to the declaration. In other cases such a declaration has been made by a state which has no history of petroleum production and/or which has negligible petroleum prospectivity within its territory. In the latter case such a declaration is little more than symbolic.

(1) *Denmark*—Denmark has history as a major petroleum-producing state, and particularly so in the European context. Following initial discoveries in 1966, oil and gas were first produced from the Danish part of the North Sea in 1972. By the early 1980s significant levels of production were being achieved, and Denmark became a net exporter of petroleum in 1997. The Danish state has also played a major part in the exploitation of the nation's petroleum reserves.[5] Danish oil production levels peaked in 2005, and thereafter began to decline. By 2018 Denmark became a net importer of oil. Gas production profiles in Denmark have followed a similar trend.

Petroleum production revenues have made a significant contribution to the Danish economy and, although a decline in the rate of production is now apparent, relatively significant in-ground petroleum reserves still remain within Denmark.

In 2020 the Danish government legislated to ban new petroleum exploration licensing (starting immediately with a cancellation of the then ongoing eighth licensing round), and also to cease any ongoing petroleum production by 2050.[6]

[3] <www.assets.publishing.service.gov.uk/media/6194dfa4d3bf7f0555071b1b/net-zero-strategy-beis.pdf> accessed 3 April 2025.

[4] Oman Vision 2040 <https://mem.gov.om/en-us/About-Us/Oman-Vision-2040> accessed 3 April 2025.

[5] Nordsøfonden (also known as the Danish North Sea Fund) is a Danish state-owned company which since 2005 has conducted petroleum exploration and production activities. Nordsøfonden, TotalEnergies, and Noreco are the current partners in the Danish Underground Consortium (DUC), which holds licences representing approximately 85 per cent of oil and 97 per cent of gas production in Denmark.

[6] <www.en.kefm.dk/news/news-archive/2020/dec/denmark-introduces-cutoff-date-of-2050-for-oil-and-gas-extraction-in-the-north-sea-cancels-all-future-licensing-rounds> accessed 3 April 2025.

'We are now putting an end to the fossil era, and drawing a straight line between our activities in the North Sea and the Climate Act's goal of climate neutrality in 2050,' said Dan Jørgensen, Denmark's minister of climate and energy and public utilities. The legislation provided that existing production permits would be allowed to continue, but would be subject to the 2050 cutoff date. An initiative to explore the potential of carbon capture and storage using old oil and gas wells was intended also 'to use the new green course in the North Sea as a springboard for an active and targeted role in the global debate on the role and responsibility of oil producing countries in the fight against climate change'.

The legislation also recognized the impact which the changes could have, by providing for the introduction of a just transition initiative in the affected regions of Denmark to safeguard future employment.

(2) *Ireland*—domestic gas production to meet Ireland's energy needs came from the offshore Kinsale Head field (which commenced operations in 1978 and ceased production in 2020), and a small percentage of the country's needs is currently met by the offshore Corrib field (which commenced operations in 2015). Otherwise, Ireland relies on imports of petroleum (including gas by pipeline from the United Kingdom). Significant undeveloped petroleum reserves are believed to underlie the seas to the south and the west of Ireland.

In 2021 the Irish government enacted legislation 'for the purpose of pursuing the transition to a climate resilient, biodiversity rich and climate neutral economy by no later than the end of the year 2050 and to thereby promote climate justice, and just transition', which included a prohibition on the award of new licences for petroleum exploration.[7] 'The decision we have made today to legislate for a ban on new oil exploration and extraction will send a powerful message, within Ireland and internationally, that Ireland is moving away from fossil fuels towards a renewable future ... by keeping fossil fuels in the ground, we will incentivise the transition to renewable energy and put ourselves on a pathway to net-zero by 2050,' said Eamon Ryan, minister for the environment, climate and communications.

(3) *New Zealand*—petroleum has been produced from a number of concession areas in New Zealand (principally in the Taranaki basin), commencing in 1970. Since then reliance has grown on gas production and onshore transmission for domestic consumption.

In 2018 the New Zealand government implemented a ban on the award of new petroleum exploration permits outside the onshore part of the Taranaki basin, although existing petroleum production permits were allowed to continue. Prime Minister Jacinda Ardern announced that 'transitions have to start somewhere and unless we make decisions today that will essentially take effect in 30 or more years' time, we run the risk of acting too late and causing abrupt shocks to communities and our country'.

[7] The Climate Action and Low Carbon Development (Amendment) Act 2021.

It has not been plain sailing for New Zealand since then. The 2018 ban caused a decline in domestic gas production rates as further development investment dried up, and resulted in an increase in the quantities of imported petroleum and coal (which in turn led to an increase in associated emissions), accompanied by energy shortages and increasing energy prices. In 2024 further legislation was introduced[8] which reversed the 2018 ban. 'The lakes are low, the sun hasn't been shining, the wind hasn't been blowing, and we have an inadequate supply of natural gas to meet demand,' said energy minister Simeon Brown. The New Zealand government also announced the removal of regulatory barriers to the construction of liquefied natural gas (LNG) import facilities which had previously applied.

(4) *France*—historically there has been some (but negligible) petroleum production within France. In 2017 the French government passed legislation (which was intended to apply in respect of the French mainland and also, more significantly, to France's overseas territories) to prohibit the granting of new exploration licences, and to phase out all petroleum exploration and production by 2040.[9] This decision was taken as part of a plan to make France carbon neutral by 2050 and to curb greenhouse gas emissions.

France's domestic petroleum production was running at between 5 and 6 million barrels of oil annually at the time when the legislation was introduced,[10] and even those modest production rates have been in decline since then. Notably, the 2017 legislation also applies to French Guiana, where there had been some optimism regarding possible exploration discoveries, given growing exploration and production successes in Guyana and Suriname.

(5) *Spain*—Spain has relatively significant undeveloped petroleum reserves but historically, little has been done to exploit them. Relatively small quantities of petroleum have been produced onshore and offshore.

In 2021 the Spanish government approved a law which prohibited the awarding of new licences for onshore and offshore petroleum exploration with immediate effect, and which sought to end the remaining production of petroleum by 2042, to apply across all of Spain's territories.[11]

(6) *Greenland*—petroleum exploration began in Greenland in the 1970s on the country's west coast. A number of wells were drilled but the exploration effort was unsuccessful and the programme came to an end in 1978. A licensing round in 1992 elicited no bids, and open door licensing was introduced in 1994 (for onshore and offshore areas). Further licensing rounds then followed between

[8] The Crown Minerals Amendment Bill (revising the Crown Minerals Act 1999), due in force in 2025.

[9] Law No 2017-1839, published on 31 December 2017, modifying a number of articles from the French mining code. Permits already granted will remain in force but will not exist beyond 1 January 2040, unless a permit holder can demonstrate that termination would prevent sufficient time for the recovery of its costs.

[10] To put this in context, total annual oil production in France at the time was less than the amount of oil produced by Saudi Arabia in a day.

[11] Ley 7/2021, de 20 de mayo, de cambio climático y transición energética <www.boe.es/diario_boe/txt.php?id=BOE-A-2021-8447> accessed 3 April 2025.

2001 and 2015, with open door licensing also taking place between 2016 and 2018. Various estimates have indicated the presence of significant in-ground petroleum reserves in Greenland.

In 2021 Greenland's government declared that it would suspend all future petroleum exploration activities. This decision was ostensibly made to combat climate change and to focus instead on sustainable energy project developments. Naaja Nathanielsen, Greenland's minister for natural resources, observed that 'the government has assessed that the environmental consequences of oil exploration and exploitation are too great'.

Other concerns were expressed that development projects which did take place could deliver low returns, or could even generate losses, given the anticipated costs and technical challenges associated with operating in Arctic waters. Nathanielsen added that 'it is a decision where climate considerations, environmental considerations and economic common sense go hand in hand'. The Greenland government also stated that it would respect the terms of the then-remaining four active exploration licences (which are due to expire in 2027 and 2028).

(7) *Sweden*—Sweden has negligible petroleum reserves and minimal domestic petroleum production. In 2022 the Swedish government enacted legislation which banned the extraction of hard coal, lignite, crude oil, shale oil, and natural gas in Sweden. 'We are tightening environmental legislation by banning the extraction of fossil fuels such as coal, oil and natural gas. Breaking the entire chain of fossil fuel dependence, from extraction to use, is crucial for Sweden to continue to be a leader in the climate transition,' said Annika Strandhäll, Sweden's minister for climate and the environment.

(8) *Belize*—Belize has negligible indigenous petroleum reserves and minimal domestic petroleum production. In 2017 the government of Belize enacted a moratorium on future petroleum exploration and production in its waters.[12] In 2023 a further law was passed to necessitate a public referendum on any proposed legislative decision to end the ban.

As a gathering house for states with the ambition to make declarations regarding the cessation of petroleum sector involvement, at the Conference of the Parties (COP) 26 summit in 2021 the Beyond Oil and Gas Alliance (BOGA) was launched. The BOGA is described as: 'an international alliance of governments and stakeholders working together to facilitate the managed phase-out of oil and gas production'.[13]

The current core members of the BOGA include Costa Rica, Denmark, France, Greenland, Ireland, Portugal, Spain, and Sweden (and the BOGA has a number of

[12] Petroleum Operations (Maritime Zone Moratorium) Act 2017, s 3 provides that: 'Notwithstanding the provisions of any other law, the carrying out of petroleum operations within the limits of the maritime zone of Belize is prohibited'.

[13] <www.beyondoilandgasalliance.org/> accessed 3 April 2025.

other—what it describes as—associate members and friends).[14] The core members 'commit to end new concessions, licensing or leasing rounds for oil and gas production and exploration and to set a Paris-aligned date for ending oil and gas production and exploration on the territory over which they have jurisdiction'.[15]

Each of the above examples of state-sponsored withdrawals represents a situation where (in some cases, despite historical and current levels of petroleum production and/or the presence of (sometimes significant) in-ground petroleum reserves) a conscious decision has been made by a state to signal the end of petroleum exploration and/or production within its territory. However, the idea that these examples reflect a triumph of the more radical version of the energy transition agenda over the ambitions of continued petroleum exploration and/or production must be kept in perspective. In several of the above examples domestic petroleum production and its attendant revenues have not had a chance to form a significant part of a national economy (whether because petroleum production has not commenced, or because such petroleum production as there is forms only a relatively small part of a wider, diversified economy within the state), and in other cases such domestic petroleum production as there was has entered into a period of natural decline and inevitable cessation.

In all of the above examples concessions for petroleum exploration and/or production which had already been granted were allowed to continue. None of the concessions were terminated prematurely by a state, nor were any of the concessions forcibly amended to reflect a state's new social or economic expectations for the remainder of their intended terms.

[14] New Zealand was, an associate member of the BOGA but it ceased to be so in June 2025 as a consequence of the implementation of legislation to revoke the 2018 ban on new petroleum exploration licensing (see note 8 above).

[15] Other core members include states and sub-governments such as the Marshall Islands, Portugal, Samoa, Tuvalu, Vanuatu, and Wales. None of these states have awarded concessions for petroleum production, and the absence of meaningful indigenous petroleum reserves means they are unlikely to do so.

PART B
THE TERMS OF A CONCESSION

5

Parties, Collateral Support, Governance, Transfers

5.1 Introduction

A concession will identify the parties to it—notably, a grantor and an investor. The concession may also regulate the joint venture arrangements underpinning the concession to which a group of persons who together make up the investor are party.

A concession may describe certain situations where the provision of collateral support may be required in support of an investor's obligations.

A concession may set out a governance regime which manages the ongoing relationship between a grantor and an investor (including the appointment of a person who is designated to act as the concession's operator).

A concession will usually apply certain conditions to an intended transfer of interests in a concession by an investor (and possibly also by a grantor), and may also regulate how a change in control which takes place in respect of an investor could be addressed.

5.2 The Parties to the Concession

In its simplest (and most common) iteration a concession is entered into between two parties—a grantor and an investor. 'The grantor' is used here as a generic term to describe the duly appointed representative of the state, holding authority to award and perform (and possibly also to regulate) a concession on behalf of the state.[1]

In practice a grantor could be a state ministry or other state entity, or the state's national oil company (14.1), and the responsibilities for awarding, performing, and regulating a concession may be allocated between different state entities.[2] A number of state entities may be party to a concession.[3]

[1] As an example of this basic construction, the Suriname 2015 production-sharing contract (PSC) is entered into between the state oil company Staatsolie Maatschappij Suriname N.V. (Staatsolie) and a named contractor, with further provision (at 2.1) that Staatsolie acts 'as agent of the Republic of Suriname with respect to the petroleum industry'.

[2] The Tanzania 2013 production sharing agreement (PSA) offers a slight departure from the customary grantor/investor bilateral relationship, with two state entities as parties (the government (represented by the minister for energy and minerals) and Tanzania Petroleum Development Corporation (TPDC)). The minister has authority to award exploration and development licences, and awards an exploration licence to TPDC, which in turn appoints the investor to carry out petroleum operations on its behalf.

[3] The Brazil 2017 PSA is entered into on the state side by: the federal government (acting through the ministry of mines and energy); the National Agency of Petroleum, Natural Gas and Biofuels (ANP), acting as regulator and inspection authority; and Pré-Sal Petróleo S.A. (PPSA), acting as manager.

The investor in a concession may be one person, or (more commonly) the investor entity will represent the collective interests of several persons (the 'investor parties') who are acting in consortium. This consortium may also include a representative of the state in some circumstances (10.8).

The presence of several persons acting in consortium as the investor may require some careful management where a grantor wishes to terminate a concession because of a breach of its terms by one of the investor parties (6.6), in respect of the several liabilities of the investor parties (11.3), and in respect of a proposed transfer of interests by, or a change in control in respect of, one of the investor parties (5.6).

5.3 The Investor Parties' Joint Venture Arrangements

Where several persons together constitute the investor, those persons will regulate their internal relationship through some form of joint venture arrangement. The investor parties as they exist at the outset of a concession will be identified in the preamble to the concession. The definition of an investor party in a concession will also usually include a reference to each investor party's successors in title and lawful assignees. A concession may also regulate changes in the identity of the investor parties over time (5.6).

In the incorporated joint venture model a concession may be held as an investor by a single incorporated entity, as a joint venture company in which the investor parties are each shareholders, with their interests being regulated by the terms of a shareholders' agreement. Alternatively, in the unincorporated joint venture model the investor parties will each be a direct party to a concession and they will regulate their internal relationship through a joint operating agreement.

In either of the incorporated or unincorporated joint venture models the concession represents the vertical relationship between a grantor and an investor, and the joint venture arrangement represents the horizontal relationship between the investor parties.

It is possible for a representative of the state (such as a national oil company (14.1)) to be one of the investor parties (possibly through being the beneficiary of the exercise of the rights created in respect of state participation under a concession (10.8)). Because of the possibility of initial or subsequent state participation a grantor may wish to ensure that the terms of the joint venture arrangement are written to reflect the state's current and prospective interests. This may be effected by a requirement for the investor to secure the grantor's approval of any of: the initial draft of the joint venture arrangement, subsequent amendments to the joint venture arrangement, or of any person appointed to act as the operator of the joint venture arrangement,[4] or by a right

[4] The Equatorial Guinea 2006 PSC provides (at 6.2) that: 'Within forty-five (45) days following the Effective Date, the Contractor shall provide the Ministry with a draft of the Joint Operating Agreement which shall be based upon the current model form operating agreement from the Association of International Petroleum Negotiators (AIPN). The Joint Operating Agreement and all amendments thereto shall be subject to the prior approval of the Ministry. The identity of the Technical Operator and any change thereto shall be subject to the prior approval

of the grantor to attend meetings which are held under the joint venture arrangement in the capacity of an observer.[5]

The grantor may require that the investor parties will only use a form of joint venture arrangement which has been approved by the state. Model joint operating agreements have been issued by the upstream regulatory authorities of a relatively small number of states, mandated for use within their territories:

Bangladesh—the Bangladesh PSC includes a model joint operating agreement for use between the members of a consortium holding the PSC.

Brazil—the Brazil PSA includes a model consortium agreement for use between the members of a consortium holding the PSA.

Denmark—Energistyrelsen (the Danish energy agency), which issues licences for upstream activities, has issued and maintains a model joint operating agreement for operations in Denmark.

Greenland—Naalakkersuisut (the Greenland government), which issues licences for upstream activities, first issued a model joint operating agreement in 2002, which has been prescribed for each licensing round held in Greenland since then.

Iceland—Orkustofnun (the Icelandic national energy authority), which issues licences for upstream activities, first issued a model joint operating agreement in 2012 for the second licensing round.

Norway—Sokkeldirektoratet (the Norwegian Offshore Directorate, formerly the Norwegian Petroleum Directorate), which issues licences for upstream activities, has issued and maintains a model joint operating agreement for operations in Norway.

When a state-mandated form of joint venture agreement is required to be used it is not uncommon for the investor parties also to enter into a further arrangement between themselves which supplements or interprets the mandated form. Such a further arrangement might also require a grantor's approval.

It may be a jurisdictional requirement of the state that an investor (or each of the investor parties) must be a company which has been incorporated in the state.[6] Adopting

of the Ministry in accordance with the Hydrocarbons Law. The National Company shall be appointed as the Administrative Operator under the Joint Operating Agreement.'

[5] The Zanzibar 2024 PSA provides (at 3 (d)) that: 'The Minister and ZPRA shall be entitled to attend the meetings of the committees pursuant to the Joint Operating Agreement as observers in a non-voting capacity ... Members and observers attending a meeting pursuant to the Joint Operating Agreement may be accompanied by advisers and experts to the extent reasonably necessary to assist with the conduct of such meeting. Such advisers and experts shall not vote but may contribute in a non-binding way to discussions and debates of the committees.'

[6] The Equatorial Guinea 2006 PSC provides (at 17.1) that: 'Within the one (1) Calendar Year following the Effective Date, to the extent that they have not already done so, each of the Parties comprising the Contractor (other than the National Company) shall incorporate an Affiliate under the laws of Equatorial Guinea and shall assign all of its rights and obligations in and under this Contract, the Joint Operating Agreement and any other agreement relating to Petroleum Operations to such Affiliate.' The Tajikistan 2008 PSC provides (at 2.8) that: 'The

such a requirement could be helpful in the popular demand for the greater localization of petroleum operations under a concession (10.2).

Some concessions recite several percentage participating interest shares in the concession, allocated to each of the investor parties, which together will add up to 100 per cent.[7] This can be helpful in identifying the several liability of each of the investor parties (11.3), effecting the possibility of termination of a concession in respect of one of the investor parties and the subsequent reallocation of that investor party's interests in the concession (6.6), and identifying the interests of one of the investor parties in a concession which could be the subject of a transfer or a change in control (5.6). A concession may also prescribe certain minimum percentage participating interests which must be held by each of the investor parties from time to time.[8]

These percentage participating interest shares should also be replicated in the corresponding provisions in the joint venture arrangement, and changes over time to the interests should be tracked to ensure a continuing symmetry of interests between a concession and a joint venture arrangement.

5.4 Collateral Support

'Collateral support' describes the procurement by an investor, in favour of a grantor, of some form of additional support for the satisfactory performance by the investor of its obligations under the concession. These obligations could be of payment or of wider performance. Such collateral support is provided by another person, which may or may not be related to an investor, and is ostensibly intended to enhance the continued performance of the concession by an investor, to protect against the occurrence of financial or operational difficulties which could inhibit the originally intended manner of performance by the investor.

Collateral support is typically intended to operate such that it can only be called upon by a grantor to remedy a breach of an investor's obligation in the concession, and not so that it can be applied electively by the collateral support provider (at the investor's request) to make good a prospective default of the investor.

Operator ... for Petroleum Operations shall be a Petroleum Operating Company established by the Contractor in accordance with the legislation of Republic of Tajikistan.'

[7] The Somalia 2019 PSA provides (at 3.1.2) that: 'The Contractor shall consist of the following Contractor Parties holding the respective following interests: --------------- with an interest of ------------- %, being the Operator, --------------- with an interest of ------------- %, and --------------- with an interest of ------------- %.' This formulation was dispensed with in the Somalia 2023 PSA. The Afghanistan 2013 EPSC provides (at 2.4) that: 'As of the Effective Date, the Participating Interests of the Contractor Entities are: Dragon Oil: 40%. Ghazanfar: 20%. TPAL: 40%. If a Contractor Entity transfers or assigns all or part of its Participating Interest under the provisions of this Contract, the Participating Interests of the Contractor Entities shall be revised accordingly.'

[8] The Brazil 2017 PSA provides (at 30.5) that: 'The Operator and the other members of the Consortium shall have, respectively, at least a thirty-percent (30%) and a five-percent (5%) share in the Agreement throughout its effectiveness.' The Guyana 2023 PSA provides (at 27.6) that: 'The Contractor may not make an assignment that creates a participating interest representing less than five percent (5%) of the total contract for a Non-Operator interest or less than thirty-five percent (35%) for an Operator interest.'

A concession will ordinarily not require a grantor to procure collateral support in respect of the grantor's performance of its concession obligations.

Where a concession is awarded to a consortium of persons acting together as an investor a grantor may make an assessment of the creditworthiness of each of the investor parties at the point when the concession is awarded. This could result in some of the investor parties being required to procure collateral support, and in others not being so required. In contrast to this piecemeal approach it is more typically the case that collateral support is required to be procured in respect of an investor as a single entity, with less focus on individual creditworthiness. In this case the investor party which is appointed to act as the operator under the concession (5.5) would assume the primary responsibility for the provision of the collateral support. Arrangements would then be made to reallocate that provision between the investor parties, under the terms of their joint venture arrangement. An assessment of creditworthiness could also be made by a grantor in respect of an incoming person who would become an investor party when an investor party transfers its interests under a concession (5.6).

The position of a grantor on the need for the provision of collateral support by an investor could vary over time. As a grantor seeks to attract new inward investment, either at the outset of the operational lifetime of the state's upstream sector or as the sector matures and declines, there could be a temptation for a grantor to lower the bar for prospective investors in order to attract investment, by applying less stringent collateral support requirements.

The forms of collateral support which customarily apply in respect of a concession are bank guarantees and corporate guarantees.[9]

A bank guarantee, which can be used to address shorter-term liquidity concerns in respect of an investor, is issued by a bank or other financial institution. Bank guarantees take various forms and the associated nomenclature is often applied imprecisely. A demand guarantee (also called a 'performance bond') is essentially an unconditional undertaking by a bank to pay a specified amount to a named beneficiary (such as a grantor), sometimes with reference to an underlying obligation (such as certain commitments in a concession), but often with no reference to the need for a grantor to evidence any default in respect of that underlying obligation as a precursor to payment. For this reason a demand guarantee can be construed as a primary obligation, and is truly abstract. A standby letter of credit fulfils a similar function to a demand guarantee, although it employs a different vernacular in its operative provisions because it is essentially a documentary credit.

A corporate guarantee is a form of surety which is given to a grantor (as the beneficiary) by an entity (which could be the parent company of the investor party which has been appointed to act as the operator (5.5)) in respect of an investor's commitments under the concession. The guarantor promises to be responsible for the debt or default

[9] The Brazil 2017 PSA provides (at 11.7) that, in respect of the costs of the exploration period obligations, the investor can procure any (or any combination) of an irrevocable letter of credit, a performance bond, an oil pledge agreement, or an escrow deposit.

of an investor, and the guarantor's liability will not ordinarily come into existence unless and until the investor has failed to perform the underlying obligation (for which reason a corporate guarantee could be said to be a secondary obligation). A corporate guarantee may present difficulties in enforcement since (in contrast with a bank guarantee) it might not be honoured on demand and without question by the guarantor, such that further enforcement action by the grantor might be necessary.

A bank guarantee may be procured by an investor as security for certain defined payments under a concession. An investor's payment obligations will initially relate to the performance of the exploration period obligations, where an investor may have an obligation to pay liquidated damages for a failure to perform an exploration period obligation or a right to pay a monetary amount in replacement for the need to perform an exploration period obligation (8.2).

A corporate guarantee may be applied to the entirety of an investor's obligations under a concession and not just those which apply during the exploration period (and, reflective of this, a corporate guarantee is sometimes described as a 'general performance guarantee').

The liability of an investor to meet the costs of decommissioning assets or equipment which have been used in the performance of the petroleum operations (8.5) may also be the subject of the provision of specific collateral support.

There is no industry-wide standard or model form corporate guarantee and so the terms of a guarantee will need to be negotiated between a grantor and an investor's guarantor. That said, most guarantees tend to follow a relatively formulaic structure. A guarantor (whether it is a bank or a corporate entity) will invariably have its own form of document which it prefers to use. In some concessions the required forms of the various collateral support documents will be appended.[10]

An investor may seek to moderate a concession's obligation to provide collateral support in various ways. Where a bank guarantee is given in respect of the costs of the exploration period obligations (8.2) the guarantee might not be provided for the entirety of the exploration period obligations but only in respect of the next-following period of exploration phase activity. This is done to reduce the size of the guaranteed amount, and so the cost to the investor of procuring the guarantee from a bank.

Alternatively, where the collateral support takes the form of a bank guarantee for a defined monetary amount (such as the entirety of the exploration period obligations costs), the size of the guaranteed amount may be reduced by defined increments against the ongoing proof of work which has been done by an investor in satisfaction of the exploration period obligations.[11] This proposition is more suited to the situation

[10] The Afghanistan 2013 exploration and production sharing contract (EPSC) appends a pro-forma financial guarantee and a pro-forma general performance guarantee. The Uganda 1999 PSC appends a pro-forma bank guarantee (and the Uganda 2015 PSC appends a pro-forma general performance guarantee).

[11] The Afghanistan 2013 EPSC provides (at 8.2) that: 'During the Exploration Phase, the amount of the Financial Guarantee shall be reduced at the end of each Contract Year by the amount actually expended on the Minimum Exploration Program.'

where the exploration period obligations relate to a lengthy period of time for their performance and/or to obvious reductions in work obligations which can be the subject of quantified translation to the amount of the guarantee (and correspondingly this proposition is less suited to the situation where there are limited exploration period obligations, such as the drilling of a single exploration well).

The requirement of an investor to procure collateral support under a concession should not be conflated with the requirement of the investor parties to procure collateral support in respect of their obligations to each other under the joint venture arrangement. These are separate obligations, and they are created in favour of separate beneficiaries and should not overlap (despite the concern which may be felt by an investor party that two sets of collateral support are seemingly being procured in respect of what is essentially a single set of petroleum project commitments).

5.5 Concession Governance

A concession may provide for how it is intended to be administered by an investor over its lifetime, and for how a grantor is to be involved in that administration.

A concession will usually appoint one of the investor parties to act as a designated operator, principally for the purposes of performing the petroleum operations (6.2) under the concession. This role is distinct from the role of the operator under the joint venture arrangement but it is customary for the same person to be the operator under both the concession and the joint venture arrangement.

The operator under the concession will be primarily responsible for liaising between the investor and the grantor, for incurring expenses in connection with the performance of the petroleum operations, for providing collateral support in favour of a grantor, and for entering into contracts and commitments which relate to the performance of the petroleum operations and the concession generally.

The person appointed to act as the operator may be agreed between the investor parties (subject to the grantor's approval), or that person could be selected directly by the grantor. The selection and the appointment of a replacement operator during the lifetime of the concession may also require the grantor's approval.

A concession might contain certain grounds for the removal of the operator by the grantor, usually relating to a defined default, although this prospect is commonly conflated with a default of the investor party which has been appointed as the operator which leads to the removal of that investor party from a concession (6.6).

The operator will act as the de facto agent of the investor, and acts and omissions of the operator will be deemed to be those of the investor so that they cannot later be disclaimed by the investor. Because of the power of the operator to bind the investor, the role of the operator under the concession is something which will ordinarily be closely controlled by the investor parties under the joint venture arrangement.

A concession may also provide for the operator's role to be displaced by a form of state participation when a development project is underway. This replacement operator may be a state entity, or a separate joint venture entity in which the state entity is a shareholder (10.8).

A concession may also make provision for the governance of the ongoing relationship between the grantor and the investor, and the management of the concession through the constitution of a consultative committee (variously called the 'management committee', the 'joint management committee', or the 'advisory committee') to consider various matters in relation to the concession.[12] This management committee is made up of a defined number of representatives from the grantor and the investor (and may include representatives of the state other than the grantor).

Where this formulation is adopted a concession will provide for how the management committee is constituted, where and how often it meets, the scope of its powers, and how it makes, records, and implements its decisions.[13]

A concession might provide a mechanism to address the inability of a grantor and an investor to agree upon a certain issue at the management committee.[14] If agreement still cannot be reached then a formal dispute under a concession could be raised (11.4).[15]

The management committee will consider various matters in relation to a concession such as the formulation of any necessary policies and procedures, the review and approval of work programmes and budgets and later amendments thereto (8.6), decommissioning plans (8.5), insurance proposals submitted by an investor (11.3), and procurement and contract management issues (10.3).

It is not automatically the case that decisions of the management committee will formally bind a grantor, despite the presence of the grantor's representatives on the management committee, and this could be so even if the grantor has voting control in respect of the decisions of the management committee. There may still be a need to

[12] The Suriname 2015 PSC provides (at 8.7) a comprehensive list of responsibilities of such a committee.

[13] The Trinidad and Tobago 2023 PSC provides (at 9.2) that: 'The mandate of the Coordination Committee is to assist Contractor in its activities under this Contract by providing a forum for continuous dialogue and flow of information between Contractor and the Minister regarding Contractor's planned activities and progress related to the Contract Area. The Coordination Committee shall review proposals for revisions to agreed Work Programmes and budgets and periodically evaluate Contractor's progress in respect of approved Work Programmes, budgets, marketing and local content initiatives and other matters related to Petroleum Operations under this Contract.' The Gambia 2022 licence provides (at 3.2.1) that: 'the Joint Operating Agreement shall establish a management committee for the purposes of controlling and supervising the conduct of Petroleum Operations, ensuring co-operation between the Parties, overseeing and supervising the implementation of Petroleum Operations and the compliance with Work Programmes and Approved Development and Production Plans, (the "Management Committee"). The Joint Operating Agreement shall establish the functions and the procedures of the Management Committee.'

[14] The Bangladesh 2023 PSC provides (at 30.1) that: 'The Parties shall make good faith efforts to settle amicably through consultation ... deadlocks in decisions of Joint Management Committee' and also (at 12.2.4) that: 'Where unanimous agreement cannot be reached despite discussion between Petrobangla and Contractor, the matter shall be promptly presented to the Secretary of the Energy and Mineral Resources Division of the Government of Bangladesh for consultation and the opinion of the Secretary shall be used to assist the Joint Management Committee to arrive at a unanimous decision.'

[15] The Suriname 2015 PSC provides (at 8.2.3) that: 'If the Operations Committee fails to reach a decision on disputed matters, then Contractor shall proceed with Petroleum Operations to fulfill its obligations, responsibilities, and duties under this Contract in accordance with good international oil field practices. Any Party may submit such matter to expert determination or to arbitration, as applicable, in accordance with Article 42.'

forward matters requiring the grantor's approval under the concession to the grantor outside of the management committee, and for this reason the real value of the management committee in conducting the business of a concession is sometimes questioned.

The terms of a concession may also be supplemented by further operational and administrative provisions which are to be agreed between a grantor and an investor.[16]

5.6 Transfers and Changes in Control

An investor party may change over time, through a transfer of its interests under the concession to another person. A concession will typically regulate the ability of an investor party to effect such a transfer. A mechanism in a concession which (by object or by effect) purports only to regulate a prospective transfer of interests by the investor as a single entity may be ineffective.[17]

A grantor is less likely to change over the lifetime of a concession (except perhaps in consequence of a wider sectoral regulatory reform programme).

A partial transfer of its concession interests by an investor party during the exploration period may enable the investor party to fund its remaining share of the exploration period costs (and the costs of any subsequent development project), and may also reduce the investor party's risk profile.

A transfer of interests by an investor party will typically be conditional upon a grantor's prior approval of the proposed transferee. A grantor may have unfettered approval rights in respect of the proposed transferee which could be applied in a grantor's absolute discretion.[18] Where a grantor has such rights the grantor may also take into account any unwritten political or other reservations which the grantor (or the wider state) might have in respect of the proposed transferee.[19]

[16] The Angola 2008 PSC provides (at 9) that: 'Sonangol and Contractor Group may sign a document (hereinafter referred to as "Petroleum Operations Procedures Document") which will regulate and interpret the contents of this Agreement, which shall be in accordance with the provisions of this Agreement and the Law.' The Mozambique 2006 EPC provides (at 34) that: 'It is understood that any written agreement which may at any time be concluded between the Concessionaire on the one hand and the Government on the other, as may be required or desired within the context of this EPC shall be deemed to have been approved to the same extent as if it was originally included in this EPC.'

[17] The Somalia 2023 PSA recognizes the distinction (at 43.1.3): 'In the event that the Contractor, or any entity making up the Contractor (the "Transferor") proposes to sell, assign, transfer or otherwise dispose of any part of its Participating Interest or any of its rights under this Agreement to any Person.'

[18] The Brazil 2017 PSA provides (at 30.1) that: 'The Contractors' rights and obligations under this Agreement may be subject to Assignment, in whole or in part, subject to the Contracting Party's prior authorization, based on ANPs' opinion.'

[19] As an example of how the grantor's concerns could be vocalized, the Pakistan 2000 PSA provides (at 7.2.3) that: 'The prospective assignee or transferee should not be a company incorporated in a country with which the Government for national security or policy reasons has restricted economic relations or which is known to be hostile or unfriendly.' The India 2010 PSC provides (at 28.1) the requirements which apply in respect of a proposed transfer of interests by an investor party to a third party: '[T]he prospective assignee or transferee is not a company incorporated in a country with which the Government, for policy reasons, has restricted trade or business' and that in respect of a proposed transfer of interests to an affiliate: 'the prospective Affiliate is not a company incorporated in a country with which the Government, for policy reason, has restricted trade or business,' and also that in either case: 'the assignment or transfer will not... be contrary to the interests of India.'

Alternatively, a grantor's approval rights may be qualified to apply only where a grantor has sustainable concerns regarding the financial and/or technical capability of the proposed transferee and its suitability as a replacement for the transferring investor party.[20]

Although it will not be spelled out in the terms of a concession, it is possible to conceive of a situation where a grantor's approval could be withheld for reasons relating to a grantor's desire to make changes to the terms of a concession, or to how a concession is being operated by an investor (which might be so where the grantor feels that the investor's historical performance has not met expectations). Equally, however, if this leverage is applied by a grantor then an investor might also have an interest in discussing changes to the terms of a concession, if those changes could also afford some benefit to the investor.

A concession might apply a less rigorous approval regime where an investor party wishes to transfer its interests to an affiliate (as the term 'affiliate' is defined in the concession or by reference to the governing law (11.2) of the concession). This could also include an affiliate of the grantor where a state participation right (10.8) has been exercised. This regime would apply for as long as the affiliate-transferee remains an affiliate of the transferring investor party. The transferring investor party may be required to assume continuing liability for the acts and omissions of the affiliate transferee as a condition of the transfer.

A transfer by an investor party of its interests under a concession does not equate to an automatic transfer of operatorship if the transferring investor party is also the appointed operator under a concession (5.5). A grantor will ordinarily reserve the right to approve a replacement operator, which might not be the proposed transferee.

A change of an investor party under a concession will usually also be mirrored by a change of the same person within the underlying joint venture arrangement, in the pursuit of continuing symmetry. A grantor's prior approval (or disapproval) of a proposed transferee under a concession could also have a bearing upon the approval process of the same transferee under the joint venture arrangement. Although a concession and a joint venture arrangement have different perspectives, in practice it may be difficult for a party to a joint venture arrangement to approve a proposed transferee which has been rejected by the grantor in respect of a concession, and equally for such a party to reject a proposed transferee which has been approved by the grantor in respect of a concession.

A concession may give a grantor (or its nominee) a pre-emptive right to acquire the interests of an investor party which are proposed to be transferred. If a grantor exercises this right it will have to be reconciled with the application of any pre-emption rights under a joint venture arrangement.[21]

[20] The Guyana 2023 PSA provides (at 27.4) that: 'Approval shall not be unreasonably withheld by the Minister. Consent shall be given where: ... the Assignee meets the qualification requirements set out by the Minister during the licensing round. These requirements include: i. financial competence; ii. technical competence; and iii. an established record of environmental, health, and safety compliance.'

[21] The Tanzania 2013 PSA provides (at 27) that: 'TPDC has the right of first refusal to acquire the participating interest that any member of Contractor Party intends to assign to a non-Affiliate' and that '[i]n the event of TPDC not exercising the right of first refusal referred to in the preceding paragraph, such right shall pass to any Affiliate of TPDC'.

A concession will rarely impose conditions upon the ability of a grantor to transfer its interests, although such conditions are not entirely unheard of.[22] A possible limitation which could apply is that a grantor can only transfer its interests to another state-owned entity.[23]

Where a state participation right exists within a concession (10.8) a grantor may be permitted to transfer that right to another person. Such a transfer might not be subject to an investor's approval, such that a grantor can freely transfer the state participation right.[24]

A transfer of interests under a concession by an investor party will usually be without prejudice to any accrued liabilities of the transferring investor party which have arisen under the concession. A transferring investor party will usually also be subject to a continuing liability to maintain any collateral support which it has procured in respect of its ongoing and prospective liabilities (5.4), unless adequate replacement collateral support has been procured by the proposed transferee, and the transferring investor party will also be subject to any continuing confidentiality obligations (11.8).

A transfer of interests under a concession by an investor party may trigger an exposure of the transferring investor party to pay some form of capital gains tax or transfer tax to the state if there has been some improvement in the value of the transferred interests (based on the positive difference between an assumed base cost of the transferred interests and the value of the transferred interests which is realized by the transfer).[25] These tax liabilities could be recited in a law of the state, or a concession could contain a mechanism which levies a bespoke contractual form of a capital gains tax.[26]

[22] The Somalia 2023 PSA provides (at 43.2.2) that: 'the Federal Government may not assign or otherwise transfer all or any of its rights, benefits or obligations hereunder without the Contractor's prior written consent (such consent not to be unreasonably withheld, delayed or conditioned) unless the Federal Government can satisfy the Contractor of such proposed assignee's status and ability to observe and perform the Agreement'.

[23] The Cameroon 2007 PSC provides (at 23.2) that: 'The STATE may assign all or part of its rights and obligations arising under this Contract ... to a government body or unit, provided that the latter remains bound by the terms of this Contract'.

[24] The Angola 2008 PSC provides (at 38.7) that: 'In the event of Sonangol not exercising the right of first refusal referred to in the preceding paragraph, such right shall pass to the associates of Sonangol which enjoy the status of national company as provided for in Article 31.3 of the Petroleum Activities Law.'

[25] The Afghanistan 2013 EPSC provides (at 16.7) that: 'Nothing contained in the Contract shall excuse or exempt the Contractor or any Contractor Entity (or any Affiliated Entity of a Contractor Entity) from any obligation that may otherwise exist under Afghanistan Law to pay any tax on the sale or transfer of any tangible or intangible property, including such Person's direct or indirect interest in this Contract or any asset owed by it directly or indirectly in whole or in part'. The Somalia 2023 PSA provides (at 42.1.7) that the contractor will pay 'the capital gains tax (at a rate of 20% of the difference between the (recoverable and non-recoverable Petroleum Costs incurred by an assignor and the total acquisition price to be paid by an assignee), which capital gains tax shall apply to both cash and non-cash based transfers of direct and indirect assignments or other transfers, but shall not apply to those within the same group of companies'.

[26] The Trinidad and Tobago 2023 PSC provides (at 31.6) that: 'For each assignment or Transfer made by any entity or entities comprising Contractor, the following rates shall apply to the amounts or value of the consideration: (a) For every dollar of the first One Hundred Million United States Dollars (US$100,000,000.00): 1% (b) For every dollar of the next One Hundred Million United States Dollars (US$100,000,000.00): 1.5% (c) For every dollar thereafter: 2%' and (at 31.10) that: 'The assignment or transfer amount payable under Article 31.6, shall be paid to the Minister within thirty (30) working days of notification of the amount payable to the Minister.' The Egypt 2021 concession agreement provides (at 9 (d)) that: 'CONTRACTOR shall pay to EGAS as an assignment bonus on the date of approval of each assignment requested by CONTRACTOR or any of the CONTRACTOR Members to any assignee pursuant to Article XXI, according to the following: (i) During any Exploration period, in case CONTRACTOR/ CONTRACTOR Member assigns in whole or in part of its rights, privileges, duties and obligations to any assignee other than an Affiliate Company of the same CONTRACTOR/CONTRACTOR Member, CONTRACTOR or CONTRACTOR Member, as the case may be, shall pay to EGAS the sum equivalent

A grantor could say that applying a liability to taxation in this circumstance is defensible because the improvement value of the transferred interests was generated by the incurrence of costs in the various stages of exploration, appraisal, and development into production which could later be reimbursable in favour of the investor party under a concession's fiscal terms (whether as cost recoverable items (9.3) or as tax-deductible expenses (9.5)), and so ultimately will be borne by the state. This notion also explains the provision which sometimes appears in a PSC in particular that the accrued petroleum costs pool which is available to an investor for cost recovery (9.3) will be reduced by the attributed value of any improvement in the transferred interests.[27] This allows a grantor to tax the transaction and improves the overall economics of the PSC from a grantor's perspective, but it could also lead to a debate between the transferring investor party and the proposed transferee as to how the incidence of this provision should be adjusted in their agreed purchase consideration.

A concession might also seek to legislate for what happens if an investor party undergoes a change in control during the term of a concession. Whilst the identity of the investor party in the concession will not change, a change in control could see an investor party becoming owned by a person in respect of whom a grantor has certain reservations.

What constitutes a change in control for these purposes may be defined in a concession (relating to how high into the corporate structure of an investor party the change in control is intended to go, and also to what circumstances of a purely internal investor party group reorganization would be disregarded).[28]

The change in control may need to be notified to a grantor and thereafter a concession may create a requirement for any of the approval of the change in control by a grantor[29] (which will not always be a tenable proposition, principally for commercial

to ten percent (10%), valued in U.S. Dollars, of the total Minimum Expenditure Obligations of the then current Exploration period during which the assignment is made and according to the assigned percentage. (ii) During the Development Period, in case CONTRACTOR/ CONTRACTOR Member assigns in whole or in part of its rights, privileges, duties and obligations to any assignee other than an Affiliate Company of the same CONTRACTOR/ CONTRACTOR Member, CONTRACTOR or CONTRACTOR Member, as the case may be, shall pay to EGAS the sum of ten percent (10%), valued in U.S. Dollars, of the value of each assignment deal whichever is applicable.'

[27] The Gabon 1995 PSC provides (at 42.3) that: 'If, due to partial assignment of its interest, the assignor earns a financial profit, this will be deducted from the Petroleum Costs' and that: 'For application of the preceding paragraph, the term "financial profit" refers to the difference, if positive, between the assignment price and the non-reevaluated amount of the Petroleum costs not yet recovered by the assignor and computed, in the case of partial assignment, proportionally to the percentage interests assigned'.

[28] The Sao Tome and Principe 2018 PSC provides (at 19.2) that the grantor's right to terminate the concession for an unapproved change in control 'does not apply if the change of Control is the direct result of an acquisition of shares or other securities of a publicly traded company on a recognized stock exchange'.

[29] The Bangladesh 2023 PSC provides (at 33.1) that: 'any party comprising the Contractor may enter into transaction which may result in change in the management or share or interest or ownership and/ or control of the Company(ies) or the relationship with any guarantor of the Company(ies) with prior written approval of the Government provided that the Government is satisfied on: a) Technical and Financial strength of the participating company (transferee); and b) Details of shareholder agreement'. The Somalia 2023 PSA provides (at 43.1.11) that: 'Any change of Control over one of the entities constituting the Contractor is, to the extent not already required by application of other provisions of this clause 43, subject to prior written approval by the SPA, which approval shall be granted within thirty (30) days of request. If the SPA has reasonable grounds for refusal (such to be notified to the Contractor), the SPA may refuse grant of approval within the same period of time. In case of expiry of the period of thirty (30) days following request to the SPA without the SPA either approving or refusing grant of approval, the approval shall be deemed granted by the SPA.'

and confidentiality reasons), a pre-emptive right of a grantor to acquire the interest of the investor party which has undergone the change in control (where, as is often the case, a concession is worded to treat a change in control as being equivalent to a direct transfer of an interest), or even a right of a grantor to terminate a concession against the investor party which has undergone the change in control (6.6).[30]

[30] The Afghanistan 2013 EPSC provides (at 2.1) that: 'The Ministry shall have the right to terminate this Contract only in respect of the relevant Contractor Entity upon notice to the relevant Contractor if, without the prior approval of the Council of Ministers and subsequent approval of the Ministry, such Contractor Entity shall, during the life of this Contract, undergo, directly or indirectly, a change of control (it being understood that for this purpose "control" of the Contractor Entity means the power, directly or indirectly, to direct or change its management or policies, whether through ownership of shares or other voting securities or by any other means).'

6
Scope and Duration

6.1 Introduction

A concession will identify the activities which are to be undertaken by an investor during its lifetime. The concession's scope is typically created as a list of permissible activities, often with the support of a list of expressly excluded activities, and performance of the concession's scope may entail the provision of certain assistance from a grantor.

A concession will have an intended duration, which (after signature of the concession) is typically broken up into defined exploration and production periods. Issues relating to the declaration of commerciality in respect of a discovery which is made by an investor, the development of a discovery, and how a marginal discovery is dealt with, will also be relevant to determining a concession's duration.

6.2 The Concession's Scope

A concession's scope reflects the objectives of a grantor (and of other state entities) in respect of the business of a concession. The concession will typically describe the activities to be undertaken by an investor, and the rights which an investor has and the obligations which an investor is subject to in undertaking those activities, in a provision which is sometimes described as a 'scope' or 'purpose' clause.[1] This is not always so. Some concessions outline the operational mechanics of the investor/grantor relationship, with the provisions which are considered below being located in various different places within the concession and not under a single provision which is described as a concession's scope.[2]

A concession's scope (however it is described) reflects the award to an investor of an exclusive right[3] to conduct petroleum operations in a concession area (7.2) for a concession's duration, typically with those operations to be conducted at the investor's sole risk and expense. This means that the investor will finance the entirety of each stage of the petroleum operations and will assume the risk of failure by not being reimbursed

[1] The Bangladesh 2023 production-sharing contract (PSC) (at 2) includes a provision headed 'Scope'.

[2] The Afghanistan 2013 exploration and production sharing contract (EPSC) takes such an approach.

[3] The Afghanistan 2013 EPSC provides (at 2.1) that: 'Subject to the terms and conditions set forth in this Contract, the Ministry grants to the Contractor the exclusive right to conduct Hydrocarbons Operations Within ... the Contract Area for the duration of this Contract'.

the costs of doing so by a grantor (or any other state entity) if the operations fail to discover or to produce petroleum in commercial quantities.

The phrase 'petroleum operations' will differ in meaning between concessions but it relates principally to the activities of petroleum exploration and appraisal, development and production (possibly also including the activities of petroleum processing, transportation, and storage), and the eventual decommissioning of the associated infrastructure.[4] A concession may also envisage the need for a further licence or lease to be awarded by a grantor (or by another state entity) for exploration, development, or production activities within a concession area.[5] Petroleum, which is an inherent part of the envisaged petroleum operations, will be defined in a concession, either expressly by reference to various forms of crude oil, natural gas, and liquids,[6] or indirectly by a law of the state which defines petroleum.[7]

Because the conduct of an activity by an investor which is beyond the concession's scope could lead variously to a liability of an investor to pay damages to a grantor for a breach of the concession (11.3), the irrecoverability of costs which have been incurred by an investor under a production-sharing contract (PSC) (9.3), or even the termination of the concession (6.6), the intended scope of the petroleum operations (including any specifically excluded activities) should be made clear in a concession. Improper definition, or application, of the concession's scope could become an issue where a grantor and an investor have been complicit in extending a concession's scope over time (to include matters such as the conduct of petroleum marketing and processing, midstream activities, or the development of midstream infrastructure), but without formally documenting these changes within the expressed ambit of the concession. Allowing the informal modification of a concession in this way may generate a constitutional basis for an investor's activities which could be called into question in the future.

The right which an investor enjoys to conduct petroleum operations might not be as exclusive as it first seems, since a concession may also apply a qualification to permit a grantor (or its nominee, or another state entity) to intervene to conduct its own activities (such as seismic surveys or wider exploration activity, or the development of

[4] The Bangladesh 2023 PSC provides (at 2.1) that: 'This is a Production Sharing Contract. The object of this Contract is for the Contractor to undertake the Exploration, Appraisal, Development and Production of Petroleum in the Contract Area at Contractor's sole risk and expense and subject to the right of the Government and Petrobangla to share in production according to the terms of Article 14.' The Qatar 2002 development and production sharing agreement (DPSA) relates only to the appraisal of discovered areas and subsequent development and production from those areas, with no provision for exploration by the investor. The definition of 'petroleum operations' (at 1.1.85) covers 'any and all operations carried out by or on behalf of the CONTRACTOR pursuant to this Agreement for the purposes of appraising, developing, producing, collecting, treating, processing, storing and transporting Petroleum from the Contract Location to the respective Delivery Points in the State of Qatar.'

[5] See the Zanzibar 2024 production sharing agreement (PSA) (at 3 (a) and 8 (j)), and the India 2010 PSC (at 11.2).

[6] The Somalia 2023 PSA provides (at 1) that: '"Petroleum" means all hydrocarbons (including Crude Oil and Natural Gas), whether capable of being produced from conventional and unconventional Reservoirs, including shale oil, oil shale, shale gas, coal bed methane gas, tar sands, and other sources of hydrocarbon reserves.'

[7] The Guyana 2023 PSA provides (at 1.1) that: 'The definitions in Section 2 of the Act are incorporated into this Agreement and, as a result, shall serve all purposes and effects' (and the Act in question includes a definition of petroleum).

mineral interests other than petroleum) within a concession area.[8] This qualification may be subject to the condition that a grantor's activities will not interfere with the investor's rights or obligations.[9]

What might be included within a concession's scope can also be determined by what is necessary in practice for an investor to be able to produce commercial quantities of petroleum. Thus a concession's scope might include the investor's construction and/or operation of roads, pipelines, storage facilities, and port facilities if such infrastructure items are required.[10] On the other hand, ancillary activities and infrastructure items may be excluded from a concession's scope.[11]

A concession's scope may be defined (in part, or substantially so) by reference to the incorporation of the terms of a law of the state by which an investor will be bound, which contains certain relevant provisions which might not be set out at length in the concession.[12] This approach helps to create a series of standards which are consistent across all the concessions which incorporate such a reference.

A concession's scope may also be defined by reference to a number of obligations which are required to be performed by a grantor, in support of an investor's obligations. These obligations might relate to a general commitment by a grantor to offer assistance to an investor in managing the business of a concession (including in respect of an investor's dealings with other state entities) or to more specific expectations such as a grantor's obligation to issue or to procure the issue of certain permits necessary for the performance of the petroleum operations, to procure access and egress rights for an investor in respect of land belonging to other persons, or to make land available to an investor for the development of any necessary facilities. Beyond such assistances a

[8] The Somalia 2023 PSA provides (at 14.1.3) that: 'The Contractor has been granted the right, subject to Law, to freely access and operate within the Contract Area any facilities associated with Petroleum Operations and to perform or cause to be performed any infrastructure work required for carrying out, under normal economic conditions, Petroleum Operations and related activities, such as transportation and storage of equipment and substances extracted, establishment of equipment of telecommunications and lines of communication, as well as production and supply of energy required for Petroleum Operations on the basis that: 14.1.3.1 Permission may be granted to other Persons to search for and mine minerals, other than Petroleum, so long as they do not unreasonably interfere with the Petroleum Operations, and 14.1.3.2 Easements and rights of way may be granted to other Persons for the benefit of land adjacent to the Contract Area.'

[9] The Afghanistan 2013 EPSC provides (at 5.6 (c)) that: 'The Ministry shall use its reasonable efforts to ensure that operations of third parties do not obstruct or interfere with the Hydrocarbons Operations within the Contract Area.'

[10] The Senegal 2012 PSC provides (at 3.2) that: 'Subject to the Minister's authorization, which shall not unreasonably be withheld, the Contractor shall have the right to build at its own expense all facilities necessary to the Oil Operations and in particular, but not limited to, any roads, pipelines, storage facilities, port facilities, both inside and outside the Contract Area.' The Bangladesh 2023 PSC provides (at 16.1) that: 'Contractor shall have the right to construct and to operate one or more Pipeline(s) or alternative transportation facilities within or from the Contract Area to one or more points in Bangladesh for the purpose of transporting Petroleum, from any Production Area to Measurement Point(s) in Bangladesh, at Contractor's option or jointly with other parties. For the purpose of this Contract, a Pipeline shall include related facilities.'

[11] The Turkmenistan 1997 PSA provides (at 15.4) that: 'Should a new Main Pipeline for Petroleum export be considered for construction as technically appropriate and economically viable, it is envisaged by the Parties hereto that the construction, financing, operation and maintenance of the new Main Pipeline (the "New Main Pipeline"), pumping stations and related terminal facilities shall be carried out through a separate pipeline company (the "Pipeline Company") and, as such, shall not be included within the meaning of Petroleum Operations under this Agreement and any related Licences.'

[12] The Guyana 2023 PSA provides (at 2.1) that: 'This Agreement constitutes an agreement made under Section 12 of the Act consistent with the Act and the Regulations.'

grantor may be reluctant to expose its own capital to the risky business of petroleum exploration (unless doing so is effected as part of a state participation exercise (10.8) or is undertaken as an exclusive operation (10.7)). A limited exception to this is where a grantor has undertaken to fund the preparation of a multi-client survey (10.5) which may be relevant to a concession.

It is also a basic expectation of a concession that a grantor will review and approve the various submissions which are made by an investor in accordance with the requirements of a concession. A concession may provide for a grantor to charge certain administrative fees to an investor for doing so.[13] A grantor might defend this proposition on the basis that the state has a nascent petroleum economy which lacks the funds to apply a competent administrative function without the assistance of such an imposition, but this proposition will not have the capacity for infinite application as the petroleum economy matures.[14]

It is arguable that a fully defined scope of permitted activities in a concession, accompanied by the implication that any other activities are thereby excluded, make it unnecessary for a concession to then go on to describe any activities which are intended to be excluded from the scope.[15] Despite that, a concession might choose also to list certain activities which are excluded from its professed scope.

These excluded activities may relate to the investor's conduct of anything other than the defined petroleum operations in the concession area, and to the investor's exploration for or the production by the investor of mineral interests other than petroleum from the concession area. The excluded activities could also reference the conduct of activities by the investor outside the concession area, and to activities and investments which take place beyond a defined point (which is sometimes defined in a concession as a delivery point), such as petroleum refining, petroleum marketing, and petroleum transportation which is not a direct part of the petroleum operations.[16]

A concession's scope (as it is established by the permitted activities and, possibly, also qualified by the excluded activities) may need to be further modified in certain circumstances as a result of the performance of certain petroleum operations (such as by what might be needed to facilitate the development of a gas commercialization project (13.3)).

[13] The Turkmenistan 1997 PSA provides (at 6.1.2) that the contractor will be subject to 'the obligation to pay compensation and dues to the Government (or its agencies) and to Competent Body in return for specific services or facilities rendered in favour of Contractor'.

[14] The Somalia 2019 PSA provides (at 13.3.1) that: 'The Contractor has the obligation to pay the following administrative fees to the Ministry of Petroleum for approvals or decisions by the Minister of Petroleum when submitting the requests for such approvals and decisions.' This formulation was dispensed with in the Somalia 2023 PSA.

[15] The Gambia 2022 licence provides (at 2.3) a positive statement of the investor's obligations without the addition of excluded items.

[16] The Somalia 2023 PSA provides (at 2.3) that: 'The Contractor is not authorised to carry out Petroleum Operations in any part of Somalia outside the Contract Area', and (at 2.4) that: 'The Agreement does not authorise the Contractor to conduct Petroleum Operations beyond the Delivery Point.'

6.3 The Concession's Duration

A concession will define when it comes into effect between the parties, how long it is intended to subsist for, and how and when it will come to an end.

A concession will be entered into (principally[17]) between a grantor and an investor but it is possible that a concession might be signed but stated only to be fully effective between the parties when a number of defined conditions precedent have been satisfied or waived. Conditions precedent are not universal in concessions,[18] and the more likely route is that the items which could otherwise be cast as conditions precedent are addressed between the parties before signature of the concession takes place, or as matters to be attended to (within certain time periods) after signature of the concession. These items may relate to the following matters:

(1) The provision of collateral support in respect of the costs of performing an investor's exploration period obligations under a concession (8.2) (which may come into force simultaneously with the signature of the concession).
(2) An investor's payment of a signature bonus (9.4) or other monetary amount which is due under a concession (which could be made simultaneously with the signature of the concession).
(3) The entry by the investor parties into a joint venture arrangement between themselves (5.3) (which may come into force simultaneously with the signature of the concession) or the approval of the joint venture arrangement by a grantor (which could take place prior to the signature of the concession).

It may also be a requirement that some form of state ratification is necessary in respect of a concession once it has been entered into between the parties. Notwithstanding the signature of the concession, it would only become legally effective between the parties after that ratification has been secured.[19] Such ratification could be a condition precedent or a condition subsequent to the full effectiveness of the concession.

A concession will subsist from the concession's signature date (or later its effective date) until the eventual date of termination of the concession. In the longest case (and subject to possible extension or renewal—see below) a concession could terminate upon the expiry of a defined production period (6.5) and when decommissioning (8.5) has thereafter been completed (although the reality of the unpredictability of depletion

[17] See note 3, Chapter 5.

[18] The Somalia 2019 PSA (at 3.1) creates conditions precedent relating to an investor's payment of the signature bonus and first-year rentals, and to the provision of collateral support by an investor. In the Somalia 2023 PSA the first two of these conditions precedent were dispensed with. The Turkmenistan 1997 PSA provides (at 33.1) for the creation of conditions precedent relating to legal registration of the PSA and to the further issue of an exploration licence.

[19] The Cyprus 2007 PSC provides (at 24) that: 'This Contract shall become effective upon the date on which it is approved by the Council of Ministers, such date herein referred to as the Effective Date, and this Contract shall then be binding for the Parties.'

by production and the permanent cessation of production means that a concession may come to an end before the scheduled end of a production period).

A concession will typically recite two particular time periods—the exploration period and the production period (see below)—which are internal to a concession's duration. Woven into those time periods are the activities of exploration and appraisal (8.2) and development and production (8.4), for which certain defined periods of time for the conduct of the relevant activities by an investor are specified. All of these internal time periods may be capable of further extension individually, and such extensions will extend a concession's overall duration. The overall term of a concession could also be extended on a day-for-day basis because of the occurrence of a force majeure event (11.5).

A gas discovery could bring its own durational requirements to a concession, in recognition of the reality that it can take additional time for an investor to develop a market for the gas (13.3).

Whilst the different phases of activity which are envisaged by a concession in the performance of the petroleum operations are ostensibly sequential, they are not exclusive of each other. Depending upon how a concession is applied (and unless the concession governs a single asset development) the activities of exploration, appraisal, development, production, and even decommissioning could all be occurring at the same time in different parts of a concession area during the term of a concession.[20] This means that the end of the production period and the completion of the associated decommissioning in one part of a concession area will not signal the end of the concession if petroleum exploration or production is continuing in another part of the concession area (although the relinquishment of a concession area (7.6) could limit the conduct of simultaneous activities).

A concession may be extended towards the end of its scheduled term, to allow for continued petroleum production by an investor. It is possible for the extension of an existing concession to be distinct from a renewal of the grantor/investor relationship through the grant of a fresh concession in respect of the same concession area. The true distinction between extension and renewal can sometimes become blurred, depending on the manner in which the underlying transaction is documented and effected. A systemic lack of flexibility by a grantor in allowing the possibility of the extension or the renewal of concessions towards the end of their lifetimes could stifle the appetite of investors to make further investments (such as more exploration drilling or production enhancements) which those investors might not be around to see the benefit of, and could be damaging to the effective exploitation of the state's patrimony over the longer term.

The extension or the renewal of a concession will typically be a matter for further agreement between the parties, rather than being applied as an automatic right.[21]

[20] The Ethiopia 2011 PSC recognizes (at 2.1.1) that: 'This Agreement shall consist of an Exploration Period, and a Development and a Production Period, both of which may run concurrently.'

[21] The Qatar 2002 DPSA provides (at 4.2) that: 'Either Party shall have the right, upon at least eighteen (18) months notice to the other Party prior to the expiry of the term of this Agreement, to make a request for an extension to the term of this Agreement for a period not to exceed five (5) years. Any such request shall be given due

This further agreement between the parties may necessitate a consideration of whether the same definition of a concession area will continue to apply, and whether any modification of the fiscal terms (9.1), or any of the other terms of the concession, is required. The extension or the renewal of a concession can also trigger a liability of an investor to pay a further signature bonus (9.4).

An investor may also require that the extension or the renewal of a PSC will not eliminate the investor's accrued but unrecovered cost pool (9.3).[22]

6.4 The Exploration Period

The exploration period is a defined period of time during which an investor is required to perform the exploration obligations which are defined in the concession (8.2), which could include the associated activity of appraisal in respect of a discovery. The exploration period generally starts on a defined day after the date when the concession becomes effective between the parties. Performance of the exploration period obligations by an investor may be preceded by the conduct of an environmental assessment and/or a social impact assessment[23] which will consume part of the exploration period.

consideration by the other Party, taking account of relevant circumstances, including, the fact that the Facilities may continue to be technically viable and that long term demand for the supply of Petroleum may continue to exist. Any extension of the term of this Agreement (after such due consideration by the Parties) shall be on such terms and conditions as the GOVERNMENT and the CONTRACTOR may agree.' The Suriname 2015 PSC provides (at 3.7) that: 'On expiration of this Contract, the Parties may negotiate the terms and conditions of a revised agreement with respect to the Contract Area or part of it, if they wish to continue Petroleum Operations. Failure to reach an agreement shall not give rise to a dispute and shall not be subjected to arbitration in accordance with Article 42 and marks the end of the Contract.'

[22] The Nigeria 2021 PSC (which was a renewal of an existing PSC) provides (at 5.2) that: 'From the Effective Date, the CONTRACTOR shall continue the conduct of petroleum operations commenced under the 1993 PSC in accordance with the terms of this Contract.'

[23] The Afghanistan 2013 EPSC provides (at 6.2) that: 'As soon as practicable following the Effective Date and prior to commencing any Exploration Operations that would be subject to review under the applicable environmental laws of Afghanistan, the Contractor shall carry out a Baseline Environmental Assessment to determine the then prevailing situation relating to the environment in the portion of the Contract Area where the Contractor intends to commence Exploration Operations' and also (at 6.3) that: 'As soon as practicable following the Effective Date and prior to commencing any Exploration Operations, the Contractor shall prepare and submit to the Ministry for approval a Social Impact Assessment relating to communities in or immediately adjacent to the portion of the Contract Area where the Contractor intends to commence Exploration Operations.' For these purposes 'Baseline Environmental Assessment' means 'a report containing a description of the environment in the subject area prior to the commencement of Hydrocarbons Operations, including the then existing flora and fauna, soil, air quality, underground and surface water, landscape aesthetics, farming conditions, and socio-economic conditions in local communities', and 'Social Impact Assessment' means a report 'assessing the probable impacts on affected communities of proposed Exploration Operations or Development and Production Operations, as applicable, including mitigation strategies and plans for community engagement and development, benefit sharing, labor welfare, resettlement and rehabilitation, and resolution of grievances.' The Bangladesh 2023 EPC provides (at 36.5) that: 'The Contractor shall cause a person or persons with special knowledge on environmental matters, to carry out two environmental impact studies in order: (a) to determine at the time of the studies the prevailing situation relating to the environment, human beings and local communities, the flora and fauna in the Contract Area and in the adjoining or neighboring areas; and (b) to establish the likely effect on the environment, human beings and local communities, the flora and fauna in the Contract Area and in the adjoining or neighboring areas in consequence of the relevant phase of Petroleum Operations to be conducted under this Contract, and to submit, for consideration by the Parties for minimizing Environmental Damage and carrying out Site Restoration activities.'

An investor ideally wants the longest possible exploration period, so that it can schedule its performance of the exploration period obligations at its own pace and with the greatest amount of flexibility. On the other hand, a grantor will prefer that the concession contains a shorter exploration period, so that the investor can make an early assessment of the prospectivity of the acreage and can proceed to the possible relinquishment and re-awarding of some part of the concession area (7.6). In between these two objectives the exploration period must, at a minimum, be of sufficient duration to allow an investor to properly perform the exploration period obligations. And an investor may also require that a concession will take account of seasonal and weather conditions which apply to the concession area—year-round exploration activities might be impossible to achieve, depending upon where they are to be performed.

The starting point for the overall duration of the exploration period can (depending on how a concession is structured) be between four and twelve years but the exploration period is rarely described as being a single period of time. Rather, the exploration period will consist of a number of sequential fixed time periods (commonly known as 'exploration phases'), which may be of equal duration. Alternatively the exploration period may be structured as a longer initial exploration phase, followed by a series of shorter extension phases, exercisable at an investor's option (and where the surrender of a concession (6.6) could result if an option to trigger a further extension phase is not exercised by an investor).[24]

However the exploration period is structured within a concession, an extension to an exploration phase may be allowed by a grantor to facilitate the completion of the drilling and the appraisal of an exploration well which has been commenced but not completed within an exploration phase. This allows the exploration well to be completed and the results shared with the grantor and analysed between the parties as a precursor to further activity by the investor.

A particular flexibility which might be engineered in a concession is a right for an investor to accelerate the commencement of the next scheduled exploration phase within the exploration period if the investor has completed its applicable obligations, thereby enabling the investor to complete its exploration period obligations as soon as possible. It is not typically the case that a grantor has such an acceleration right, since its exercise could unduly prejudice the investor's interests.

The exploration period (and the timings of the exploration phases) may be fixed and absolute, or they may each be capable of being extended on a day-for-day basis because of the occurrence of a force majeure event (7.5).[25]

[24] The Bangladesh 2023 PSC provides (at 4.1) that: 'The Exploration Period shall be for a period of maximum nine (9) consecutive Contract Years from the Effective Date, consist of Initial Exploration Period and Subsequent Exploration Period. The Initial Exploration Period shall be for six (6) consecutive Contract Years and Subsequent Exploration Period shall be for three (3) consecutive Contract Years' and that: 'If the Minimum Exploration Program consists of only Geological and Geophysical survey with no commitment for exploration drilling, the Initial Exploration Period shall be limited to four (4) consecutive Contract Years.'

[25] The Suriname 2015 PSC provides (at 3.3) that: 'In case of unforeseen delays which are not an event of Force Majeure, Contractor may, at least sixty (60) Days prior to the expiration of any phase of the Exploration Period, request Staatsolie to extend the duration of such phase for a maximum of one (1) Calendar Year in order to complete ongoing drilling operations.'

A concession typically precludes an investor from performing any of the petroleum operations (including exploration) without first having acquired certain permits and approvals from a grantor (or from other state entities). The time taken to secure these permits and approvals may consume part of the exploration period (unless the exploration period is timed to start only when the permits and approvals have been secured by the investor). The exploration period may be extended in the investor's favour if these permits and approvals are not forthcoming in a timely manner. The frustration of the investor's intent in this regard may also be the subject of a claim for force majeure relief.

In some concessions the phrase 'exploitation period' is applied to describe whatever happens after the exploration period has concluded, with that phrase being intended to encompass the activities of development and production.

6.5 Development and the Production Period

'Development' describes the steps which are taken by an investor to promote a commercial discovery (8.3), through the design, installation, commissioning, and operation of the assets or equipment which are needed for the production of petroleum, as a precursor to the commencement of production.

'Production' describes the production of petroleum in commercial quantities from a developed discovery. A concession may identify a particular development period, as a defined period of time in which an investor will undertake the development activity under a concession, but such a development period may also be part of the production period.

A concession will typically recite a defined period of time in which an investor is authorized to effect the production of petroleum from a developed discovery. The production period can be for any period between 10 and 30 years. From an investor's perspective (or, more likely, to reflect the requirements of an investor's lenders) a lengthy production period could be necessary to enable an investor to secure an adequate return on its often significant level of capital investment.

It is not axiomatic that the production period will start only when the production of petroleum in commercial quantities commences. The production period typically starts earlier in time—which could be as far back as when an investor's declaration of a commercial discovery is approved by a grantor (8.3) or to when a field development plan (8.4) is approved by a grantor. In either case these approvals will be forthcoming some time prior to the actual start of the production of petroleum. It is from such an earlier point in time that the clock will start to run on an investor's production period, and for this reason an investor will want the production period to be as long as possible because it also has to encompass development activities.

The commencement of the production period will also not bring the exploration period to an end. A grantor and/or an investor may still wish to continue exploration in the remainder of a concession area, notwithstanding the making of an early discovery in the concession area which is capable of moving into production.

An issue to consider is what happens where there is still viable petroleum production taking place from a concession area at the point when a concession is due to end naturally at the end of a scheduled production period. An investor may require a right to continue the production period beyond its scheduled end,[26] and this is particularly likely in the case of what has been a relatively short production period to begin with.

Such a right of continuation is unlikely to be awarded automatically to an investor (particularly where there has been a relatively long production period), because a grantor might at that time prefer to see a concession come to an end and the concession area be taken over by the grantor (or its nominee)[27] or be re-awarded through a fresh concession.[28] This fresh concession would essentially be a concession for continued production only, and it could trigger the liability of an investor to pay a further signature bonus (9.4).

6.6 Surrender, Termination, and Suspension

A concession may contain a right for an investor to surrender the concession at any time. Although described as a surrender, this is effectively a unilateral termination right for an investor.[29] An investor may choose to surrender a concession for economic reasons (principally, because the exploration period activities have failed to make a discovery) or for strategic reasons (such as where the imposition of sanctions makes it untenable for an investor to maintain the concession, or where an investor is effecting a wider withdrawal from the petroleum business).

[26] The Bangladesh 2023 PSC provides (at 4.6) that: 'If Commercial Production of an Oil Field or Gas Field remains possible beyond the applicable term specified in Article 4.5, Petrobangla may grant the Contractor an additional ten (10) years extension on terms and conditions to be mutually agreed between Petrobangla and Contractor.'

[27] The Suriname 2015 PSC provides (at 3.6.3) that: 'Contractor may, upon at least three hundred and sixty-five (365) Days prior notice to Staatsolie, elect to abandon a Commercial Field. Within one hundred eighty (180) Days of receipt of Contractor's notice, Staatsolie may, upon notice to Contractor, elect to assume responsibility for such Commercial Field. In such case, Contractor shall, acting as a reasonable and prudent Operator, transfer and deliver the Commercial Field and all associated facilities to Staatsolie in working order and as a going concern ("as is, where is").'

[28] The Suriname 2015 PSC provides (at 8.2.3) that: 'On expiration of this Contract, the Parties may negotiate the terms and conditions of a revised agreement with respect to the Contract Area or part of it, if they wish to continue Petroleum Operations. Failure to reach an agreement shall not give rise to a dispute and shall not be subjected to arbitration in accordance with Article 42 and marks the end of the Contract.'

[29] The Tajikistan 2008 PSC provides (at 29.1) that: 'At any time, if in the opinion of Contractor, circumstances do not warrant continuation of the Petroleum Operations, Contractor may, by giving written notice to that effect to the Ministry, relinquish its rights and be relieved of its obligations pursuant to this Contract, except such rights and obligations as related to the period prior to such relinquishment.' The Ethiopia 2011 PSC provides (at 2.5.1) that: 'The Contractor may terminate this Agreement by giving the Minister one hundred eighty (180) days prior written notice. A surrender of all the area included in the Contract Area shall constitute a termination of this Agreement.'

A concession may provide that an investor's surrender right will not apply for a defined period (such as until the full duration of the exploration period has passed and all of the requisite obligations have been performed by an investor according to the terms of the concession), where a grantor wishes to lock in an investor for a defined period of time.[30]

An investor's surrender of a concession will typically be effected without prejudice to any accrued or contingent liabilities of the investor and without prejudice to the investor's obligation to procure and to maintain collateral support (5.4) for certain of its ongoing obligations (such as the anticipated costs of decommissioning (8.5)).

The relinquishment by an investor of the entirety of the concession area will also lead to the effective termination of a concession by a form of surrender, subject to the ongoing legacy issues which arise as a consequence of relinquishment (7.6).

Termination of a concession could otherwise arise by the natural expiry of its scheduled duration, or by mutual agreement between the parties, or by the act of one of the parties which is entitled to terminate the concession because of the occurrence of a defined event. Such events include the following:

(1) A concession may be terminated by one party because of the other party's unremedied breach of a term of the concession (where a definition of the breach includes the failure of a party to make a monetary payment when due). This termination right may apply only in favour of a grantor in respect of a breach by an investor or it may apply equally in respect of a breach by a grantor.[31] This event may be subject to a test of materiality in respect of the alleged breach (and whether or not a breach is material for these purposes could become the subject of a dispute between the parties where a concession does not define such materiality).

(2) A concession may be terminated by a grantor where it requires an investor to ensure that the information which was provided in a licensing round which led to the award of a concession (2.5) was accurate and that information is subsequently proved not to be so.[32]

[30] The Uganda 1999 PSC provides (at 3.4) that: 'Licensee, on giving to the Government not less than ninety (90) days notice in writing (the "Surrender notice"), may ... Surrender its rights and be relieved of its obligations in respect of the whole of the Contract Area if its minimum work and financial obligations under Article 4 hereof in respect of the relevant Exploration Period have been fulfilled in accordance with Section 51 of the Act'. The Suriname 2015 PSC provides (at 3.2.2) that: 'Contractor shall have the right to withdraw from this Contract at the end of each phase of the Exploration Period, provided that, subject to Sub-Article 5.4, the Minimum Work Obligations for such phase have been fulfilled'.

[31] The Qatar 2002 DPSA provides (at 30.2) that: 'the CONTRACTOR shall have the right to terminate this Agreement by notice to the GOVERNMENT if the GOVERNMENT fails to fulfil any of the GOVERNMENT'S material obligations under this Agreement and such failure has a material and adverse effect on the rights of the CONTRACTOR under this Agreement'. The Somalia 2023 PSA provides (at 39.3.1) that: 'Subject to the provisions of the Act and clause 39.3.2, the Contractor may terminate the Agreement by giving the Federal Government written notice: 39.3.1.1 if the Federal Government fails to make a material payment to the Contractor (if any), as required under the Agreement for a period exceeding thirty (30) days from the date of such payment became due; or 39.3.1.2 if the Federal Government is in material breach of any other obligation under the Act, Regulations or the Agreement not remedied within ninety (90) days after notice from the Contractor giving reasonable details of the breach by Federal Government and demanding remedy thereof'.

[32] In the Suriname 2015 PSC the recitals observe that: 'Contractor represents that it possesses the financial ability, technical competence and professional skills necessary to perform operations for the Exploration,

(3) A concession may be terminated by a grantor as a reaction to an investor's insolvency (or, more likely, as a reaction to the insolvency of an individual investor party). 'Insolvency' for this purpose will be determined according to a defined statutory test.

(4) A concession may be terminated by a grantor in respect of a particular investor party because of a change in control of that investor party which was not notified to or approved by the grantor in accordance with the requirements of the concession (5.6).

(5) A concession may be terminated (by either party or by the affected party) because of a prolonged period of force majeure (11.5) affecting the concession.[33]

(6) A concession may be terminated automatically or by a grantor where the exploration period (8.2) has elapsed and all of the requisite obligations have been performed by an investor according to the terms of the concession but either no discovery has been made or there has been no declaration of commerciality made in respect of a discovery (8.3).[34] In practical terms the same effect could be achieved in this circumstance by an investor's surrender of a concession but these actions might be rights rather than obligations to which an investor is subject, and a more predictive termination provision might be preferred by a grantor.

(7) A concession may be terminated by one party because of the other party's failure to comply with the terms of an arbitral award or a court judgment which has been made in respect of the concession.[35]

Development, Production, transportation and marketing of petroleum and is prepared to utilize such technical competence and financial ability as is necessary to fulfill its obligations under this Contract'. In the Trinidad and Tobago 2023 PSC the recitals observe that: 'AND WHEREAS, Contractor submitted a bid on the day of 20 ... AND WHEREAS, Contractor has represented to the Minister that it has the requisite technical and financial capabilities to carry out Petroleum Operations and wishes to assist the Government in thoroughly evaluating the Petroleum potential and promptly and efficiently developing Petroleum discovered in the Contract Area. AND WHEREAS, the Ministry selected the Contractor as the preferred bidder for Block .... and entered into negotiations with the Contractor to finalize the terms and conditions of the Production Sharing Contract.' In the Zanzibar 2004 PSA (at 4 (d)) the grantor has a termination right if the Contractor '[d]oes not have the necessary technical competence or financial capacity or professional skill to adequately perform the Contractor's duties and obligations under the Act and this Agreement' and also if the Contractor did '[i]ntentionally submit false information to the Government, ZPRA or ZPDC'. The Pakistan 2000 PSA provides (at 7.4 (c)) for a termination right in favour of the grantor if 'Contractor has knowingly provided false information to the Government which was in any manner a material consideration in the execution of this Agreement'. Similar provision exists in the India 2010 PSC (at 30.3) and in the Afghanistan 2013 EPSC (at 25.4 (a)).

[33] The Somalia 2023 PSA provides (at 38.5) that: 'If the performance of an obligation is suspended due to Force Majeure for more than sixty (60) months, either Party may terminate the Agreement by notice in writing to the other Party, without further obligation.' The Afghanistan 2013 EPSC provides (at 30) that: 'If this Contract is subject to Force Majeure for more than ninety-six (96) consecutive Months, either the Ministry or the Contractor shall have the right, upon notice to the other, to terminate this Contract with respect to the part or parts of the Contract Area affected.' The Trinidad and Tobago 2023 PSC provides (at 34.4) that: 'Contractor may terminate this Contract upon a three (3) month written notice to the Minister if the fulfilment of the obligation of either Party under this Contract is affected by Force Majeure during the Exploration Period or any extension thereof for a continuous period exceeding three (3) years without further obligation and liabilities of any kind.'

[34] The Suriname 2015 PSC provides (at 40.2.2) for termination 'if Contractor does not submit an application for the declaration of a Commercial Field pursuant to Sub-Article 10.3, at the end of the Exploration Period, unless otherwise agreed to by Staatsolie.'

[35] The Suriname 2015 PSC provides (at 40.3.4) for termination 'upon failure of Contractor to comply with any final decisions from any arbitration proceeding conducted pursuant to Article 42.'

A concession is unlikely to allow for its termination at any time at the convenience of a grantor, since to do so is effectively an act of expropriation (11.6).

Termination of a concession by a grantor will require careful consideration where the termination event complained of (such as an unremedied breach, an insolvency event, or a change in control) is relevant only in respect of one of the investor parties and not in respect of an investor as a single entity. Termination of the concession would be unwelcome to those investor parties who were innocent of the termination event. This issue could be addressed by provision in a concession that termination applies only in respect of a particular investor party and not in respect of an investor as a whole.[36] This then necessitates the consideration of a further issue—what happens to the interests of the terminated investor party? The concession may be silent on this, or it may provide that the interests revert to the grantor, or it may provide that the interests are to be reallocated between the other investor parties pro rata to their existing interests.[37]

The termination provisions in a concession will usually provide that the fact of termination is without prejudice to any accrued or contingent liabilities of the parties (where a concession might also provide for some apportionment (by reference to the effective termination date) of annualized costs (such as rentals (9.4) and training costs (10.2)). It will be a matter for provision in the concession as to whether an investor party should be obliged to pay its share of the exploration period obligations costs (8.2) which are unexpended at the effective date of termination.

Termination of a concession will also trigger the automatic termination of any ancillary exploration, development, or production lease or licence (6.2), and may also trigger an obligation of an investor to transfer assets or equipment which have been used in the performance of the petroleum operations to a grantor (10.4).

A concession might provide that where it is producing petroleum at the time of its termination, a grantor can elect to continue with the concession in its own name[38] or that, despite its termination, the investor will continue to produce petroleum and will

[36] The Uganda 1999 PSC provides (at 27.6) that: '[W]here, in respect of a liability which is a several liability, one or some only of the persons constituting Licensee is in breach of the provisions hereof or has so failed in compliance ... or ... where the bankruptcy, liquidation or composition relates to one or some only of the persons constituting Licensee ... the Government ... may, upon giving thirty (30) days written notice of its intention to do so, terminate the Participating or Joint Venture Interest herein, and in any related Licences, of the person or persons in breach, or which have failed in compliance, or, as the case may be, have become bankrupt, gone into liquidation or made a composition as aforesaid ("the Defaulting Party") but nothing in this paragraph shall affect the rights and obligations of any other person who constitutes Licensee which shall remain in full force and effect.'

[37] The Afghanistan 2013 EPSC provides (at 25.10) that: 'If the Contract is terminated ... the Participating Interest of the terminated Contractor Entity shall be transferred to the other Contractor Entities in the proportions which their Participating Interests bear to the aggregate of the Participating Interests of all such Contractor Entities (unless otherwise agreed by the Contractor Entities).' The Sao Tome and Principe 2018 PSC provides (at 20.4) that: 'Where this Contract is terminated with respect to only one Contractor Party, the State shall have the option to assume the interests, rights and obligations of such defaulting Contractor Party under this Contract. If the State elects not to exercise this option, the interests, rights and obligations shall be assigned to the remaining Contractor Parties who shall be liable jointly and severally.'

[38] The Pakistan 2000 PSA provides (at 7.13) that: 'Where any Gaseous or Liquid Reservoir is capable of continued Commercial Production upon the termination of this Agreement, GHPL may at its sole discretion elect to: (a) negotiate a new production sharing agreement with respect to Contract Area, or (b) take over Petroleum Operations of the Contract Area.'

otherwise continue to perform the concession until alternative provision has been made for the continuation of the petroleum operations (whether by the grantor or by another person).[39] The termination provisions in a concession may also include a mechanism for final accounting between a grantor and an investor,[40] and also for some form of handover of the business of the concession from an investor to a grantor.[41]

It should be evident that if the concession is a PSC and the PSC is terminated at a time when an investor has accrued but unrecovered petroleum costs (9.3) then those costs will be lost to the investor, but this point should be made clear in the PSC.[42] This position is understandable where the PSC has been terminated for an investor's default, but could be difficult for an investor to accept where the PSC has been terminated against the grantor by the investor.

Suspension of the operation of a concession because of the occurrence of an event of force majeure is possible (B7.5). A concession may also give a grantor a right to suspend the operation of a concession, which would apply, for example, where a grantor has health, safety, or environmental concerns relating to the performance of the petroleum operations or concerns about the risk of reputational damage to the grantor (or the state) by the continued operation of the concession, or where an event has occurred which would generate a right of a grantor to terminate the concession. The grantor may then proceed to terminate the concession if an event which led to the grantor's suspension is still continuing after the end of a defined suspension period.

[39] The Afghanistan 2013 EPSC provides (at 25.6) that: 'In the event of termination or revocation . . . the Ministry may require the Contractor, for a period not to exceed one hundred eighty (180) Days from the effective date of termination, to continue, for the account of the Ministry, Liquid Hydrocarbons or Natural Gas production activities until the right to continue such production has been transferred to another entity.'

[40] The Sao Tome and Principe 2018 PSC provides (at 20.6) that: 'Without prejudice to all other rights of the State, the Contractor shall upon the termination of this Contract permit inspection, copying and auditing of its accounts and records for the Petroleum Operations by the National Petroleum Agency and/or its agents.'

[41] The Pakistan 2000 PSA provides (at 7.12) that: 'At least one (1) Year prior to termination of Production from any Lease, Contractor shall submit to the GHPL a plan for the smooth transfer of Petroleum Operations to GHPL if Commercial Production is likely to continue.' The Ethiopia 2011 PSC provides (at 2.5.5) that: 'In the event of surrender of an Appraisal Area or a Development Area or termination of this Agreement, the Minister may require the Contractor to continue, for the account of the Government, Petroleum Operations for properties currently producing or capable of producing Petroleum until the right and responsibility for continuing such operations have been transferred to another person or the Government or an agency thereof but for a period not to exceed one hundred eighty (180) days after the date this Agreement would otherwise terminate with respect to all or any portion of the Contract Area concerned.'

[42] The Gabon 1995 PSC provides (at 44.3) that: 'The Administration's decision to terminate the Contract, under the provisions of Articles 44.1 and 44.2, is communicated to the Contractor in writing with return receipt; the latter automatically forfeits all its interests deriving from the Contract and its right to recover its Petroleum Costs.'

7
The Concession Area

7.1 Introduction

What is described in a concession as the 'concession area' (or otherwise as the 'area', or the 'contract area') is an expression of the location (whether onshore, or offshore, or both) in which an investor's rights and obligations which together make up a concession's scope (6.2) are to be exercised and performed.

The concession area will be defined in a certain manner at the outset of a concession, but the definition of that area is dynamic rather than static. The physical measure of a concession area will be subject to modification throughout the lifetime of a concession by the possibility of extension or subdivision, and by the ongoing process of relinquishment. The economic profile of a concession area may be modified by the activities of unitization or joint development.

Definition of the concession area can be considered in the abstract but it should also be considered more widely, as one part of a trinity which includes what a concession says about the definition of the exploration period obligations and the timings for their performance (8.2). Together, these three elements shape where, how, and when an investor will be responsible for the initial exploitation of the state's patrimony.

7.2 The Meaning of the Concession Area

A concession will set out a definition of the concession area as it exists at the outset of the concession.

The concession area is a positive delineation, in that it defines an area of exclusivity for the performance of the petroleum operations (6.2) by an investor. The concession area may be part of a wider award of contiguous concession areas in other proximate concessions by a grantor (whether effected simultaneously through a licensing round or as the subject of a bespoke concession award (2.5)). Consequently, the concession area is also a negative delineation, in that it defines the adjacent and subjacent areas into which an investor's activities ordinarily cannot stray.

A concession may also make it clear that creation of a concession area does not create any direct property rights in favour of an investor in respect of any surface, seabed, or subsoil areas.[1]

[1] The Bangladesh 2023 production-sharing contract (PSC) provides (at 3.2) that: 'Except for the rights expressly provided by this Contract, no right is granted in favour of the Contractor to the surface area, sea-bed, subsoil or to any natural resources or aquatic resources.'

The dimensions of a concession area may be defined by the terms of a state's petroleum law (2.2) or by a grantor in the terms of a licensing round (2.5), and this definition is often made by reference to prescribed 'blocks',[2] but that definition could be modified in respect of a particular concession by negotiation between a grantor and an investor. Block sizes tend to be larger in offshore frontier areas, and correspondingly tend to be smaller in developed offshore areas, shallow water areas, and onshore areas.

The concession area (as it is defined in a concession at the outset) should be sized to be large enough to give an investor sufficient options as to where it will undertake the exploration period obligations (8.2) within the timings of a concession, but it should not be so large that it gives the investor an almost impossible task of realizing meaningful exploration and appraisal. Neither should the concession area be so large that it diminishes a grantor's ability to award a number of other contiguous concessions with their own concession areas (and with their own exploration period obligations) to other investors.

A larger concession area increases the chance that a discovery which is made will reside within a single concession area. This will avoid the expense, effort, and associated risks of a scheme for the unitization of a discovery which extends over multiple concession areas (7.7).

It also follows that a larger concession area will increase any rental payments which might be due from an investor to a grantor (9.4). It might be a temptation for a grantor to raise revenue for the state by enlarging a concession area in this manner, but this could be a false economy because of the possible adverse effect on the state's interests which such an award could entail.

7.3 Initial Description of the Concession Area

A concession will usually describe the concession area by the use of a narrative such as geographical references and surface area coordinates and possibly also with the addition of a map. A concession might legislate for which definition will prevail in the event of a discrepancy between the narrative and the map.[3]

A concession area could be described two-dimensionally by the use of surface area coordinates or three-dimensionally, with surface coordinates and provision that the

[2] On the UK continental shelf, standard blocks are sized to be 250 square kilometres (reflecting a block which is sized to be 25 kilometres by 10 kilometres). In the Ghana 2000 petroleum agreement 'a Block' is sized to be approximately 685 square kilometres. In the Pakistan 2000 production sharing agreement (PSA) the reference unit (which is provided for at 1.71) is the 'Section' which means 'an area of thirty (30) seconds latitude by thirty (30) seconds longitude, based on a general block system as provided for in the Rules' and the PSA also provides (at 1.4) that: '"Appraisal Area" means an area of no more than 150 contiguous Sections selected by Contractor, subject to the limitations of the Contract Area, whereby the Sections are connected and have in common at least one side of thirty (30) seconds latitude or longitude and that is sufficient in the reasonable opinion of the Contractor to cover the vertical projection to the surface of any discovered reservoirs of a Discovery.'

[3] The Equatorial Guinea 2006 PSC provides (at Annex B) that: 'This map is included for illustrative purposes only and in the event of any discrepancies or conflict, the Contract Area shall be defined by the geographical coordinates specified in Annex A.'

concession area extends downwards from a defined reference point to include certain subjacent stratigraphic layers.[4]

In the interests of maximizing the sizing of the areas which are available to be awarded by a grantor the definition of the concession area might also impose a depth limitation. A concession area may be described such that it starts at a defined stratigraphic layer and then extends downwards but only to a further defined stratigraphic layer (all within the same set of surface area coordinates).[5]

In such a case the concession may prohibit the conduct of activities by the investor beyond the defined vertical axis of the concession area.[6]

A concession might also provide that a concession area extends downwards only to the point where a basement (ie a rock layer which suggests that a viable petroleum system does not exist below it) has been proven to exist through the investor's exploration activities.

A concession might also provide that once a discovery has been made, and an area for development has been identified, the base of that development area (8.4) will be limited to the lowest vertical point of the discovery, thereby freeing up the stratigraphic layers which lie below that point for relinquishment (7.6) and the possible award of a separate concession by the grantor.

The limitation of a concession area to a particular stratigraphic layer is particularly suited to a subsurface situation where layers of petroleum (which could take different forms) are thought to exist at different depths within a single set of surface area coordinates, in respect of which separate concessions (with concession areas defined by different stratigraphic depths) may be awarded by a grantor.

The initial outline of the concession area may also be redefined by any subdivisions of the original concession area to create new smaller areas which a grantor and an investor agree to effect.[7]

7.4 Other Concession Area Issues

Several issues are relevant to defining the dimensions of, and the use of, a concession area:

[4] The concession could say, eg, that: 'The concession area means the offshore area allocated for the conduct of the Petroleum Operations: (i) shown by the two-dimensional surface coordinates in and as further illustrated by the map in Appendix A; and (ii) the stratigraphic layers subjacent thereto.'

[5] The concession may say, eg, that: 'The concession area means the offshore area allocated for the conduct of the Petroleum Operations: (i) shown by the two-dimensional surface coordinates in and as further illustrated by the map in Appendix A; and (ii) representing the stratigraphic layers subjacent thereto commencing at the depth of x meters measured vertically from the mean sea level to a maximum depth of • meters measured vertically from the mean sea level.'

[6] The Equatorial Guinea 2006 PSC provides (at 6.15) that: 'No Well may be drilled to an objective which is outside the vertical projection of the boundaries of the Contract Area.'

[7] The Brazil 2017 PSA provides (at 30.17) that: 'In the event of division of the Contract Area for any reason, a new Production Sharing Agreement shall be executed for each area resulting from the division, keeping the same terms, obligations, programs, and deadlines of the original Agreement.'

(1) *Managing competing interests*—a concession might attempt to regulate the relationship which exists between the concession area and any other area (whether surface or subsurface) in respect of which another permit has been issued by a grantor (or by another state entity) for the conduct of other operational activities where the concession area and that other area could overlap, but this is rarely addressed in any great detail within the terms of a concession.

(2) *Quiet enjoyment*—an investor might require an undertaking from a grantor that no other persons have interests in respect of the concession area, or that the boundaries of the concession area are not subject to disputes from neighbouring persons (or states) holding acreage which might otherwise impede the intended performance of the petroleum operations. The protection afforded by such an undertaking may also extend to disapply certain prohibitions which could otherwise be applied by other state entities (eg in support or environmental or other social or policy objectives) against an investor.

Extensive undertakings of this nature might not be given by a grantor in the terms of a concession.[8] A concession may state that an investor will be bound by the outcome of any disputes relating to the definition of the concession area,[9] or that in the event of a dispute relating to the concession area the investor has a right to surrender the concession (6.6).[10]

(3) *Priority usage of the concession area*—a grantor might be concerned that an investor has contiguous acreage in neighbouring states which it could use the exploration data generated under the concession to better define (and that the investor might ultimately prefer that contiguous acreage for the implementation of a petroleum production project).

It is unlikely that a concession would provide for an undertaking to be given by an investor that it will not hold contiguous acreage in neighbouring states,

[8] The Mexico 2015 PSA provides (at 2.1) that: 'CNH makes no assurance or warranty of any kind regarding the Contract Area.' The Gambia 2022 licence provides (at 2.4.1) that: 'The Government warrants and represents that... the rights and benefits afforded to the Licensee under this Licence are granted free from all Encumbrances', where Encumbrances are defined (at 1.1) as 'all liens, charges, mortgages, pledges, encumbrances, security, overriding interests, claims, options, pre-emption rights or equitable interests or any agreement to create any of the foregoing, to the extent that the foregoing would affect any of the rights or benefits whatsoever of the Licensee under this Licence, other than the liens, claims or encumbrances in favour of the Government under the terms of this Licence and/or Applicable Laws.' The Qatar 2002 development and production sharing agreement (DPSA) provides (at 37.1) that: '[I]f there has been an expansion of the Contract Location in accordance with Article 5.5 and the GOVERNMENT has reason to believe that activities in a specific area of the expanded Contract Location will result in a dispute over a boundary line with a neighbouring state or states, the GOVERNMENT may set limits on the conduct of the Petroleum Operations within that specific area of the Contract Location.' The Liberia 2013 PSC provides (at 34.1) that: 'The STATE certifies and guarantees that there is no other applicable agreement with respect to the petroleum rights within the Delimited Area.' The Sao Tome and Principe 2018 PSC provides (at 24.2) that: 'The State warrants the Contract Area that is the subject matter of this Contract is within the territorial jurisdiction of the Democratic Republic of Sao Tome and Principe.'

[9] The Danish 2018 licence provides (at 2(3)) that: 'Where the area covered by this License ... is not within, or is withdrawn from, Danish sovereignty under rules of international law, including any international treaties, the Licensee shall be bound by any resulting restriction of the area.'

[10] The Afghanistan 2013 exploration and production sharing contract (EPSC) provides (at 25.9) that: 'If, after the Contractor has signed this Contract, the State declares or designates a portion of the Contract Area or the Supplemental Exploration Area as disputed, prohibited or unauthorized in accordance with the Hydrocarbons Law, then the Contractor shall be entitled to terminate or renegotiate this Contract. The Contractor shall also be entitled to damages for losses incurred due to such declaration or designation.'

but a concession could make some provision for how that contiguous acreage is to be managed by an investor.[11]

(4) *Managing directional drilling*—a concession might say something about the consequences of directional drilling from a concession area which strays into adjacent acreage, or from adjacent acreage which strays into a concession area (such as by providing that such drilling is prohibited from the concession area, and that drilling from adjacent acreage which strays into the concession area will be deemed to belong to the investor which holds the concession area and so will not benefit the person in the adjacent acreage).[12]

A further possibility is provision in a concession that petroleum which flows into a concession area from an adjacent concession, or petroleum which flows out of a concession area and into an adjacent concession (in each case reflecting the rule of capture), will lead to the introduction of a scheme for the consolidation of production from the two concession areas.[13]

7.5 Extension of the Concession Area

The defined concession area may be extended by enlargement to include an un-awarded adjacent or subjacent area into which extends a discovery that has been made by an investor during the exploration period. The un-awarded adjacent or subjacent area could have been a part of the original concession area which has previously been relinquished by an investor, or it could be an area in respect of which a concession has not previously been awarded.[14]

[11] The Guyana 2023 PSA provides (at 21.8, and by reference to the applicable petroleum law) that where an investor holds rights on both sides of the border in respect of a discovery which underlies the concession area and a concession area in a neighbouring state, the investor will (if so directed by the grantor) share all data, interpretations, and studies related to the discovery, and will refrain from developing that part of the discovery which underlies the concession area in the neighbouring state until a cross-border unitization treaty has first been entered into between the neighbouring states.

[12] The Equatorial Guinea 2006 PSC provides (at 6.15) that: 'No Well may be drilled to an objective which is outside the vertical projection of the boundaries of the Contract Area. Controlled direction Wells drilled within the Contract Area from adjacent terrain not covered by this Contract will be considered for all purposes of this Contract as Wells drilled from territory included in the Contract Area.'

[13] The Egypt 2021 concession agreement provides (at III (e)) that: 'If EGAS deems, or upon application by CONTRACTOR, it is recognized by EGAS that Crude Oil or Gas is being drained or might be drained from an Exploration Block under this Agreement into a development block on an adjoining concession area held by the same CONTRACTOR or another contractor, such Exploration Block being drained or which will be drained from shall be considered as participating in the Commercial Production of the Development Block in question and the Exploration Block being drained shall be converted into a Development Lease with the ensuing allocation of costs and production ... between the two concession areas.'

[14] The Gabon 1995 PSC provides (at 17.5) that: 'If, during the course of the year following the granting of an Exclusive Exploitation Authorization, the dimensions of the Deposit appear to be greater than those of the Exploitation Area, the Minister of Hydrocarbons will grant ... an additional surface area such that the entire Field may thus be covered'. The Bangladesh 2023 PSC provides (at 8.11) that: 'If any Discovery extends beyond the Contract Area into an adjacent area that is not currently under contract with Petrobangla and is considered 'open' the Contractor shall be entitled to define with seismic and other approved technical means, the limits of such Discovery. The Contractor and Petrobangla shall endeavor to obtain a supplemental agreement to modify the relevant terms of the Contract Area to include the entire Discovery'.

The implementation of such an extension may be required by a grantor, or it may be undertaken at the request of an investor. In either case, where the extension has been effected an investor may be required to make additional rental payments to a grantor (9.4) in respect of the extension area.

A grantor may prefer that where a discovery extends into an un-awarded adjacent or subjacent area then an investor should apply for the award of a separate concession in respect of the extension area (for which a further signature bonus (9.4) may be payable by an investor), rather than that the existing concession area will be automatically enlarged to accommodate the discovery.

Extension of a concession area into an adjacent or subjacent area in respect of which another concession has been (or will be) awarded is considered at 7.7, where such an extension may result in the unitization of the two concession areas.[15]

Where an investor wishes to build infrastructure which would be located outside of a concession area (such as an export pipeline, a processing facility, or a storage facility) to effect the petroleum operations, the definition of the concession area could be extended to include the location of this infrastructure (and changes might also need to be made to the concession's scope (6.2) to facilitate this). It may be necessary to provide some form of authority for the installation and operation of the infrastructure, and also to permit cost recovery of the associated costs where the concession is a PSC (9.3). Alternatively, an investor could enter into an ancillary arrangement with a grantor in relation to the provision of such infrastructure.[16]

7.6 Relinquishment

The dimensions of the concession area will also be determined by application of the concession's relinquishment provisions (which are also sometimes described as 're-sizing', 'surrender', or 'reduction' provisions). Relinquishment is typically (but not always[17]) mandated by the terms of a concession, providing for the return to the grantor of certain parts of the original concession area over time. Consequently, it is common

[15] The Afghanistan 2013 EPSC provides (at 22.1) that: 'If the Contractor identifies a proposed Field within the Contract Area that appears to extend beyond the Contract Area to other areas of Afghanistan over which other parties have the right to conduct exploration, development and production operations, the Contractor shall notify the Ministry and the other party of the proposed Field ... The Ministry may require that the development of the proposed Field and the production of Hydrocarbons from such proposed Field be carried out in collaboration with the other parties.'

[16] The Uganda 1999 PSC provides (at 13.2) that: 'It is understood by the Parties hereto that the construction, financing, operation and maintenance of an export pipeline, pumping stations and related seaboard terminal or other facilities shall be carried on through a separate pipeline company ("the Pipeline Company") which shall be responsible for the handling and transportation of Petroleum from the Delivery Point in Uganda to the ocean port of loading. In such event, the operations of the Pipeline Company will not be included within the meaning of Petroleum Operations under this Agreement and any related Licences.'

[17] Early forms of production-sharing agreements in Angola made no provision for relinquishment.

to find that the definition of a concession area is stated to be subject to the effect of periodic relinquishments under the concession.[18]

A concession area is ordinarily sized at the outset to represent a geographical scope which is beyond what an investor could conceivably expect to explore and appraise in its entirety within a defined exploration period. This is also partially reflective of the likelihood that the application for the award of a concession will have been made by an investor on the basis of relatively little existing geological and geophysical data, such that the concession purposefully reflects an area in which an investor has ample opportunity to select what it thinks will be the best sites for exploration. As the results of an investor's exploration and appraisal activities become apparent the investor will focus its ongoing attention on certain parts of the concession area. This should be acceptable to a grantor as long as the concession also contains a mechanism to prevent the unused parts of the concession area from becoming dormant and being sterilized for long periods of time through inactivity by the investor. Relinquishment is that mechanism.

The ultimate intention of a relinquishment provision is that the concession area will be re-sized to a final iteration where only development and production activities are being undertaken by an investor, with no fallow areas. The key to successful relinquishment is that it achieves a balance between a grantor's aversion to the dormancy of the state's patrimony, and an investor's need for sufficient time and space to carry out the required exploration and appraisal activities. The prospect of relinquishment could also encourage an investor to focus its attentions on meaningful exploration and appraisal.

Relinquishment benefits a grantor, which may choose to re-award a relinquished part of a concession area to another investor (or to a state entity, including a national oil company (14.1)) for exploration under a fresh concession. Relinquishment also benefits an investor, since it will be relieved of the obligation to make rental payments (9.4) to a grantor in respect of the relinquished area, although this will be a relatively modest benefit.

If a concession does not contain a relinquishment provision an investor may be required to commit to more onerous exploration period obligations (in terms of duration and extent) as a condition of being awarded a concession which relates to an inalienable concession area, to give comfort to a grantor that the adverse consequences of extensive amounts of dormant, unexplored acreage will thereby be minimized.

Relinquishment may be expressed to be mandatory or voluntary. Typically (but not always[19]) a concession will provide for both options.

Mandatory relinquishment compels an investor to relinquish defined percentage parts of a concession area at periodic intervals. A concession may provide that the percentage of a concession area which is to be relinquished will be determined only

[18] The Angola 2008 PSC provides (at 1.7) that: '"Contract Area" means on the Effective Date the area described in Annex A ... and thereafter the whole or any part of such area in respect of which Contractor Group continues to have rights and obligations under this Agreement.'

[19] The Azerbaijan 1996 PSC provides (at 29.5) that: 'Contractor shall have no unilateral right to relinquish a part of the Contract Area. In the event Contractor decides not to develop any portions of the Contract Area, the Parties will discuss the possibility of partial relinquishment on mutually agreed terms.'

according to its original and then its residual concession area definitions,[20] or that the percentage of a concession area which is to be relinquished will be determined according to its original concession area definition.[21] The second proposition results in relatively greater relinquished areas. If this approach is adopted the percentages specified for the area to be relinquished could be lower, to offset the potentially greater extent of the relinquishment.

A concession might also provide that at the end of the exploration period (6.4) an investor must finally relinquish the parts of a concession area which are not then sanctioned for development. If no such development areas exist then the entirety of a concession area will effectively be surrendered by relinquishment by the investor.

Mandatory relinquishment may also be applied by a grantor as a sanction for an investor's failure to perform an obligation under a concession,[22] or in response to a delay by an investor in commencing or carrying out development or production operations.[23] Relinquishment may also apply where an approved development has not started within a defined period of time,[24] or where there has been a cessation of petroleum production from a defined area for a defined period of time (which could also be subject to certain qualifications).[25]

An investor may prefer to defer mandatory relinquishment for a period of time, in the interests of having a greater choice over the parts of the concession area in which it elects to conduct its exploration and appraisal operations. Rather than provide for a relinquishment of (say) 25 per cent of the concession area at the end of each of the first and the second exploration phases (6.4), the concession may provide that an investor will instead relinquish (say) 50 per cent of the concession area at the end of the second exploration phase. A grantor may be willing to accept this flexibility (and the accompanying continued rental payments), unless a grantor is keen to re-award relinquished parts of a concession area as soon as possible.

[20] See the Afghanistan 2013 EPSC (at 4.1).

[21] See the Bangladesh 2023 PSC (at 5.1).

[22] The Qatar 2002 DPSA provides (at 8.9) that: 'This Agreement may be terminated by either Party upon notice to the other Party, and if so terminated, the CONTRACTOR shall be deemed to have relinquished all its rights to proceed with the Project, if the CONTRACTOR fails'.

[23] The Somalia 2023 PSA provides (at 6.8.1) that: 'Unless otherwise agreed in writing, if the Contractor fails to commence the development of a Commercial Discovery ... or if ... the Contractor considers the Commercial Discovery does not merit development, the SPA may request the Contractor to relinquish the area corresponding to such Commercial Discovery and the Contractor shall forfeit any rights relating to any Production therefrom.'

[24] The Egypt 2021 concession agreement provides (at III (e)) that: 'In the event Commercial Production Commencement of Oil or Gas has not started from any Oil or Gas Development Lease in accordance with the items specified in the granted Development Lease, the CONTRACTOR shall immediately surrender such petroleum reserves to EGAS and relinquish the relevant Development Lease'.

[25] The Trinidad and Tobago 2023 PSC provides (at 5.6) that: 'Upon the written request of the Minister, the Contractor shall relinquish its rights to conduct Petroleum Operations in a Production Area where Contractor has ceased, voluntarily or intentionally, normal Production of such Production Area for more than one hundred and eighty (180) consecutive days, provided however, Contractor shall not be required to relinquish its rights where: (i) such cessation is as a result of Force Majeure; (ii) the Minister has specifically provided his approval for such cessation; or (iii) the Contractor is undertaking scheduled maintenance under an approved Work Programme and budget within the timeframe specified in the relevant approval.' The Egypt 2021 concession agreement provides (at III (e)) that: 'In case the production has stopped from any well, and the reproduction hasn't started within a period of maximum one (1) year from the date of such stop, a revision for the Development Lease block(s) will take place in order to relinquish the Development Block(s) not contributing to production from such Development Lease'.

Relinquishment may also be voluntary, such that an investor can relinquish all or any part of a concession area at any time. Voluntarily relinquished areas can be credited to count towards an investor's mandatory relinquishment obligation, so that an investor is not exposed to double jeopardy.[26]

A voluntary relinquishment of the entirety of a concession area (which may be subject to an investor's compliance with the conditions set out below, and possibly also to certain timing restrictions) would essentially be a surrender right for an investor in respect of a concession (6.6).

Voluntary relinquishment should not be capable of being exercised by an investor to avoid performing the concession's requirements. Consequently a concession will usually provide that voluntary relinquishment cannot be applied where the concession's exploration period obligations (8.2) are still to be completed.

Relinquishment by an investor (whether mandatory or voluntary) will be subject to a number of conditions:

(1) Relinquishment may be deferred from application in respect of a part of the concession area where an exploration period obligation is still to be performed by an investor or where appraisal works are underway (8.2), or where the consideration of a field development plan is underway (8.4).
(2) Relinquishment may be deferred where an investor wishes to consolidate discoveries which have previously been made in a concession area but not declared as commercial during the exploration period (including marginal discoveries) in order to make a later declaration of commerciality (8.3). Such a deferral could be made for general purposes,[27] or more specific conditions to the deferral could apply.[28]
(3) Relinquishment of a part of a concession area where petroleum operations have been carried out may be subject to an investor's completion of any decommissioning activities which are required in relation to those operations (8.5), and may also be subject to an investor's provision of collateral support (5.4) for the costs of those activities (if collateral support has not already been procured).

[26] The Bangladesh 2023 PSC provides (at 5.3) that: 'Contractor may at any time relinquish voluntarily its rights hereunder to conduct Petroleum Operations in all or any part of Contract Area upon giving Petrobangla at least ninety (90) days prior written notice. Such voluntary relinquishments during the Exploration Period shall be credited toward the relinquishments required by Article 5.1.'

[27] The Guyana 2023 PSA provides (at 8.1) that: 'If an accumulation of hydrocarbons discovered in the Contract Area is deemed by the Contractor not to be of potential commercial interest at the time of the discovery but is likely to become commercial within five (5) years of the discovery date, the Contractor may request to the Minister an authorization to postpone the Declaration of Commercial Discovery and retain the Discovery Area for up to five (5) years.'

[28] The Brazil 2017 PSA provides (at 13.4) that: 'If the main accumulation of hydrocarbons discovered and assessed in a Contract Area is Natural Gas, the Consortium Member may request to ANP an authorization to postpone the Declaration of Commercial Feasibility in up to five (5) years, in the following cases: a) lack of market for the Natural Gas to be produced, expected to be created in less than five (5) years; b) lack or inadequacy of infrastructure for handling of the Natural Gas to be produced by the Consortium Member, expected to be implemented in less than 5 (five) years.'

(4) A concession may require that a relinquished part of a concession area must be sufficiently sized to permit the conduct of petroleum operations in its own right by another person. Relinquishment, says the concession, cannot be configured such that it would result in a relinquished area which is not readily capable of being re-awarded by a grantor under a new concession because of its irregular size or shape (a principle which is sometimes called the 'ragged edge' rule).[29]

(5) An investor may insist on having any necessary rights of access over a relinquished part of the concession area to allow petroleum operations to be performed in the un-relinquished parts of the concession area (which seems sensible enough, but which could pose difficulties where the relinquished part of the concession area has been awarded to another investor as part of a fresh concession which contains a quiet enjoyment provision (7.4) in favour of that investor).

(6) A grantor's approval will ordinarily be required for a proposed relinquishment (which relates to the approval of a voluntary relinquishment or the parts of a concession area which an investor proposes to relinquish as part of a mandatory relinquishment).

(7) An investor may require confirmation that, where the concession is a PSC, any exploration expenditures which have been incurred in the relinquished part of the concession area will be cost recovered (9.3) against future production revenues from any un-relinquished parts of the concession area.

7.7 Unitization and Joint Development

A single discovery could underlie more than one concession area. This situation might apply in a purely domestic context (ie within the state) but it could also apply internationally across contiguous concession areas which underlie more than one state.

Rather than allowing engagement in competitive drilling between the investors in their respective concession areas, which could lead to a suboptimal development of the discovery and the unnecessary duplication of costs, some form of consolidation of the interests of the involved investors may be required. This will be effected by unitization.

In a unitization, such a discovery would be developed as a single unit by all of the involved investors, each holding agreed percentage interests according to a pre-agreed ratio which reflects their understanding of the extent to which the discovery

[29] The Afghanistan 2013 EPSC provides (at 4.2) that: 'To the extent that the boundaries of the original Contract Area permit, each individual portion being relinquished shall: (i) be not less than twenty percent (20%) of the area being relinquished at such time; (ii) be not less than fifty percent (50%) of the largest individual portion being relinquished at such time; (iii) have a longest side not more than three times as long as the shortest side; and (iv) have sides parallel to the boundaries of the original Contract Area.' Less prescriptively, the Cameroon 2007 PSC provides (at 5.4) that: 'The shape and size of the parcels relinquished pursuant to this Article 5 shall, to the extent reasonably possible, be of simple configuration and of a size sufficient to allow the granting of a new petroleum contract.'

underlies their respective concession areas, and the investors would express their interests through a unitization and unit operating agreement with an agreed single operator of the unit. A unitization could be described as 'greenfield' (where the discovery which underlies the concession areas has not been developed in any of the concession areas) or as 'brownfield' (where development of (and the production of petroleum from) the discovery which underlies the concession areas has commenced in at least one of the concession areas).

A concession may recognize the need for a collaborative effort to develop such a discovery but without being prescriptive as to whether unitization is the preferred approach for doing so.[30]

A concession may contain a unitization provision which offers guidance as to which process is to be followed. An investor may suggest a proposal for the unitization of a discovery for a grantor's approval, or the unitization of a discovery may become a mandatory requirement of an investor at the request of a grantor.[31] The terms of the resultant unitization agreement will usually be subject to approval by a grantor (or by another state entity). A dispute under a concession may arise between an investor and a grantor concerning the proposed basis for unitization. If a basis for unitization proves impossible to agree, a concession may provide a default solution.[32]

Unitization will not change the definition of a concession area but it will result in the economic amalgamation of a concession area with other concession areas as part of a scheme of common operation for the single discovery. Unitization will not result in the termination of individual concessions and the re-creation of a common concession in respect of the resultant unitized area. Unitization is intended to respect the continuation of the ring-fencing of the underlying concession areas (9.3) whilst at the same time facilitating improved operational coordination between the concessions.

Negotiating and documenting a unitization can be time-consuming and expensive (including the need to involve various experts), and disputes relating to the relevant arrangements are not unheard of.[33]

[30] The Afghanistan 2013 EPSC provides (at 22.4) that: 'The Contractor shall collaborate with other parties in preparing a collective proposal for common development and production of the deposits of Hydrocarbons for approval by the Ministry.' On the other hand, the Bangladesh 2023 PSC expressly provides (at 34) for unitization as the preferred means of collaboration for the development of a single discovery.

[31] The Tanzania 2013 PSA provides (at 32) that: 'Where a Petroleum accumulation in the Contract Area extends beyond the boundaries of the Contract Area into another contract area or a licence area, the Contractor shall not develop such petroleum accumulation without seeking an agreement with the contractor or the licensee in the other area. An agreement on the development of the petroleum accumulation to be carried out as a single unit shall be submitted to the Minister for approval. In case no such agreement is submitted, the Minister may direct the relevant parties to enter into an agreement to this effect.'

[32] The Indonesia 2018 PSC provides (at 2.3.1) that: 'If during the Exploration Period, Petroleum is discovered in a field in the Contract Area which straddles in the other contract area which in the judgment of SKK MIGAS, such field cannot be produced commercially by the Contract Area on its own, other than through unitization of the field with the part of such field located substantially in other contract area adjacent to the Contract Area, then if the POD of such field is approved by the Minister, the part of the field located in the Contract Area will be declared as a Limited Commercial Contract Area. Upon the commencement of commercial production of Petroleum from such Limited Commercial Contract Area, CONTRACTOR shall have the right to the Petroleum produced from the Limited Commercial Contract Area only.'

[33] The arbitral decision in *Eni Ghana Exploration and Production Limited and Vitol Upstream Ghana Limited v Republic of Ghana and Ghana National Petroleum Corporation (GNPC)* SCC Case No U2021/114, concerning the potential unitization of the Sankofa field in Ghana was widely reported in 2024.

Examples of unitization within a state are relatively common. The need for unitization in a domestic context can be obviated by the sizing of a concession area such that the single discovery exists within the ambit of a single concession area (see above) but this ambition will be incapable of realization where a discovery straddles the boundary between two or more neighbouring states. A concession may also legislate for how unitization is intended to operate on an international basis, should the need arise.[34]

A proposal for the cross-border unitization of a discovery could be useful in addressing onshore and/or maritime boundary delineations and disputes between neighbouring states. This may in turn necessitate the entry of the states into a treaty to ratify their positions,[35] or alternatively a unitization agreement may allow for the joint exploitation of petroleum reserves for the mutual benefit of the states but without compromising their respective territorial claims, which would remain intact for further determination.

In the international context, examples of cross-border unitizations include the Ekanga/Zafiro field between Nigeria and Equatorial Guinea (2002), the Sunrise and Troubadour fields between Australia and East Timor (2003), and the Grand Tortue Ahmeyim field between Mauritania and Senegal (2018).

Unitization applies in respect of a single discovery which underlies more than one concession area, but it is possible that two or more concession areas could contain several proximate but unconnected discoveries. An option for consolidation in this situation is joint development (sometimes also described as 'pooling'), where the involved investors agree to work together under a contract-based joint venture to develop the discoveries, contributing development costs and taking produced petroleum revenues according to a pre-agreed ratio which reflects the contributions made by their respective discoveries.[36]

Like unitization, joint development does not change the definition of a concession area but it will result in the economic amalgamation of the relevant concession areas.

[34] The Egypt 2021 concession agreement provides (at III (e)) that: 'In case Petroleum reserves exists in one of the geological structures, that extends between this Area which is located in the exclusive economic zone of the A.R.E and the exclusive economic zone of one of the neighboring states, then the CONTRACTOR under this Agreement shall notify EGAS, as a government's representative, of the existence of this Petroleum reserves as a preparation for the competent authority to take all required procedures to reach an agreement on the modalities of the exploitation of such petroleum reserves'.

[35] The Guyana 2023 PSA provides (at 21.7) that: 'The Contractor shall not enter into a unitisation agreement with the holders of rights to a Petroleum Reservoir under Article 21.6 until a until a unitisation treaty is entered into between the Government and the neighbouring State pursuant to Section 45(4) of the Act.'

[36] The Bangladesh 2023 PSC provides (at 8.10) that: 'If any Discovery extends beyond the Contract Area into one or more adjacent areas held by one or more of Petrobangla's other contractor's or any other entity, Petrobangla and Contractor and any other relevant contractor or contractors or entities in the adjacent areas shall meet and endeavor to agree on the most efficient method for jointly appraising the Discovery and on possible joint Development, Production and storage, and if appropriate, transportation of Petroleum from such accumulation and on the manner in which the costs and proceeds derived therefrom shall be equitably apportioned.' The Zanzibar 2024 PSA provides (at 30 (d)) that: 'Where a petroleum accumulation in the Contract Area is in proximity to another petroleum accumulation in another area, the Minister may, in order to ensure efficient petroleum operations, require the petroleum accumulations to be developed and produced in a coordinated manner in order to ensure optimum petroleum recovery and optimum use of the relevant petroleum infrastructure.'

A further variation on this theme is where the involved investors jointly develop and then share access to common infrastructure for petroleum production.[37] This principle could also be reflected by provisions in a concession which oblige an investor to offer rights of access to its infrastructure to third parties (which could in turn encourage more infrastructure-led exploration (12.3)).[38]

Joint development applies in both domestic and international contexts. Examples of cross-border joint development agreements include the Malaysia–Thailand Memorandum of Understanding (1979), the Timor Gap Treaty between Australia and Indonesia (1989), and the Treaty on the Joint Development of Petroleum and Other Resources in Respect of Areas of the Exclusive Economic Zone of Nigeria and Sao Tome and Príncipe (2001).

[37] The Suriname 2015 PSC provides (at 10.10) that: 'Where otherwise non-commercial volumes of Petroleum in the Contract Area would, if exploited together with deposits in an area adjacent to the Contract Area, be commercial, subject to Sub-Article 2.4.3, Staatsolie may require Contractor and the contractor of that adjacent area to share facilities, provided always that such sharing does not compromise operational integrity the commerciality of operations in the Contract Area, or economics associated with a Development' and (at 29.4.1) that: 'Where Staatsolie and Contractor agree that a mutual economic benefit can be achieved by constructing and operating common facilities, the Contractor shall use its utmost efforts to reach agreement with other producers on the construction and operation of such common facilities.' The Somalia 2023 PSA provides (at 18.4) that: 'Where the SPA and the Contractor agree that a mutual economic benefit can be achieved by constructing and operating common facilities, the Contractor shall use its best endeavours to reach agreement with other contractors on the construction and operation of such common facilities.'

[38] The Zanzibar 2024 PSA provides (at 29 (a)) that: 'The Contractor, [and ZPDC where ZPDC is party to joint operations pursuant to Article 9] shall provide access to third parties for use of its petroleum facilities in the Contract Area for conduct of petroleum operations where such access will not be to an unreasonable detriment of the petroleum operations of the Contractor or other users who have already been granted a right of use. The Contractor shall provide such third party access on reasonable terms and conditions.' The Bangladesh 2023 PSC provides (at 16.5) that: 'Priority in the use of Pipeline built by Contractor will be given to transportation of Petrobangla's and Contractor's Petroleum from the Contract Area or any other area in Bangladesh held by Contractor. Spare capacity in the Pipeline can be assigned to third parties for the transport of their Petroleum by receiving a tariff at a negotiated rate if the quality of such Petroleum is compatible with Petroleum from the Contract Area, subject to agreement of the parties concerned. Such tariff received shall be shared between Petrobangla and Contractor at a negotiated rate.' The Pakistan 2000 PSA provides (at 16.5) that: 'The Government may, while according its approval for a pipeline or terminal stipulate such conditions as are reasonable and necessary to secure a rational system for transportation of Petroleum. The Government may in accordance with applicable rules, for example, but without limitation: (a) require that Contractor and any other contractor under a production sharing agreement or a petroleum concession agreement with the Government install jointly owned transportation facilities; and (b) grant to GHPL or its nominee or any third party access to transportation capacity at approved tariffs on a non-discriminatory basis.'

8
The Investor's Obligations

8.1 Introduction

A concession will create a series of work obligations for an investor which relate principally to three areas of activity: (1) exploration (and the subsequent appraisal of a discovery); (2) development and production (assuming exploration has been successful and a commercial discovery has been declared); and (3) decommissioning (when the production of petroleum from a discovery ceases).

Within these work obligations a concession will provide for the determination of work programmes and budgets, which will further regulate an investor's performance of the petroleum operations.

A concession will provide a mechanism for determining whether a petroleum discovery which has been made and appraised by an investor is sufficiently commercial to be developed and to move into production, and may also deal with a discovery which is regarded as 'marginal'.

A concession may also require an investor to comply with certain standards (including environmental protection and corporate behaviour standards) in the performance of its obligations.

8.2 Exploration and Appraisal

A grantor and an investor will commonly have imperfect knowledge regarding the level of in-ground petroleum reserves in a concession area at the time when a concession is entered into between them (apart from what an investor has been able to learn from a purchased data package (2.5), or unless an investor has other data from a contiguous concession which could be extrapolated for the benefit of the concession area). Consequently, the first activity of an investor relates to the exploration for petroleum within the concession area, followed by the appraisal of any discovery which is made as a consequence of that exploration.

During the exploration period an investor will be required to conduct certain exploration and appraisal activities which are defined by the concession. An investor's exploration period obligations should be viewed three-dimensionally, since they are bounded also by the extent of the concession area in which they are to be performed (7.2), and the period of time which is afforded to an investor by the concession for the performance of those obligations (8.2).

'Exploration' is a shorthand term for the activities of drilling wells and generating and processing seismic data. These activities are of vital importance to a grantor because they represent the creation of value—although these activities are principally intended to facilitate the discovery of commercially viable quantities of petroleum, they also realize invaluable geological and geophysical data for the grantor and this will remain a benefit even if the exploration activity proves to be unsuccessful. The grantor can take the data which is generated in respect of a particular concession area and use it to develop a better understanding of the state's patrimony.

An investor has a different perspective, and will be less focused on the generation of data for wider interpretive purposes. An investor's principal aim is to make a petroleum discovery which is capable of being commercialized so that revenues can be generated to recover the investor's exploration costs and thereafter make a profit. In pursuit of this, an investor will want the greatest amount of flexibility in a concession in respect of how it is required to perform its exploration period obligations (including the ability to accelerate, delay, or even disapply those obligations).

The operational activities relating to exploration which an investor must undertake during the exploration period as a whole, and in respect of each exploration phase, (sometimes also called 'minimum work obligations' or 'commitment wells') which are recited in a concession may be derived from the commitments which were made by an investor during a licensing round, where those obligations were contestable items (2.5).[1]

An investor has an interest in reducing the scope of the exploration period obligations because they represent the incidence of costs which might not be recovered if a commercial discovery is not made as a consequence (although, paradoxically, the conduct of more exploration could also increase the investor's chances of making a discovery).

The exploration period obligations typically relate to any (or more typically to a combination) of drilling an exploration well (or wells) to a defined target depth (and/or to a defined target distance in the case of horizontal drilling) in a location or locations which will be further agreed between a grantor and an investor (and possibly drilling a further appraisal well thereafter), generating new seismic data, processing and/or reinterpreting existing seismic data, and preparing technical studies.

Issues which arise for debate in the negotiation of a concession in respect of these obligations relate to whether the requirement to drill an exploration well includes any of the activities of deepening, side-tracking, or testing an exploration well which has already been drilled as an acceptable substitute activity for the requirement to drill a further exploration well, and whether drilling an appraisal well equates to drilling an exploration well in its own right. These possibilities can be spelled out in

[1] The Afghanistan 2013 exploration and production sharing contract (EPSC) provides (at 6.4) that: '[T]he Contractor undertakes to carry out and comply with the work commitments established by the Winning Bidder's Exploration Program.'

the concession, or left for discussion between the parties at the appropriate time. The former is the preferred course.

Exploration period obligations should be drafted with sufficient detail in a concession. Requiring an investor to drill an exploration well should, for example, address whether an investor is expected to commence or to complete drilling within the relevant exploration phase (and consideration could also be given to what 'commence' will mean for these purposes[2]).

In some concessions an investor's exploration period obligation is defined not by the need to complete a series of tasks but by the requirement of an investor to complete what are defined as 'work units'. Each defined exploration period obligation is ascribed a number of work units (where each such unit could have an ascribed monetary value), and an investor is required to complete a number of work units within a defined time period to meet its exploration period obligations.[3] In theory, this approach gives more flexibility to an investor, which can select the manner in which it chooses to complete the necessary work units rather than being bound by defined exploration period obligations. However, an applicable work programme and budget (8.6) could still impose some constraints on an investor's discretion.

The performance by an investor of the exploration period obligations within an exploration phase should not be determinative of whether an investor can proceed to the next exploration phase. An investor's liability for a failure to perform a particular exploration period obligation to the extent required by a concession should be assessed in its own regard as a potential breach of contract, and the failure to perform such an obligation should not have the capacity to disapply a requirement for the investor to continue with the performance of any further obligations. In some concession formulations an investor's exploration period obligations are described as an 'unless' clause (meaning that an investor cannot proceed with its planned activities under a concession unless the investor has first performed a particular exploration period obligation in accordance with its requirements), but this construction should not be used by an investor as an option right to permit a performance failure.

[2] In *Vitol E&P Limited v Africa Oil and Gas Corporation* [2016] EWHC 1677 (Comm) the English courts were called upon to offer a definition of 'spudding' a well.

[3] The Trinidad and Tobago 2012 production sharing contract (PSC)provides (at 1.67) that: '"Work Unit" means the numerical representation of the cost of the work obligations specified in the Work Programme under the Petroleum Regulations (Competitive Bidding) Order 2012 for one or more phases of this Contract or under an appraisal programme or relative to a retained exploration area'. In the Trinidad and Tobago 2023 PSC the definition (at 1.79) had changed to say: '"Work Unit" means the numerical representation of the cost of the work obligations specified in the Work Programme under Article 7 or under an appraisal programme or relative to a retained exploration area and calculated in accordance with Annex "E"'. The Pakistan 2000 PSA provides (at 3.3) that: 'The minimum work (the "Minimum Work") to be carried out shall be as follows: (a) INITIAL TERM: (i) Phase One: Contract Years 1 and 2: __*__ Work Units plus 3 Work Units per Grid Area in the Original Contract Area, for each of Contract Years 1 and 2. (ii) Phase Two: Contract Years 3 and 4: __*__ Work Units plus 5 Work Units per Grid Area in the Contract Area, for each of Contract Years 3 and 4. (iii) Phase Three: Contract Year 5: _ _*__ Work Units plus 7 Work Units per Grid Area in the Contract Area. * Work Unit offered as Bid Obligation at the time of award' and (at Annex III) that each Work Unit has an ascribed value of US$10,000, and (at Annex III) that: 'the following equivalency applies in order to equate work that has been carried out with Work Units' with the attribution of work units to specified exploration period obligations.

The failure of an investor to perform an exploration period obligation according to the concession's requirements (which failure is not excused by force majeure (11.5), or which failure has not been authorized by a grantor or is otherwise permitted by the concession) has a number of potential consequences:

(1) A grantor may treat the failure as a breach of the terms of a concession, giving the grantor a right to suspend and/or to terminate the concession (6.6).
(2) Whether or not a grantor terminates a concession, the failure may expose an investor to a liability to pay damages (whether general damages or liquidated damages) to a grantor for its breach of contract.[4]
(3) A grantor may have a right to enter into the concession area and (at its own expense, to be reimbursed by an investor) complete the unperformed obligation.[5]
(4) An investor may be obliged to pay to a grantor a monetary sum which reflects the unspent element of the exploration period obligation's associated costs. This formulation offers no remedy to a grantor where an investor has spent the exploration period obligation's associated costs but has still failed to complete the exploration period obligation, and so this formulation could be revised to say that an investor will pay to a grantor the greater of the unspent element of the exploration period obligation's associated costs and a defined monetary amount (as liquidated damages).

Where an investor becomes obliged to make a monetary payment a grantor may also call on any collateral support which has been provided by an investor in respect of its obligations under a concession (5.4) as surety for the payment which is due.

The exploration period obligations in most concessions are relatively inflexible, in that they are required to be performed without regard to extraneous economic circumstances affecting an investor (such as the impact of a low petroleum price or a high contracting cost environment). That said, experience has shown that global market conditions which adversely affect all sector participants can lead to informal discussions between a grantor and an investor about the rescheduling of exploration period obligations and their associated costs, notwithstanding the absence in a concession of a formal mechanism to facilitate this, in the interests of keeping the concession alive between the parties. This was a widespread practice as a consequence of the interruption of project development and operational activities resulting from the

[4] The Kenya 2014 PSC provides (at 8.5) that: 'If ... the contractor has not fulfilled its minimum work obligations under sub-clause 5(1) hereof, and/or its minimum expenditure obligations under sub-clauses 5(1) and 5(5) hereof, the contractor shall pay to the Government the minimum monetary obligation in respect of the work not carried out multiplied by the discount rate, as defined in sub-clause 5(5) and calculated on the last month of that exploration period, and/or the shortfall, if any, between the amount expended, in accordance with sub-clause 5(5), and the minimum monetary obligation for that exploration period, multiplied by the discount rate, as defined herein above.'

[5] The Kenya 2014 PSC provides (at 25 (4)) that: 'The Cabinet Secretary may require the contractor to perform an obligation under this contract by giving reasonable written notice, and if the contractor fails to comply with the notice, the Cabinet Secretary may execute the obligation for which the contractor shall pay forthwith amounts expended by the Cabinet Secretary in the execution of the obligations.'

Covid-19 pandemic in 2020. The grantor may be less willing to be accommodating to an investor in this manner, however, where an investor's difficulties relate to any of private financing difficulties, problems within the investor party consortium, or disappointing results from an earlier part of the exploration period's activities which lead to an investor's reluctance to proceed further.

From a grantor's perspective a concession describes a fixed set of exploration period obligations which must be performed by an investor without fail (subject only to the availability of force majeure relief (11.5) or a specific authorization by a grantor or otherwise under the terms of a concession), up to a maximum amount of scheduled expenditure and according to a defined schedule.

An investor may be less impressed by a requirement for absolute performance, however. An investor wants to make a petroleum discovery which is capable of being commercialized, but it will also want the greatest amount of flexibility in how and when it performs the exploration period obligations so that it can maximize costs savings, and improve the prospect of making a return on its incurred costs. An investor may seek to moderate a grantor's preferred positions in the concession in several ways:

(1) A concession might permit an investor to be deemed to have completed the performance of a particular exploration period obligation where circumstances beyond the investor's control have prevented the required performance (such as a provision that the investor can be deemed to have drilled a well to a required target depth or distance where the initial attempt to do so has been abandoned because the drilling encountered an impenetrable geological layer or dangerous downhole conditions). This could also be supported by a requirement that the investor has first incurred a certain minimum level of expenditure in doing so. A concession may also require the investor to drill a substitute well at its own expense.[6] In these circumstances it will always be an issue as to whether the investor can unilaterally deem that the particular circumstances have arisen, or whether the grantor's approval is also required for that determination.

(2) A concession might deem the investor to have completed the performance of a particular exploration period obligation where, in drilling a well, the investor encountered a viable petroleum system before the agreed target depth or distance was reached.[7]

[6] The Angola 2008 PSC provides (at 15.12) that: 'If any obligatory Exploration Well is abandoned due to technical difficulties, and at the time of such abandonment the Exploration Expenditures for such Well are less than ______________ U.S. dollars (U.S.$ ______________), then Contractor Group shall have the option either to: (a) drill a substitute Well at the same or another location in which case the Exploration Expenditures for both the original Well and the substitute Well shall be credited against Contractor Group's minimum Exploration Expenditures set forth in paragraph 8 of this Article.'

[7] The Cameroon 2007 PSC provides (at 6.5) that: 'The CONTRACTOR may interrupt a Drilling which has not reached the depth and/or deepest geologic objective envisioned by the corresponding minimum Work Programme if the CONTRACTOR has encountered petroleum bearing strata, which, according to the CONTRACTOR, constitute a Discovery. In such case, the well drilled shall nonetheless be considered an Exploration well within the framework of the corresponding minimum Work Programme.'

(3) A concession might oblige an investor to continue drilling a well if the target depth or distance has been reached but further drilling is required to facilitate the penetration and/or testing of a prospective petroleum system.[8]

(4) A concession might give an investor an option to pay an agreed monetary amount to a grantor rather than perform a particular exploration period obligation, so that the investor can effectively buy out an unperformed obligation.[9] This buy-out option makes particular sense to the investor if the performance of previous exploration period obligations has indicated no or a negligible chance of future success, where the investor believes that taking the risk and the (additional) expense of drilling what would almost certainly be another unproductive well would defy commercial logic.

(5) The making of a commercial discovery (8.3) could obviate the investor's obligation to perform the remainder of the exploration period obligations, or those obligations could remain due for performance by the investor. A grantor will have a preference for the latter formulation, since the continued performance of those obligations will continue to generate more data for a grantor and could lead to another discovery.

(6) The investor may require flexibility in a concession which allows for the extension of a particular exploration phase (6.4), or an extension of the allotted time for the performance of a particular exploration period obligation, at the investor's request.

(7) Where, in a particular exploration phase, the investor has performed work which is in excess of the required obligation for that exploration phase (such as by conducting a seismic survey over a wider area than was initially required, or by carrying out additional well testing or appraisal works) the excess work can be carried forward and credited towards satisfaction of the exploration period obligations for a future exploration phase.[10] This construction may be difficult to apply in practice to discrete and identifiable work products, but it is more readily applicable where a concession adopts a work units formulation

[8] The Trinidad and Tobago 2023 PSC provides (at 7.5 (b)) that: 'In the event that an Exploration Well attains the minimum depth requirement in a prospective zone, Contractor shall be required to continue drilling to a depth which will ensure penetration of and allow for the proper evaluation of the entire prospective zone, provided such further drilling is operationally and technically feasible. Such further drilling shall be credited against any other outstanding Work Units in that current phase of the Exploration Period on a dollar for dollar basis.'

[9] The Angola 2008 PSC provides (at 15.7) that: '[I]f Contractor Group relinquishes its rights under this Agreement before drilling the minimum number of Exploration Wells undertaken by it under this Article, Contractor Group shall be obligated to pay Sonangol an amount equal to ____________ U.S. dollars (U.S$ ______ ____________) for each such Exploration Well not drilled.'

[10] The Guyana 2023 production sharing agreement (PSA) provides (at 11.6 (c)) that: 'Additional line kilometres of seismic and additional Exploration Wells beyond the minimum work obligation required for any phase of the Exploration Period may be carried forward to satisfy the respective work obligations of a subsequent phase of the Exploration Period provided that the work commitments for the current phase of the Exploration Period have been satisfied. The Contractor may request the recognition of such additional exploration work be credited against any work commitments in the subsequent phases of the Exploration Period.' The Zanzibar 2024 PSA provides (at 5(d)) that: 'Where in any Exploration Period, the Contractor has carried out more than the minimum work obligations specified in paragraph (b) of this Article, for that period the Contractor shall be permitted to credit such excess work obligation as satisfying work obligations specified in that paragraph for the next succeeding Exploration Period.'

(see above). Such a carry forward mechanism might also lend itself more readily to an investor's obligation to fund a defined amount in respect of exploration period activities as the true definition of an investor's exploration period obligations. Such a carry forward mechanism could also be applied so that any excess work is credited towards satisfaction of the exploration period obligation in another concession (although this formulation is inconsistent with the notion of the ring-fencing of a concession (9.3)).

A grantor may require that an investor's performance of the defined exploration period obligations must be completed regardless of the associated cost to the investor of doing so. An investor may seek to moderate a grantor's position by requiring that a concession will apply a monetary cap to the costs which the investor is expected to incur in the performance of the exploration period obligations, to protect the investor from being obliged to incur limitless expense. If, says an investor, the monetary cap is reached and the exploration period obligations remain unperformed according to their definition then the exploration period obligations will be deemed to have been completed. This construction is rarely accepted by a grantor however, which has as its primary objective the successful performance of the required works by the investor, rather than the expenditure of money.

However, a grantor might also wish to structure the exploration period obligations so that an investor must incur a defined minimum amount of expenditure (often called the 'exploration period obligations costs') in their performance. This construction benefits a grantor because it establishes a minimum financial threshold for an investor's obligation, which ensures a certain level of quality and commitment in the performance of the exploration period obligations. The exploration period obligations costs also establish a baseline amount to be applied for the payment of liquidated damages by an investor for a failure to perform the relevant obligation (see above). A concession may make clear that the principal purpose of so stating the costs is to establish a liability of an investor for a performance failure, rather than to have them taken as a proxy for the required performance which could be applied as an election by the investor.[11]

Where a minimum expenditure formulation is adopted a concession may state what expenditures will count, and will not count, towards satisfaction of the investor's expenditure obligation. A grantor will want to make it clear that the amount of the exploration period obligations costs are not offset, for example, by an investor's rental payment (9.4) or training payment (10.2) obligations under a concession.

A concession may provide that if an exploration period obligation is performed and the corresponding exploration period obligation's costs are not fully expended then the exploration period obligation will be deemed to have been completed, without an

[11] The Cameroon 2007 PSC provides (at 6.5) that: 'It is understood that the monetary value of the work referred to in Articles 6.1, 6.2 and 6.3 above which should reflect the reality of the cost of the work programme are shown in this Contract for reference purposes only and solely for determining the indemnity due pursuant to Section 30 of the Petroleum Code. It does not constitute a minimum expenditure obligation, the CONTRACTOR's obligation being defined only in the work obligations of the minimum Work Programme set forth in said articles.'

investor obligation to account to a grantor for the unspent balance of the exploration period obligation's costs. Alternatively, the amount of the unexpended exploration period obligation's costs could be carried forward and credited towards the exploration period obligations costs for the next exploration period obligation, or, in some circumstances, become due for payment by the investor to the grantor.

If a discovery of a viable petroleum system is made during the exploration period the next question to consider is whether that discovery merits appraisal. 'Appraisal' (sometimes also called 'delineation' or 'evaluation') describes the activities which are undertaken in assessing whether a petroleum discovery which has been made during the exploration period is a candidate to be declared as a commercial discovery.

Where an investor notifies a grantor of the existence of a discovery a concession may give an investor additional time to prepare and propose a plan for the appraisal of the discovery, for the grantor's approval.[12] This additional period of time, and the conduct of the appraisal plan's activities, could overrun the end of a scheduled exploration phase or of the exploration period as a whole (which might then be extended accordingly).

Whether a discovery should qualify for appraisal can be determined by an objective test in a concession, relating for example to the achievement of defined flowrates of petroleum over a particular period of time in well testing during exploration drilling, or it can be something for a grantor to consider in its discretion.

If, at the end of the exploration period (or at the end of the period of appraisal of a discovery which is made), an investor is of the opinion that there are no commercially viable quantities of petroleum in the explored part of a concession area (whether or not discoveries have been made by an investor) the investor can take steps to plug and abandon any drilled wells and will carry out any site remediation which has become necessary as a consequence of its activities (8.5). The explored part of the concession area may also become the subject of relinquishment by the investor (7.6).

8.3 Commerciality and Marginality

If the activities which were undertaken by an investor during the exploration period have resulted in a discovery which, when appraised, contains what could potentially be regarded as commercially viable quantities of petroleum then this may lead to a declaration that the discovery is 'commercial'. In some concessions the term 'commercial well' is used to indicate a discovery which could go forward for appraisal.[13] This is not the same as a commercial discovery, and the risk of confusion is obvious.

[12] The Suriname 2015 PSC provides (at 10.3.2) that the contents of an appraisal report will include: 'a. geological and geophysical conditions; b. areal extent, thickness and depth of pay zones; pressure, volume and temperature of the reservoir fluid; c. Crude Oil and Natural Gas reserve estimates; d. fluid characteristics, including, gravity, sulfur percentage, sediment and water percentage of the fluid; e. anticipated production performance; f. an assessment of the commerciality of the field.'

[13] The Angola 2008 PSC provides (at 15.4) that: '"Commercial Well" means the first Well on any geological structure which after testing in accordance with sound and accepted industry Production practices, and verified by SONANGOL, is found through analysis of test results to be capable of producing, from a single reservoir not less than an average rate of ________ Barrels of Crude Oil per day (______ b/d).' Similar provisions apply in the

An investor may (whether directly, or after consideration at a meeting of the management committee (5.5)) make a declaration of commerciality in respect of a discovery if the investor believes that the discovery demonstrates the existence of commercially viable quantities of recoverable petroleum which are sufficient to support the profitable exploitation of the discovery. Even if a declaration of commerciality is not made, a grantor should still be able to secure the data which was generated by the exploration works, which might be of some value to the grantor.

A concession may also prescribe the creation of a specific geographical area around the nucleus of a commercial discovery (8.3). Such a development area (sometimes called an 'exclusive exploitation area') represents the delineation of a part of the concession area in which an investor is deemed to have performed certain of its exploration period obligations (8.2), whilst leaving the rest of the concession area open to the performance by the investor of any remainder of its exploration period obligations.

What constitutes 'commerciality' for these purposes may have an objective definition in a concession[14] or this could be a matter for the subjective determination of an investor.[15] There might not be automatic alignment between the aspirations of an investor and a grantor concerning the commerciality of a discovery (arising, eg, where a grantor believes that a particular discovery is commercial and merits development but an investor is less sanguine). If there is a dispute between the parties recourse may be had to the dispute resolution provisions of the concession (11.4) to determine the matter.[16]

Egypt 2021 concession agreement (at I (i)), where a further distinction is made between a 'Commercial Gas Well' (which is a well capable of producing at an average rate of not less than 15,000,000 standard cubic feet of gas per day) and a 'Commercial Oil Well' (which is a well capable of producing at an average rate of not less than 3,000 barrels of oil per day)).

[14] The Afghanistan 2013 EPSC provides (at 1.1) that: '"Commercial Discovery" shall mean a Discovery which, as determined in accordance with the provisions of Section 7.1, can be produced commercially, based on consideration of all pertinent operating and financial data, such as Hydrocarbons volumes, recoverable reserves, production levels and other relevant technical and economic factors, according to Good Oil Field Practice.' The Egypt 2021 concession agreement provides (at III (c)) that a 'Commercial Discovery', whether of oil or gas, 'may consist of one (1) producing reservoir or a group of producing reservoirs which is worthy of being developed commercially'. The Kurdistan Iraq 2007 PSC provides (at 1.1) that a commercial discovery 'means a Discovery which is potentially commercial when taking into account all technical, operational, commercial and financial data collected when carrying out appraisal works or similar operations, including recoverable reserves of Petroleum, sustainable regular production levels and other material technical, operational, commercial and financial parameters, all in accordance with prudent international petroleum industry practice'.

[15] The Trinidad and Tobago 2023 PSC provides (at 13.1) that: 'If a Discovery is made in an Exploration Well, Contractor shall: (a) immediately notify the Minister of such Discovery; (b) within thirty (30) days thereafter provide the Minister with all available information regarding the Discovery, including a preliminary classification of the Discovery as Crude Oil or Natural Gas; and (c) within ninety (90) days after such Discovery, also notify the Minister whether or not it considers the Discovery of Crude Oil or Natural Gas to have commercial potential.' The Guyana 2023 PSA applies (by reference to the applicable petroleum law) a definition of a commercial discovery as 'any discovery, which a licensee, in its sole judgment, considers economic to develop and produce'. The Cyprus 2007 PSC (at 1.2) describes a Commercial Field as 'a Discovery that, in the judgment of the Contractor, can be produced commercially'.

[16] The Afghanistan 2013 EPSC provides (at 7.1 (k) (iii)) that: 'In the event that no agreement is reached between the Ministry and the Contractor within one hundred and eighty (180) Days from the date of submission of the report and proposed Development Program and Development Program Budget pursuant to Section 7.1 (i), the Ministry or the Contractor may refer the matter for determination pursuant to Article XXIV.'

In determining the commerciality of a discovery an investor will, at a minimum, wish to take into account the costs which it has incurred in making the discovery and actual and prospective volumetric, operating, and financial data related to the discovery (and also the fiscal terms of the concession (9.1)). This also assumes that an investor would analyse the economics of a discovery on a stand-alone basis, whereas in reality an investor might also wish to realize revenues from a discovery which could cover an investor's sunk costs in respect of its other unsuccessful exploration activities within the concession area. An investor may also consider the commerciality of the discovery in comparison with other exploration and development leads with better prospects elsewhere (in other concessions, and possibly also in other states) which it might prefer to pursue.

The creation of a commercial discovery may also result from the consolidation of a number of adjacent previous petroleum discoveries[17] and an investor might wish to assess the commerciality of a discovery by reference to any previous discoveries which have not been declared commercial in their own right but which could become so by consolidation with the addition of the latest discovery, to be developed on a combined basis.[18]

From a grantor's perspective, the test for whether a discovery is commercial may be determined as something which affords an acceptable level of state take (9.2), regardless of the investor's ambitions. Ordinarily a grantor has an interest in seeing a declaration of commerciality being made in respect of a discovery because that will (or should) lead to petroleum production revenues and a profit element.

An investor's declaration of commerciality may be subject to approval by a grantor, such that in practical terms the declaration of commerciality will be made as a joint determination between a grantor and an investor. The need for a grantor's approval of a consequent field development plan (8.4) may also give a grantor a form of veto right.

The preceding discussion assumes that determining whether or not a discovery is commercial is a binary decision. There is also a middle ground to consider however, which is represented by a discovery which is regarded as 'marginal'.

A marginal discovery may have no obvious meaning beyond being a discovery which an investor does not regard as being sufficiently remunerative to develop as a commercial discovery (but perhaps only narrowly so). It is not axiomatic that a grantor will see marginality through the same lens, because the grantor may have different economic and strategic perspectives which will produce a different result.

17 The Angola 2008 PSC provides (at 7.1) that: 'In the event of Commercial Discoveries in deposits which underlie and overlie each other, such deposits shall constitute a single Development Area, and such area shall be defined or redefined as necessary, within the boundaries of the Contract Area, to incorporate all underlying and overlying deposits.'

18 The Somalia 2023 PSA provides (at 7.4.1) that: 'If following the initial evaluation in accordance with clause 6.4.1.4 the Contractor determines that a Discovery is a Discovery Not Currently Warranting Appraisal, or, if following Appraisal in accordance with clause 6.7 the Appraisal demonstrates that the Discovery, although substantial, is not then, either alone or in combination with other Discoveries, commercially viable, but is likely to become so within five (5) Calendar Years, the SPA may, at the request of the Contractor, declare a Retention Area in respect of those Discovery Areas.'

An investor may consider the marginal discovery as being capable of generating revenue which is sufficient to allow an investor to recover its costs but with the discovery thereafter leaving relatively little else for recovery by a grantor. An investor may, however, be willing to proceed with the development of such a discovery so that it can at least recoup its sunk costs, whereas a grantor might be less enthused by such a development. On the other hand a grantor may be desperate to see petroleum production from the state's patrimony such that a grantor might require an investor to make a declaration of commerciality even in respect of a marginal discovery.

An investor might not want to immediately relinquish a marginal discovery (7.6), preferring instead to wait until the end of the overall exploration period to do this, so that it can then make a decision about combining the development of the marginal discovery with the development of other discoveries, to achieve a better economy of scale. However, a grantor may employ a more aggressive 'use it or lose it' philosophy, compelling the swift relinquishment of a marginal discovery, so that the grantor can appoint another investor (or another state entity, including a national oil company (14.1)), perhaps more suited to, or more willing, to undertake the development of a marginal discovery. A grantor may also elect to take over such a relinquished discovery as an exclusive operation (10.7).[19]

A particular paradox to note is that if an investor relinquishes a marginal discovery that discovery could cease to be regarded as marginal by another investor as it no longer has to bear the associated exploration and appraisal costs (since those costs were incurred, and written off, by the relinquishing investor). This will reduce the prospect that the discovery is marginal in the eyes of a successor investor which picks up the discovery under a re-awarded concession.

Alternative fiscal terms for a marginal discovery may also be applied under a concession in an investor's favour (by further negotiation between a grantor and an investor).[20] This could transform a discovery from marginal to commercial.

[19] The Egypt 2021 concession agreement provides (at III (c) (iv)) that: 'If Crude Oil or Gas is discovered but is not deemed by CONTRACTOR to be a Commercial Discovery of Oil or Gas under the above provisions of this paragraph (c), EGAS shall ... have the right ... at its sole cost, risk and expense, to develop, produce and dispose of all Crude Oil or Gas from the geological feature on which the well has been drilled.'

[20] The Ghana 2000 petroleum agreement provides (at 8.9) that: 'If Contractor informs the Minister that the Discovery is not commercial then ... contractor shall relinquish such Discovery Area, provided, however, that in appropriate cases, before declaring that a Discovery is not commercial, Contractor shall consult with the other Parties and may make appropriate representations proposing minor changes in the fiscal and other provisions of this Agreement which may, in the opinion of the Contractor, affect the determination of commerciality. The other Parties may, where feasible, and in the best interests of the Parties agree to make such changes or modifications in the existing arrangements.' The Kenya 2014 PSC provides (at 31(1)) that: 'Where the contractor determines that a discovery is marginal or non-commercial, the contractor may propose a modification to this contract, based on an alternative economic evaluation and after consideration the Cabinet Secretary may accept or reject the proposed modification.'

8.4 Development and Production

'Development' describes the activities which are undertaken in progressing a discovery which has been declared or agreed to be commercial towards the point where the production of petroleum from the discovery can begin.

After a declaration of commerciality has been made in respect of a discovery an investor may be required to prepare and submit a field development plan (FDP) to a grantor, with this FDP forming a key part of the development agenda. The FDP may have a broad stated purpose.[21] Alternatively a concession may go into some detail about the required content of the FDP, including an assessment of a discovery's geological and geophysical characteristics, the estimated petroleum in place (which may also be indicated by the provision of an independently-prepared resource estimation report), petroleum production project development options and costs, and possibly also the provision of an environmental assessment or a social impact assessment.[22] A longer period of time might be required for an investor to prepare and submit an FDP for a technologically complex field, or where gas commercialization is in prospect (13.4). As part of the production activity a grantor may afford access to state-owned infrastructure for the benefit of an investor and its development aspirations,[23] with these possibilities being reflected within the FDP.

After the submission of an FDP there may be some dialogue between a grantor and an investor (relating, eg, to a grantor being satisfied that the FDP makes technical and economic sense and complies with any necessary environmental standards). Revisions to an investor's proposed FDP may be required by a grantor, with a consequent impact on the timing of a subsequent development project.

Once the FDP has been approved (whether by a grantor alone, or with the input of other state entities) an investor can begin implementing the development of the discovery, in turn leading to the eventual commencement of petroleum production operations.

A concession may identify a particular development period, as a defined period of time in which an investor will undertake the development activity under a concession, but the development period may also be part of the production period (6.5).

[21] The Kenya 2014 PSC provides (at 29 (1)) that: 'This field development plan shall be based on sound engineering and economic principles and in accordance with best petroleum industry practice and considering the Maximum Efficient Rate of production appropriate to the commercial discovery.'

[22] The Afghanistan 2013 EPSC requires (at 7.1 (i)) the submission of an environmental impact assessment and a social impact assessment where a notification is made to the grantor of a discovery which may be of commercial interest. The Somalia 2023 PSA provides (at 8.2.4.5) that the development plan which is to be submitted by the contractor must include 'a detailed social and environmental impact assessment (prepared in accordance with the then applicable international standards, requirements and guidelines and the Best International Practice) for the Commercial Discovery, which identifies current and possible social and environmental issues and concerns and contains a plan for ensuring social and environmental compliance during the life of the Field.'

[23] The Tajikistan 2008 PSC provides (at 13.7) that: 'The Contractor shall have the right to use existing pipeline and terminal facilities belonging to or under the control of the State or the Ministry. The State and the Ministry shall assist in making these facilities available to the Contractor on terms with regard to access and tariffs that are no less favourable than those available to others including the Ministry and any other State enterprise. Priority shall be given in the use of such pipelines and facilities to Petroleum produced within Republic of Tajikistan.'

'Production' connotes the period of time in a concession's lifecycle which sees the production of petroleum in commercial quantities from a developed discovery. The potential duration of the production period is considered elsewhere (6.5).

Once production has commenced a concession may have something to say about the rate of production of petroleum from the discovery which an investor maintains over time. A concession might simply oblige an investor to produce petroleum from the discovery but such an obligation could be qualified to require an investor's compliance with good and prudent oil and gas field practice (8.7), rather than that the rate of production is to be construed as an absolute obligation. This qualification may be applied to ensure that a discovery is preserved and exploited by the investor in the most prudent manner and for as long as possible.

Sometimes the phrase 'maximized economic recovery' (or some variant of that term) is used to describe the rate of petroleum production which an investor should aspire to, where the definition of the phrase requires an investor not to undertake activities which might result in an excessive loss of pressure or in a decline in production, or which might result in irreversible damage to the discovery.[24] The test for maximized economic recovery might also be set as a variable amount in a concession.[25]

A concession might also specify certain commercial circumstances when an investor is required to reduce the rate of petroleum production. This could relate to an absolute or a partial curtailment of production during periods of low petroleum prices or where the state has made a commitment to reduce petroleum production rates (such as where the state is a member of the Organization of the Petroleum Exporting Counties (OPEC), which could impose production quotas on its members). An investor, when faced with this prospect under a concession, may require a corresponding extension to the production period (6.5) to later recover its position. An investor may also require that a curtailment of production is made rateably across all concessions and impacts all investors (including a state nominee where a state participation right has been exercised (10.8)).[26] Whether an investor has a right to impose a production curtailment

[24] The Afghanistan 2013 EPSC provides (at 7.2 (b)) that: 'The Contractor shall produce Liquid Hydrocarbons from the Contract Area at the Maximum Efficient Rate' and (at 1.1) that: '"Maximum Efficient Rate" shall mean the maximum rate of production of Hydrocarbons in a Field, without excessive rate of decline of production or excessive loss of reservoir pressure, and in accordance with Good Oil Field Practices'. The Kenya 2014 PSC provides (at 2 (1)) that: '"[M]aximum efficient rate" means the rate at which the maximum ultimate economic petroleum recovery is obtained from a commercial field without excessive rate of decline in reservoir pressure, and consistent with best petroleum industry practice.' The Tanzania 2013 PSA provides (at 9 (j)) that a proposed development plan for a potentially commercial discovery shall 'be designed to ensure the recovery of the maximum quantity of Petroleum from the proposed Development Area which the economics of the Development shall justify and it shall be designed in compliance with best international petroleum industry practices'. The Uganda 1999 PSC provides (at 7.8) that: 'Licensee shall use its best efforts to produce Crude Oil from each Development Area at the Maximum Efficient Rate' and (at 1.1) that: '"Maximum Efficient" means the maximum rate of production of Crude Oil from a Development Area, without excessive decline of production or excessive loss of reservoir pressure, in accordance with good oilfield practice'. The Guyana 2023 PSA provides (at 16.5) that: 'The level of production set shall be consistent with the maximum efficient recovery of resources which conforms to sound reservoir engineering principles in accordance with Best International Industry Standards and Practices.'

[25] The Turkmenistan 1997 PSA provides (at 12.6) that: 'The Maximum Efficient Rate of production for Crude Oil and the production rate for Non-Associated Gas shall be established in the Development Plan for each Development Area. Such rates shall be reviewed and approved annually, at the time of submission by Contractor of the annual Work Programme and Budget to the Management Committee.'

[26] The Kurdistan Iraq 2007 PSC provides (at 16.2) that: '[I]n the event the production rate of the individual wells and Reservoir of a Petroleum Field is to be set below the Maximum Efficient Rate ("MER") for the Reservoir,

at its own behest during a low petroleum price environment will be a matter for negotiation.[27]

A concession may provide for the freedom of an investor to dispose of produced petroleum,[28] or it may impose certain restrictions on an investor's ability to do so.[29] Temporary restrictions on an investor's petroleum disposal rights may also be applied as part of a grantor's reserved rights under the concession to requisition certain quantities of petroleum production during times of war or national emergency.[30]

8.5 Decommissioning

The decommissioning of the various assets or equipment which have been used by an investor in the performance of the petroleum obligations (including wells and subsea infrastructure) will be an issue when the permanent cessation of the production of petroleum from a discovery has occurred or when a concession has come to an end (unless a grantor requires that any such assets or equipment should remain in place). A concession may make provision for an investor's required decommissioning activities (although older concessions tend to contain less prescriptive decommissioning provisions[31]). A concession may require an investor to prepare a detailed decommissioning plan and an associated budget in respect of the assets or equipment in the concession area which are to be, or which have been, used for petroleum production activities.

as provided for in the Development Plan, as a consequence of a decision by the GOVERNMENT or any federal or international regulatory body, the GOVERNMENT undertakes to allocate any such reduction fairly and equitably among the various operators (including the GOVERNMENT) then producing in the Kurdistan Region, pro rata their respective production rates.'

[27] The Brazil 2017 PSA provides (at 16.9) that: 'The Consortium members may request ANP to approve, upon prior request, the interruption of Production in one Field for a maximum period of one year', but with a further proviso (at 16.11) that: 'Interruption of Production shall not entail suspension of the term of the Agreement.' The Suriname 2015 PSC provides (at 2.4.3) that: '[N]othing contained in this Contract shall be construed or interpreted to require Contractor to develop or produce or continue to produce Petroleum from a Commercial Field, which, in Contractor's opinion, does not provide it with an acceptable rate of return.'

[28] The Pakistan 2000 PSA provides (at 12.3) that: '[E]ach Foreign Contracting Company (and its registered branch in Pakistan) shall be entitled to export its share of the Petroleum acquired by Contractor under this Agreement'. The Tajikistan 2008 PSC provides (at 21.1) that: 'The Contractor, Contractor Parties, any purchaser from such parties and their respective carriers shall, for the duration of this Contract, have the right to export without any export duties, levys, rents, taxes or similar, from any export point selected by the Contractor for such purpose, the share of Petroleum to which the Contractor is entitled under this Contract.'

[29] The Pakistan 2000 PSA provides (at 11.1) that: 'Contractor hereby agrees to refrain from exporting Petroleum produced from the Contract Area to countries with which the Government for national security or policy reasons has officially restricted its international relationship.'

[30] The Trinidad and Tobago 2023 PSC provides (at 26.1) that: 'In case of war or imminent expectation of war or grave national emergency (as provided for in Section 36 of the Act), the President may requisition all or a part of the Petroleum Production from the Contract Area and require Contractor to increase such Production to the extent required' and (at 26.2) that: 'In the event of any requisition as provided above, the President shall indemnify Contractor in full for the period, during which the requisition is maintained, including all reasonable damages, if any, which result from such requisition.' The Mozambique 2006 EPC provides (at 27.11 (a)) that: 'In the event that the Government exercises any right it may have under the laws of Mozambique to acquire for imperative reasons in the national interest Petroleum belonging to the Concessionaire, the Government shall give not less than forty five (45) days notice of the exercise of such right and of the volumes it wishes to acquire, and the Concessionaire shall supply the volumes so notified from the Petroleum to which the Concessionaire is entitled under this EPC.'

[31] The Guyana 2023 PSA (at 40) offers a comprehensive decommissioning provision.

The legal framework for effecting decommissioning may also be set out within a petroleum law of the state (and could set out decommissioning principles which are derived from international accords). The expectation of a grantor is that an investor will fund the costs of the decommissioning activities, and that the burden of those costs should not fall upon the state (at least, not in the first instance).

The decommissioning plan and budget can be submitted by an investor to a grantor at the same time as an FDP is submitted, or such submission can come later in the lifecycle of a development and production project—such as when a defined percentage of the estimated petroleum initially in place in the discovery has been produced,[32] and certainly well ahead of the intended date of the permanent cessation of production of petroleum from the discovery.

To meet the anticipated costs of decommissioning an investor may be obliged to provide collateral support (5.4) for those costs, or to contribute monies periodically into a segregated decommissioning sinking fund, which will (hopefully) mature to be sufficient to meet the costs of the decommissioning plan at the time of the performance of the intended decommissioning activities. These payments may become due from the time when the decommissioning plan and budget are approved by a grantor, from a certain time after the date of the first production of petroleum from a discovery, or from a point when the production of petroleum has reached a defined percentage level of the initial assumption of petroleum in place in the project. The later occurrence of the obligation of an investor to begin financing the anticipated decommissioning activities could improve the overall economic bargain of a concession from an investor's perspective.

Once the decommissioning plan and budget have been approved by a grantor it may be a requirement of the management committee (5.5) to consider periodically whether the plan and budget remain appropriate for the ongoing production activities, taking into account any operational changes or technological evolutions which have occurred, and the management committee will also recommend any necessary revisions to the plan and budget. The actual decommissioning activities can be undertaken at the appropriate time under the stewardship of the investor if the investor remains party to the concession, or by the grantor if the concession has come to an end and the investor's involvement has ceased.

If, at the intended time of decommissioning, a grantor has a preference not to decommission certain assets or equipment (eg because a grantor wishes to continue petroleum production from the producing part of the concession area or to undertake a field enhancement programme, in either case for its own account or through the issue of a permit or concession to do so to another person) a grantor could release an investor from its decommissioning obligations, with the accumulated

[32] The Afghanistan 2013 EPSC provides (in 7.3) that: 'The Contractor shall submit to the Ministry for approval a proposed Field decommissioning and abandonment plan (the "Decommissioning and Abandonment Plan") after exhaustion of fifty percent (50%) of Recoverable Gas Initially in Place (RGIIP)/Recoverable Oil Initially in Place (ROIIP)'.

funds to be held over for when the intended decommissioning does eventually take place.[33]

A concession may also provide for certain assets or equipment which are to be decommissioned to be repurposed for other local uses[34] or to be reused elsewhere by an investor.[35]

Care will need to be taken where certain assets or equipment to be decommissioned in the abstract under a concession are also being used to support petroleum operations in respect of other concessions. One element of decommissioning could trigger a domino effect in respect of other concessions (3.4), which a state will be reluctant to see happen.

8.6 Work Programmes and Budgets

A concession could require an investor to prepare (and thereafter perform) a work programme and budget in respect of each aspect of the anticipated petroleum operations (6.2). This requirement may apply to the activities of exploration and appraisal, development and production, and decommissioning (on an activity-specific basis and/or on an annual basis), or it could be disapplied in respect of the exploration period (where work programmes and budgets are effectively prescribed by the defined exploration period obligations and their associated costs) and apply only to the development phase onwards.[36]

Each work programme and budget will be subject to a grantor's approval (which may be subject to prior discussion at a management committee (5.5)). The work programme element of the work programme and budget will have to be approved by a grantor within a sufficient time period to allow the necessary works envisaged by an investor to take place in accordance with the timetable demanded by the concession. Some iteration may take place between a grantor and an investor, with possible revisions and resubmissions of the work programme and budget by the investor. A concession might also provide for deemed approval of the work programme and budget if a grantor's approval (or no objection by a grantor) has been forthcoming within a defined period of time after the work programme and budget was submitted for approval.

Thereafter, the performance of the work programme and budget is less likely to be subject to ongoing approval, except where subsequent amendment of the work programme and budget (perhaps arising as a consequence of slippage by an investor in the

[33] The Guyana 2023 PSA provides (at 40.17) that: 'In the event minister elects to continue the Petroleum Operations and take over the relevant facilities, the accumulated amount in the Decommissioning Fund and such additional amounts as may be estimated for Decommissioning at the time of the transfer, shall be deposited in a nominated bank account domiciled in Guyana having the Minister as beneficiary.'

[34] The Guyana 2023 PSA provides (at 40.19 (b)) that: 'The Minister may grant a departure from the requirement to remove a platform or other facility by approving partial structure removal or toppling in place for conversion to an artificial reef'.

[35] The Guyana 2023 PSA provides (at 40.19 (c)) that: 'The Contractor may apply to reuse or relocate the facility for conduction oil or gas development at another location, or for additional energy or marine-related purposes.'

[36] See the Trinidad and Tobago 2023 PSC (at 15.1).

programme or as a reaction to the results of the performance of the associated obligations) is required by an investor. A concession may also reserve a right for the operator to overspend against an approved work programme and budget with approval, up to a specified percentage of the originally approved amount.

A concession may also provide that any activities carried out by an investor must be within the ambit of an approved work programme and budget (unless a management committee (5.5) or the grantor otherwise authorizes, or unless the investor's activities are in response to an emergency). Failure of an investor to comply with this requirement may expose the investor to a liability for breach of the concession.

8.7 The Investor's Performance Standards

A concession may oblige an investor to undertake the petroleum operations (6.2) to a standard which is in accordance with some variant of a broad theme of good and prudent oil and gas field practice (which may be defined in the concession).[37] This requirement, in whatever form it takes, will set out an objective standard of behaviour which would be expected from a person similar to the investor which is operating in circumstances similar to those of a concession, and is intended to guarantee certain minimum standards of operational behaviour, health and safety management, and environmental compliance by the investor.[38] Such a provision is generalized and reference in a concession to compliance by the investor with specific standards might be preferable.

A concession may also require an investor to observe certain environmental protection standards and to undertake certain obligations (both positive and negative) which relate to the protection of the environment in the performance of the petroleum operations. These standards include the legislative requirements of the state in respect of environmental protection matters, and certain regional or international environmental standards which have been imported into the state's domestic law.

[37] The Afghanistan 2013 EPSC provides (at 1.1) that: '"Good Oil Field Practices" shall mean such practices and procedures employed in the hydrocarbons industry worldwide by prudent and diligent operators under conditions and circumstances similar to those experienced in connection with the relevant aspect or aspects of the Hydrocarbons Operations, intended principally at guaranteeing: (i) environmental protection, which calls for the adoption of methods and processes which avoid or minimize the adverse impact of Hydrocarbons Operations on the environment, including avoiding or minimizing damage to flora and fauna; (ii) operational safety, which entails the use of methods and processes that promote occupational safety and the prevention of accidents; and (iii) conservation of Hydrocarbons resources, which implies the utilization of adequate methods and processes to maximize the recovery of Hydrocarbons in a technically and economically sustainable manner, with a corresponding control of reserves decline, using principles of maximum efficient production rates and other conservation principles, and to minimize losses at the surface and avoid waste.'

[38] The Zanzibar 2024 PSA provides (at 23 (a)) that: 'The Contractor shall comply with Zanzibar laws related to Occupational Safety and Health, laws related to Environmental protection, laws related to Public and Environmental Health, Food, Drugs and Cosmetics, the Regulations and administrative decisions issued by virtue of the Laws, all other legislation at any time in force in Zanzibar as well as best international petroleum industry practices, through the implementation of necessary systematic measures.' The Bangladesh 2023 PSC provides (at 10.4) that the investor will '[c]onduct all Petroleum Operations in a diligent, conscientious and workmanlike manner, in accordance with the applicable laws and this Contract, and generally accepted standards of the international Petroleum industry designed to achieve efficient and safe exploration and production of Petroleum and prevent loss or waste of Petroleum above or below the surface and to maximize the ultimate economic recovery of Petroleum from the Contract Area.'

This requirement of an investor may be imported through the application of the governing law of a concession (11.2), but it will usually be made clearer in a concession by the inclusion of a specific provision for environmental compliance.[39]

The principal aspect of this requirement relates to ongoing environmental protection by an investor,[40] and also to the preparation of a pollution response plan,[41] and it could also require the investor to minimize harmful emissions which arise from the performance of the petroleum operations.[42] This latter point includes controls on the amount of gas which is flared by an investor (13.4).[43] As part of an investor's obligations, when an FDP has been approved and a development project is underway an investor may be required to conduct an environmental assessment in respect of a defined target area.[44] This study could later be used to assess the investor's satisfaction of the site remediation elements within an approved decommissioning plan (8.5).[45] In some circumstances such a study could also be required ahead of the performance of any exploration works.

All of these aspirations add to the definition of the requirements for the investor's compliance with good and prudent oil and gas field practice.

Ensuring that an investor takes full note of the requirement for its environmental standards compliance may be achieved by making the investor fully liable for the

[39] The Somalia 2023 PSA provides (at 20.1) that: 'During the performance of the Petroleum Operations (including, without limitation, during Decommissioning), the Contractor shall comply with environmental principles and safeguards prescribed in Law concerning environmental protection'.

[40] The Guyana 2023 PSA provides (at 44.3) that: 'In the conduct of Petroleum Operations, the Contractor shall take necessary and adequate precautions, in accordance with Best International Industry Standards and Practices, against pollution and for the protection of the environment and the living resources of the rivers and sea.'

[41] The Guyana 2023 PSA provides (at 44.4) that: 'If the Contractor's failure to comply with applicable law, the provisions of this Agreement and Best International Industry Standards and Practices results in pollution or damage to the environment, riverain or marine life or otherwise, the Contractor shall take all measures necessary in accordance with Best International Industry Standards and Practices to remedy the failure and the effects thereof and shall where pollution occurs treat or disperse it in an environmentally sound and safe manner.'

[42] The Guyana 2023 PSA provides (at 3.1 (c)) that: '[T]he Contractor must . . . take all steps necessary that these operations are carried out with as low as reasonably practicable impact on the environment. The Contractor must take reasonably practicable steps to ensure that its activities have the lowest commercially and technically possible Greenhouse Gas (GHG) operational emissions.'

[43] The Gambia 2022 licence provides (at 9.6) that: 'The Licensee shall not flare any Petroleum for the duration of the Licence, including during the testing of any Reservoir or Producing Interval without the express written consent of the Commissioner (such consent not to be unreasonably withheld or delayed), except in the case of an Emergency where the Licensee may flare such amounts of Petroleum as is reasonably required to prevent or reduce the impact of the Emergency'.

[44] The Somalia 2023 PSA provides (at 20.5) that: 'The Contractor shall conduct a strategic environmental and social impact assessment and, within ninety (90) days after the Effective Date, submit a report thereon to the SPA (and to the relevant Somali Governmental Authority being responsible at that time for the environment) for approval . . . Such environmental and social impact assessment shall establish the effect of the Petroleum Operations to be undertaken under the Agreement on the environment, human beings, livestock, wildlife or marine life, and shall include emergency and accident response plans.'

[45] The Guyana 2023 PSA provides (at 3 (h)) that the contractor will '[p]rovide all the information, environmental impact assessments and specific technical studies required for the purposes of obtaining applicable environmental licenses', and (at 16.6) that: 'The Development Plan shall be accompanied by an Environmental Impact Assessment Plan submitted under the Environmental Protection Act, 1996', and (at 40.5) that: 'The Decommissioning Plan shall be accompanied by an Environmental Impact Assessment Plan submitted under the Environmental Protection Act.'

consequences of any breaches of those standards (without the prospect of offsetting such liabilities),[46] although a concession may afford some latitude to an investor.[47]

As part of its environmental commitments, a concession may also require an investor to finance certain environmental protection initiatives at its own expense.[48]

Recent years have also seen an increasing trend towards requiring investors to comply with certain protocols regarding corporate behaviour and responsibility, which are variously paraphrased under headings such as 'sustainable development', 'ethical behaviour', 'corporate and social responsibility', and (most commonly) 'environment, social and governance' (ESG) requirements.[49]

A concession may contain a declaration by an investor that it will perform the concession in a manner which evidences compliance with certain defined protocols (where definition of the applicable protocols will be addressed in the concession). Regard might be had, for example, to the declarations of the International Petroleum Industry Environmental Conservation Association (IPIECA),[50] the International Union for Conservation of Nature[51] and its joint commitments with the International Association of Oil & Gas Producers,[52] the Equator Principles governing social and environmental issues in project financing,[53] and the Voluntary Principles on Security and Human Rights.[54] This is by no means an exhaustive list.

The protocols which are suggested above are finding their way into newer editions of joint venture arrangements between investor parties, but in the context of the terms of concessions this is a relatively unexplored area. An investor's commitment to compliance with such commitments is often made so that an investor can disclose the fact of its compliance to its shareholders and to society as a whole, as evidence of an investor's commitment to being a good corporate citizen. Without knowing the full implication of what is required, a grantor may be less willing to make a public statement of its own intention to comply with these protocols in the performance of a concession.

[46] The Guyana 2023 PSA provides (at 3.1 (j)) that: '[T]he Contractor must ... indemnify and hold the State harmless, as the case may be, from all claims, losses and damages of any nature whatsoever that are caused by the Contractor's and Subcontractors' operations. Expenses incurred by the Contractor on this account shall not be considered Cost Oil.' In furtherance of this protection of the grantor, the Guyana 2023 PSA also provides (at 29.3) that the investor will effect policies of insurance in respect of its prospective liabilities, with the grantor to be named on those policies as a co-insured person.

[47] The Somalia 2023 PSA provides (at 20.12) that: 'The Contractor shall not be liable for any pre-existing environmental conditions and any environmental damage caused by acts of Third Parties (other than the Contractor's Affiliates, contractors, sub-contractors or agents).'

[48] The Guyana 2023 PSA provides (at 44.7) that: 'The Minister and the Contractor shall establish a programme of financial support for environmental and social projects to be funded by the Contractor. The Contractor shall directly fund the amount of one million United States Dollars (US$1,000,000.00) per Calendar Year with any funded but unspent portion be carried over into the ensuing Calendar Years of the Agreement.'

[49] The Gambia 2022 licence includes (at 13.1.1) the following statement: 'Corporate social responsibility is the commitment of the Licensee to contribute to sustainable economic development, working with employees, their families, the local community and society at large to improve their quality of life in The Gambia', and provides (at 13.1.2) that: 'The Government and the Licensee shall meet annually in order to formulate the programmes of activities to be undertaken by the Licensee in relation to corporate social responsibility'.

[50] <www.ipieca.org/> accessed 3 April 2025.

[51] <www.iucn.org/> accessed 3 April 2025.

[52] <www.iogp.org/> accessed 3 April 2025.

[53] <www.equator-principles.com/> accessed 3 April 2025.

[54] <www.voluntaryprinciples.org/> accessed 3 April 2025.

9

Fiscal Terms

9.1 Introduction

The fiscal terms of a concession reflect the competing elements of state take and investor take. 'State take' describes an aggregation of the different forms of revenue which a grantor earns from a concession. As the obvious counterpoint to state take, 'investor take' represents the revenues which an investor earns from the concession, net of the costs of performing the petroleum operations, and the incidence of state take.

In constructing the fiscal terms of a concession a grantor must reconcile its desire to retain a fair measure of return from an investor's exploitation of the state's patrimony with presenting an investment opportunity which an investor will find sufficiently compelling. The fiscal terms represent a balancing of the competing interests of a grantor and an investor. An investor will require that the fiscal terms are predictable at the time of entry into the concession, and that they will remain stable for the concession's duration.

9.2 State Take

State take, as an aggregation of the rewards which flow (directly and indirectly) to a grantor under a concession (including where the concession proves to be revenue generative through the production of petroleum),[1] should be structured to realize several objectives:

(1) *Equal application*—the broad principles of state take should be applied equally to all energy sector (ie petroleum and non-petroleum) investors. A subsidy which is granted to one set of investors (eg in the form of tax exemptions or the disapplication of other fiscal terms) may be borne indirectly by another set of investors. This may act as a disincentive for certain investors, which could be detrimental to the state's overall interests.

(2) *Progressiveness*—the tools used for realizing state take should be designed to be progressive. This is a linkage whereby the level of state take increases as the level of revenue which is generated in favour of an investor increases. Apart from creating an economic advantage for the grantor (compared to a measure of state

[1] Daniel Johnston, 'Government Take' [2018] JWELB 506.

take which remains relatively flat), progressiveness addresses popular concerns that exploitation of the state's patrimony by an investor is not accompanied by the accrual of satisfactory returns to the state. Progressiveness may also reduce the temptation for a grantor to unilaterally re-regulate the economic bargain with an investor through some form of expropriation (7.6) if a grantor feels that it is not making a fair return from a concession.

(3) *Reliability*—the manner in which state take is realized should be transparent and readily understandable by investors, and the use of those tools should be effected in a manner which offers certainty and stability to investors. A concession should strike the balance between preserving a state's sovereign rights to regulate its energy sector as it sees fit over time, and ensuring that agreed standards of investment protection are maintained and the scope for disputes between a grantor and an investor is minimized.

Where the concession is a production-sharing contract (PSC) the principal vehicle for effecting state take is profit sharing, net of an investor's cost recovery (9.3). Under a licence the principal vehicle for effecting state take is taxation (9.5), also with the possibility of royalty income (9.4). And, in either case, a number of other devices could apply which generate state take. All of these elements can be aggregated to demonstrate levels of return to a state which will result from the award of a concession which can be very significant.[2]

9.3 Cost Recovery and Profit Sharing in a PSC

'Cost recovery' in a PSC reflects a process whereby an investor is reimbursed for the accrued costs which it has incurred in connection with the performance of the petroleum operations from the revenues which result from the sale of produced petroleum. Although the recovered costs relate to petroleum operations generally the PSC may provide for separate cost recovery regimes for oil and gas development projects. From an accounting perspective, cost recovery is akin to tax deductible expenses (9.5), as both constructions represent the allowance of certain costs which an investor has incurred before profitability is assessed and addressed.

From a grantor's perspective cost recovery could be seen as a vehicle to encourage an investor to invest properly in the performance of the petroleum operations, so maximizing the chances of success in finding and developing a discovery and generally acting as a catalyst for investment. On the other hand, since increased cost recovery reduces the available profit share, a grantor will have a keen interest in controlling the level of costs incurred by, and which can be claimed as being recoverable by, an investor.

[2] 'The average government share of profits is just under 70 per cent. For those countries with better geology and a healthier geopolitical setting the government share of profits ... will more likely be on the order of 80-85 per cent, or more. For countries lacking such robust potential, the average government take can range around 55 per cent or less.' (Daniel Johnston, *Oil and Gas Contracts: Principles and Practice* (3rd edn, Sweet & Maxwell 2022)).

Cost recovery gives comfort to an investor that it will (or should[3]) be able to recover the accrued costs which it has incurred once petroleum production revenues start to flow and is essentially the *quid pro quo* for an investor taking exploration risk under the PSC. However, an investor's view of cost recovery could be less sanguine where certain provisions in the PSC condition the freedom of its application. A cost recovery mechanism can be characterized (and conditioned) by a number of features:

(1) *Irrecoverable costs*—costs which have been incurred by an investor in the performance of the petroleum operations will accrue in a costs pool but it is not the case that all of those costs will automatically be recoverable by the investor.

An accounting procedure which is typically attached to a PSC (7.9) could describe the categories of costs which are recoverable (and which are ineligible for recovery) by an investor.[4] A grantor will usually oversee the conduct of a periodic audit process which will identify whether costs are recoverable or irrecoverable. Where an investor's costs are not approved for cost recovery they will be borne by the investor, which will diminish the overall economic returns from the PSC from the investor's perspective.

Common examples of irrecoverable costs include an investor's liability to pay any bonuses, rental payments, or royalties incurred under the PSC, costs not regulated by an approved work programme and budget (8.6), costs incurred prior to the effectiveness of the PSC (which might include data package acquisition costs (10.5)), costs associated with the provision of collateral support (5.4) and with the investor parties' joint venture arrangement (5.3), fines or penalties which relate to an investor's mis-performance or non-performance of the PSC, fees payable by an investor to a grantor in consideration of any services provided by the grantor, liabilities of an investor to a grantor for a breach of the terms of the PSC, and the costs associated with downstream activities and the marketing of petroleum for sale (which might be beyond the scope of the PSC (6.2) in any event, although an exception might be made for gas (13.1). The PSC might also limit an investor's recovery of costs which were not incurred using good and prudent oil and gas field practice (8.7).[5] Making an assessment of this last issue could be contentious.

[3] The Azerbaijan 1996 production sharing agreement (PSA) makes the observation (at 2.2) that: '[I]n the event production resulting from Petroleum Operations, upon completion of commercial production from the Contract Area at the end of the term of this Agreement . . . is insufficient for full recovery of Contractor's Capital Costs and Operating Costs as provided hereunder, then Contractor shall not be entitled to any reimbursement or compensation for any of its costs not recovered.'

[4] The Qatar 2002 development and production sharing agreement (DPSA) provides (at 1.1.84) that costs which are not recoverable include: 'all interest on borrowings, financing fees, premiums and all other charges paid or costs incurred or accrued by the CONTRACTOR in respect of financing Petroleum Costs' but also with an interesting footnote which observes that: 'If interest costs are not cost recoverable then the CONTRACTOR will require a larger profit split to recover these costs. A larger profit split for the CONTRACTOR goes against QP's policy of keeping as high a profit split for the GOVERNMENT as possible.'

[5] The Tanzania 2013 PSA provides (at 12) that: 'Recoverable Contract Expenses may be recovered as from the date they have been prudently incurred.' The Qatar 2002 DPSA provides (at 1.1) that Petroleum Costs 'means all costs incurred or accrued after the Effective Date by the CONTRACTOR or its contractors directly related to

Disagreements between a grantor and an investor regarding the recoverability of costs (whether by principle or by quantum) are not uncommon. This is frequently an issue for contention in the negotiation (and the later administration) of a PSC, and the poor definition of costs classifications in the PSC at the outset could be responsible for generating later disputes between a grantor and an investor.

(2) *Enhanced cost recovery*—certain costs might be notionally increased under the terms of a PSC in an investor's favour (so that, eg, an investor will be able to cost-recover $125 for each incurred $100 of those costs). This 'enhanced cost recovery' is intended to give an investor an added incentive to undertake certain activities and to incur the associated costs where those activities could also benefit a grantor.[6] These enhanced costs might also be expressed to be not subject to a cap on their recoverability.

Enhanced cost recovery could apply, for example, to the costs of seismic surveys or exploration drilling (where the resultant data will accrue to benefit a grantor) or to exploration activity in particularly difficult deep-water or frontier areas which a grantor is keen to see explored. From an investor's perspective, care should be taken to ensure that the incremental element of enhanced cost recovery, which gives an investor a monetary amount in excess of its actual incurred costs, is not taxed as the investor's income.

(3) *Ring-fencing*—costs incurred in connection with the performance of a PSC are ordinarily subject to a concept called 'ring-fencing'. This means that the costs so incurred, which might otherwise be irrecoverable by an investor because of the lack of a commercial discovery and a development and production project under the PSC, cannot be recovered by an investor against the petroleum revenues generated under another PSC which an investor holds where a development project has taken place.[7] Ring-fencing could also apply within a PSC in respect of discrete development areas or activities.[8]

the conduct of Petroleum Operations ... as a result of the CONTRACTOR acting as a Reasonable and Prudent Operator'.

[6] The Kenya 2014 PSC provides (at 36(3)) that: 'An amount equal to fifteen percent (15%) of the development costs related to a development area incurred and paid during a given fiscal year shall be referred to as "Uplift" for that development area and fiscal year. Such Uplift regarding the development costs of one fiscal year shall be recoverable under sub-clauses 36(1) and 36(2) in five (5) equal installments starting in the fiscal year in which the related development costs are incurred or the fiscal year in which commercial production for that development area commences, whichever is the later. The Uplift shall be applicable only to the development costs incurred in the first five (5) fiscal years of an approved development plan starting the fiscal year of its date of approval.'

[7] The Uganda 1999 PSC provides (at 10.1) that: 'For purposes of Cost Recovery and Production Sharing, ring fencing around each Contract Area shall apply. In the event that a Licensee has more than one Contract Area, the calculations shall be done on a contract by contract basis. There shall be no consolidation.' The Trinidad and Tobago 2023 PSC provides (at 21.10) that: 'The Parties agree that for the purposes of determining Contractor's Taxable Income in Trinidad and Tobago, profits and/or losses resulting from Petroleum Operations carried out under this Contract shall not at any time be consolidated with profits and/or losses resulting from any of the Contractor's other operations in Trinidad and Tobago outside the Contract Area.'

[8] The Suriname 2015 PSC provides (at 3.5) that: 'During the entire term of this Contract, Contractor may conduct exploratory activities in all Development and Production Areas, at all depths and strata, until Contractor relinquishes these areas or this Contract is terminated. These exploration expenditures, which are the result of the above mentioned exploration activities, after expiration of the Exploration Period, shall not be cost recovered

The absence of ring-fencing could create cross-subsidization between PSCs. The economic risk profile of the PSC could thereby be enhanced for an investor, but at the expense of a grantor (which would be subsidizing an investor's unsuccessful exploration activities by allowing their costs to be offset against an investor's other revenues).

(4) *Cost recovery limits*—the more generous the cost recovery regime is from an investor's perspective, the longer it will take for a grantor to realize revenue from the PSC. Consequently, a PSC will typically not allow an investor to offset the entirety of its recoverable costs from the revenues which result from the sale of produced petroleum in respect of a defined accounting period (7.9), because of the risk that a grantor would see no share of those revenues until the investor's costs had been fully recovered. Indeed, in the extreme case, an investor's recovery of costs could be so extensive that the revenues due to a grantor through the profit shares could be virtually non-existent (apart from the recovery of any applicable bonuses, rental payments, and royalties) if a PSC is cost-saturated and remains in the cost recovery phase for the entirety of its duration.

To overcome this risk to a grantor, one option is that a PSC might apply what is called a 'first tranche petroleum' provision, wherein the revenues resulting from the sales of petroleum are applied towards reimbursement of an investor's accrued costs but with the exception that a defined percentage of the revenues is first applied between a grantor and an investor according to the agreed profit shares. This would give a grantor early access to a part of the revenues resulting from the sales of petroleum. This construction first appeared in Indonesian PSCs in the late 1980s.

The more typical protection for a grantor in this situation is to engineer the cost recovery mechanism in a PSC such that the PSC imposes a general percentage cap on the amount of costs which are recoverable by an investor in respect of a defined accounting period (often called a 'cost stop'), with provision for any unrecovered costs to be carried forward for recovery in successive accounting periods. Once the cost stop has been reached in respect of the defined accounting period then the remaining revenues are distributed between the parties according to the profit shares for the remainder of that accounting period. The cost stop mechanism does not deny the recovery of costs by an investor, but it does limit how much of those costs can be recovered by an investor within a particular period. Alternatively, some costs could be capped and other costs not so capped in this manner if a PSC applies a hierarchy order of recoverable costs.

The cost stop figure could be a flat percentage of all recoverable costs in respect of specified periods throughout the duration of a PSC or it could be applied on a sliding scale, whereby a higher percentage for recoverable costs could apply in an investor's favour in the early period of petroleum production to accelerate

through existing Commercial Fields, but shall only be recoverable from production from the newly discovered reservoirs established as the result of such exploratory activities.'

cost recovery, before then dropping down to a percentage figure which is something nearer to equilibrium with the profit shares when a specified percentage of the overall costs has been recovered by an investor.

A PSC might also provide that if any otherwise recoverable costs remain unrecovered by an investor by the end of the PSC's term then those costs will be lost to the investor and a grantor will have no obligation to reimburse them.

(5) *Individual costs*—each investor party will incur its share of the overall costs associated with the performance of the petroleum operations, but the actual costs incidence could be different between the investor parties. Some investor parties could pay for certain insurances to be put in place (7.3) whilst others might not, and some investor parties may have borrowed money to meet their share of the petroleum operations costs and may have associated financing costs and interest charges which could be cost recoverable under a PSC, whilst others will not.

Cost recovery should be accounted for under a PSC so that each investor party has its own separate costs pool which is generated according to its actual costs incurrences, rather than that the investor parties' costs are aggregated and made payable to the investor parties according to their percentage participating interests. Where an investor party has borrowed money to meet its share of the petroleum operations costs, and financing costs and interest charges are expressed to be cost recoverable under a PSC, it is possible that an affiliate of an investor party could lend money to that investor party with high financing costs and/or at a high rate of interest. To protect against the risk of abuse, a PSC could apply a deemed rate of interest to apply to such an affiliated lender, or the consent of a grantor to an affiliate lending arrangement could be required as a condition of the financing costs and interest charges being cost recoverable by an investor party.

(6) *Cost recovery hierarchy*—when recoverable costs are due to be recovered, the costs will be relatively generalized but a PSC might seek to apply some form of hierarchy to the recovery of those costs. This could be applied so that (eg) costs will be recovered by an investor in the order of annual production operating costs first, then accrued exploration and appraisal operating costs, and then accrued development project capital costs. Where a state participation right has been exercised (10.8) and the state nominee has incurred costs, a grantor could prefer that costs which have been incurred in part by the state nominee are recoverable as a matter of priority.

This hierarchy could be expressed in various ways, according to a grantor's preference.[9] Decommissioning costs could be an anomaly in this construction, since they could be incurred by an investor as part of a sinking fund

[9] The Qatar 2002 DPSA provides (at 18) that: 'The order in which costs shall be recovered is as follows: 18.6.1. firstly, Operating Costs as set out in Article 18.3; 18.6.2. secondly, Development Costs as set out in Article 18.4; then 18.6.3. thirdly, carried-forward costs as set out in Article 18.' The Tanzania 2023 PSA provides (at 18.8) that costs and expenses 'shall be recovered from the relevant account on a first in, first out basis subject to the following: (a) costs incurred in respect of Exploration Operations may be recovered on an expensed basis; (b) capital costs incurred in respect of Development and Production Operations may be recovered on an expensed basis commencing in the year in which such expenditure is incurred; (c) annual operating costs, may be recovered in

(and cost recovered as they are incurred) well ahead of the time when the decommissioning activity is actually performed (8.5).

A PSC may oblige an investor to prepare a monthly or quarterly statement of expenditures and recoverable costs (reflecting the various conditions set out above) for submission to a grantor for review and approval.

Mechanisms in a PSC which limit recoverable costs (whether by principle or by quantum) ensure that remaining petroleum production (and its revenues) are forced into the profit-sharing mechanism, thereby securing some economic returns for a grantor even though the cost recovery phase under a PSC is still ongoing.

'Profit sharing' in a PSC represents an agreed division, between a grantor and an investor, of the proceeds of sale of produced petroleum entitlements which remain after the application of cost recovery in favour of an investor. Each party has an interest in maximizing its profit share under a PSC, not surprisingly.

The profit shares division between a grantor and an investor takes the form of a percentage ratio. Although the profit shares relate to petroleum operations generally, a PSC may provide for different ratios to apply to oil development projects and to gas development projects.

The profit shares could be set as fixed percentages of agreed tranches of petroleum production volumes[10] or, to make the fiscal terms progressive (9.2), the profit shares could be represented as a sliding scale which is designed to increase a grantor's entitlements as the underlying project attains greater levels of petroleum production over time. In its simplest form this construction would account for increased levels of petroleum production but not for the true economic value of that production (since production levels could be high but petroleum prices could be low, which would offset the real gain to a grantor).[11] This structure is progressive as far as production is concerned, but it is neutral in respect of real profitability, and it could be further modified to also reflect price recoveries.[12]

An alternative method of creating a sliding scale of profit shares in order to embrace progressiveness is the use of an 'R factor' (or 'ratio factor'), sometimes also defined as an 'investment multiple'. The R factor is arrived at by dividing the revenues from a petroleum production project by the costs of that project (so that R = Revenues/Costs)

the year in which they are incurred; and (d) annual administrative overhead costs, up to the limits established in Article 2(l) of the Accounting Procedure of Annex "C" may be recovered in the year incurred.'

[10] See the Senegal 2012 PSC (at 22.3).

[11] The Pakistan 2000 PSA provides (at 6.6) for profit sharing on a volumetric basis.

[12] The Trinidad and Tobago 2023 PSC provides (at 18.14) for a grantor's entitlements to be determined by reference to production volumes and realized prices: 'The Government's share of Profit Crude Oil and/or Profit Natural Gas for a Calendar Month from the Contract Area shall be determined separately for Crude Oil and Natural Gas by reference to the applicable price class in the relevant table(s) detailed hereunder. The relevant price class shall be determined using the value of Profit Crude Oil and Profit Natural Gas calculated in accordance with Article 20 herein. The average daily Production rates referred to in the Production tiers set out in the tables hereunder shall be calculated for each Calendar Month by dividing the respective volumes of Available Crude Oil and Available Natural Gas produced from the Contract Area during that Month by the number of days in such Month.'

and then ascribing particular profit shares which are payable to a grantor and to an investor in respect of each band of the resultant R factor calculation.[13]

At the start of a petroleum production project, costs inevitably outweigh revenues and so the R factor would be low (indeed, at the very outset of a project, costs are high and revenues are non-existent and so the R factor could be zero). As the R factor increases (that is, as revenues increase (and the economic gain to the investor improves) and as revenues increasingly outweigh costs in the later stages of a project) then the profit shares in favour of a grantor increases.

A PSC could also apply the sliding scale which is outlined above in respect of the R factor to an investor's rate of return from a project (where higher rate of return percentages over time will increase a grantor's profit shares). This is sometimes described as a 'rate of return' (ROR) based system. Understanding what an investor's internal rate of return is, particularly where an investor is a consortium of investor parties who could each have different methodologies for determining this measure, could be a challenge and so the PSC may set out its own deemed investor rate of return methodology.

A PSC usually provides for quarterly calculations in arrears of the cost recovery and profit-sharing elements, based on measured levels of petroleum production from the preceding quarter and applying a valuation methodology to manage the interface between produced petroleum, petroleum sales revenues, and the interests of a grantor and an investor. There is an obvious disparity between an investor's accrued petroleum costs (which have been incurred and paid in cash) and the produced petroleum which is applied between the parties in their respective profit shares (which is a physical measure) to offset those petroleum costs. To reconcile these different measures, by normalizing them to a consistent cash basis, a PSC will contain a valuation mechanism, whereby crude oil is required to be sold on an arm's length basis by an investor and according to international market prices, and the actual sales proceeds are remitted through the petroleum accounting mechanisms of the PSC to create a cash value which will then be applied for the cost recovery quantification. If crude oil is sold other than on an arm's length basis, a PSC could recite a mechanism by which a proxy market price is derived. Similar provisions could apply in the sale of gas, except that gas which is sold under a bilateral contract might not have an international market reference price against which the fairness of the particular contract price as part of an arm's length transaction can be assessed.

[13] For examples of R factor mechanisms see the Afghanistan 2013 EPSC (at 10.1); the Bangladesh 2023 PSC (at 14.6); the Cameroon 2007 PSC (at 13.2); the India 2010 PSC (at 16.2.3); the Kurdistan Iraq 2007 PSC (at 26.4); the Mauritania 2012 PSC (at 10.3); the Mozambique 2006 EPC (at 9.11); the Qatar 2002 DPSA (at 18.6.3); the Suriname 2015 PSC (at 14.7); the Turkmenistan 1997 PSA (at 13.13); the Zanzibar 2024 PSA (at 11 (h)).

9.4 Other Options for State Take

State take also can be realized through the following devices (which can apply to most forms of concession) which provide for various monetary payments to be made by an investor to a grantor:

(1) *Signature bonus*—an investor could be required to pay a defined monetary bonus to a grantor upon the signature of a concession.[14] The extent of a signature bonus tends to be modest for unexplored acreage where there is little pre-existing geological and geophysical data and a higher level of exploration risk; the bonus tends to increase in size where the prospectivity of the acreage improves through the availability of data and the experience of previous exploration activity. The signature bonus will be payable by an investor regardless of whether or not a commercial discovery of petroleum ensues (8.3), will not be repayable if an investor subsequently surrenders the concession (6.6), and is typically not cost recoverable under a PSC. For these reasons, a signature bonus tends to be a sensitive issue from an investor's perspective, compared to most of the other fiscal terms (and especially those fiscal terms which are triggered by an investor's earnings from a concession, where an investor will at least feel that it is finally deriving some benefit from the concession). A further bonus might also be payable by an investor if an extension to the production period (6.5), or if an extension to or a renewal of a concession is agreed (6.3).

(2) *Production bonus*—this is a payment made by an investor to a grantor on the occurrence of a particular event. This could be when a commercial discovery is declared (8.3),[15] when petroleum production begins, when rates of petroleum production over a particular period reach a defined threshold, or when a defined cumulative quantity of petroleum production is achieved.[16]

    The production bonus is usually paid on a barrel of oil equivalent basis, regardless of how profitable the production of petroleum is for an investor, and is typically not cost recoverable under a PSC.

[14] The Sao Tome and Principe 2018 PSC provides (at 2.1) that: 'The Contractor shall pay to the State by deposit into the National Petroleum Account a signature bonus in the amount of US$5,000,000 (five million United States dollars) within thirty (30) days after both the execution of this Contract and delivery to the Contractor of an instrument of ratification and in immediately available funds.'

[15] The Iraq 2018 exploration, development and production contract (EDPC) provides (at 4) that: 'Within thirty (30) days from the date of Declaration of Commerciality approval, each Company shall deposit into a bank account designated by ROC its respective pro-rated Participating Interest of the non-recoverable Declaration of Commerciality bonus of fifteen million Dollars (US$ 15,000,000).'

[16] The Bangladesh 2023 PSC provides (at 20.2) that: 'Contractor shall pay Petrobangla the following Production Bonuses for Oil after a period of thirty (30) consecutive producing days, within thirty (30) days after the first date when the total average daily Production of Oil from each field separately from the Contract Area has been sustained at the rate of: a) 10,000 barrels per day, the sum of amount 500,000 Dollars ($). b) 20,000 barrels per day, the sum of amount 1,000,000 Dollars ($). c) 30,000 barrels per day, the sum of amount 2,000,000 Dollars ($). d) 40,000 barrels per day, the sum of amount 2,500,000 Dollars ($). e) 50,000 barrels per day, the sum of amount 3,000,000 Dollars ($). f) 100,000 barrels per day, the sum of amount 4,000,000 Dollars ($).'

Compared to a signature bonus, a production bonus tends to be a less emotive issue for an investor, since an investor could be enjoying revenues from the sales of produced petroleum at the time the production bonus becomes payable. Some thought will need to be given to how the level of a production bonus is set. Significant bonus payments payable on higher petroleum production levels are obviously attractive to a grantor but there is no guarantee that the higher production levels will be reached in practice, and so this could be an illusory attraction.

(3) *Rental payments*—a rental payment is a fixed payment which is made (typically annually) by an investor to a grantor. The rental payment could be a fixed monetary amount which is payable periodically for the lifetime of a concession, or it could be fixed as a monetary amount which is payable in respect of each square kilometer of the surface coordinates of the concession area (7.2). The rental payment amount could also increase during successive phases of a concession, as an investor moves from exploration to the point of earning revenues from acreage when petroleum production gets underway.[17]

A concession usually provides that any rental payment amount which has already been paid by an investor in respect of a part of a concession area which is relinquished (7.6) will not be reimbursed by a grantor, and also that the future rental payment which is payable by an investor will be adjusted to account for the effects of a relinquishment. A rental payment is similar to a signature bonus in that it is payable by an investor regardless of whether a commercial discovery of petroleum ensues, but rental payment amounts tend to be smaller than signature bonus amounts and so the issue could have less of an impact upon an investor.

(4) *Royalties*—a royalty is an ad valorem payment made by an investor to a grantor, calculated by reference to the volume of petroleum which is produced from a concession area over a particular period of time. A royalty could be payable in cash or in kind by an investor,[18] where (respectively) it represents a guarantee of

[17] The Zanzibar 2024 PSA provides (at 10 (a)) that: 'The annual surface rental fees in respect of which the Contractor is obliged to disburse to ZPRA, pursuant to Section 102 of the Act, in respect of the said Exploration License, shall be paid within the first fifteen (15) days of each Calendar Year at the following amounts for every square kilometre of the Contract Area retained:

Period United States Dollars/square km Initial Exploration Period 30
First Extension Period 60
Second Extension Period 120

The annual surface rental fees in respect of a Development License shall be 300 United States Dollars per square kilometre.' The Afghanistan 2013 exploration and production sharing contract (EPSC)provides (at 14.1) that: 'In accordance with the Hydrocarbons Regulations, the Contractor shall be liable for payment of the following annual surface rental fees to the Ministry in respect of all unsurrendered State-owned land forming part of the Contract Area: (a) for so long as a Commercial Discovery has not been declared with respect to any Field: (i) during the Initial Exploration Period, one U.S. Dollar (US$ 1.00) per hectare; (ii) during the First Extension Period, four U.S. Dollars (US$ 4.00) per hectare; and (iii) during the Second Extension Period and any extension granted pursuant to Section 3.1, eight U.S. Dollars (US$ 8.00) per hectare; (b) from the first declaration of Commercial Discovery with respect to any Field: (i) fifteen U.S. Dollars (US$ 15.00) per hectare, excluding Fields; and (ii) forty U.S. Dollars (US$ 40.00) per hectare of each Field.'

[18] The Pakistan 2000 PSA provides (at 9.2) that: 'The Royalty shall be payable in cash or kind, or partly in cash and partly in kind, at the option of the Government.'

either immediate cashflow or the provision of cost-free petroleum for a grantor to do with as it wishes. In either case the royalty also represents a payment made by an investor which, whilst determined by the production of petroleum under a concession, is payable regardless of the realization of profits from a concession by the investor.

Royalty rates could be set as a fixed percentage of produced petroleum or they could be set by reference to a sliding scale (with higher royalty rates applicable to less difficult forms of petroleum production and lower royalty rates to apply where petroleum is produced in more challenging circumstances). Royalties payable in cash by an investor are ostensibly payable from the value of the gross produced petroleum, rather than being payable after the deduction of the associated costs of production, but there is often scope for dispute between the parties on the real value of the royalty. Royalties payable in cash are usually based on a deemed wellhead sales price for produced petroleum, but because petroleum could require processing and transportation (both of which represent negative cost consequences for the investor) to another point for an actual sale to take place, the effective petroleum sales price will be lower. These extra costs could be deducted (or netted back—to give a 'netback price') from the wellhead price to determine the true royalty. How accurately these costs are defined and calculated under the concession could lead to disputes between the parties. A concession may provide that the quantity of petroleum represented by the royalty amount is deemed to be sold back by a grantor to an investor at the wellhead, at a market price which is determined under a concession.

State take can also be realized through a number of other elements which provide for indirect benefits to accrue to a grantor (or to a state) from a concession. A state participation right (10.8), a domestic market obligation (10.6), the satisfaction of local content requirements 10.3), and the provision for the transfer of assets to a grantor (10.4) each represent a vehicle by which a state can profit from a concession. These elements might be less obviously quantifiable in objective monetary terms but they represent real value to a grantor (and to a state).

9.5 Taxation

State take can also be realized through the state's decision to tax the profits which an investor earns from a concession (although the more likely approach is that taxation will be levied in respect of the individual investor parties, rather than upon an investor as a single taxable entity). States take differing approaches to allocating the incidence of income tax to an investor in a concession. The liability to income tax can be a fiscal term in a concession, as part of the overall economic package which is agreed between a grantor and an investor. A grantor will not be the taxation authority (nor its representative) for these purposes, although a concession could set out a number of relevant tax administration provisions.

An investor could be made liable to pay various specific taxes, duties, and imposts in relation to the business of a concession, but the key issue from an investor's perspective relates to whether or not income tax will be charged by the state on the profits which are earned by an investor from a concession.[19] This is relevant not least since an investor party could also have some liability to pay income tax in respect of those profits in the country of its origin. The exposure of an investor party to multiple income tax liabilities in respect of the same profits could be managed by dual tax treaties.

The possible liability of an investor party to pay some form of capital gains tax or transfer tax on a transfer of its interests is considered elsewhere (5.6).

The incidence of income tax on an investor could be a significant burden. The prospective impact of income tax and the anticipated development costs of a project (together with future petroleum price projections) will go into the wider equation which an investor applies in deciding whether a discovery is commercial (8.3). Future petroleum price projections are inherently unreliable. Development costs should be relatively inelastic, in that they will be the product of the development needs of the project and they will be set by negotiation with third-party service providers (although they are also prone to inflation over time). But income tax is a construction of the state, and a variable factor which could determine the commerciality of a discovery. This issue could present itself in respect of existing concessions and in respect of the design of future concessions.

After a concession has been entered into (and a petroleum project has been sanctioned and developed and has started production), reduced demand for petroleum (which could result from the growth in alternative sources of energy) could lead an investor to lobby the state to reduce the rate of income tax which is applicable to the investor (where the concession requires an investor to accept the incidence the incidence of income tax), or even to introduce the benefit of a tax paid provision (whether temporary or permanent) in favour of an investor to ensure the continuing viability of the project.

On the other hand, if there is a sustained increase in petroleum prices (and so in the level of the profits which are earned by an investor) then a state may wish to increase (or even introduce) the incidence of income tax on the investor in order to enhance state take. However, such a step might not be easy to effect, and it could expose the state to reputational damage in respect of how it is perceived to treat its investors where a certain expectation on the part of investors as to the incidence of income tax has become embedded.

[19] The Suriname 2015 PSC provides (at 19.1) that: 'Each Contractor Party shall pay its own income tax in accordance with Sub-Article 19.2.' The Liberia 2013 PSC provides (at 17.2) that: 'Income tax applicable to Petroleum Operations carried out under this Contract shall be thirty-five percent (35%), which shall be paid directly by the Contractor to the Government of Liberia.' The Bangladesh 2023 PSC provides (at 19.3) that: 'Contractor shall be subject to the tax laws in force from time to time in Bangladesh.'

From a state's perspective, whether or not the incidence of income tax should be borne by an investor could be determined by a concession's other fiscal terms; significant state take which is secured by non-taxation-based fiscal terms could reduce the need for a state to require that an investor also bears the incidence of income tax. The obverse could be true where non-taxation-based fiscal terms generate a relatively low level of state take.

It is common to find concessions where an investor is required to accept the incidence of income tax[20] (which could be so where income tax is the principal vehicle for, or at least a key part of, state take, or where the state's legal (and possibly religious) regime does not allow a person to be exempt from the incidence of income tax). This liability would apply also to a state entity which has exercised a participation right in respect of the concession and the joint venture arrangement and has become an investor party (10.8), unless a special arrangement for the incidence of income tax is made in respect of that state entity.

If an investor is required to accept the incidence of income tax then that tax will be payable by the investor at a defined percentage rate (or rates) on the profit (ie revenue minus defined exemptions and tax-deductible allowances and expenses[21]) which the investor realizes from the production of petroleum under the concession. Even then, however, an investor's liability to pay income tax will need to be read in a wider context:

(1) An investor's liability will be a key part of the wider fiscal terms which are agreed between a grantor and an investor in a concession—the impact of an investor's liability to pay income tax could be ameliorated by the presence of other economic benefits for the investor under a concession.
(2) An investor will require stability in respect of several items: the rates of tax applicable to the profits generated by the investor through the performance of the petroleum operations; the exemptions and allowances which could be applied to offset an investor's tax liability; and the procedural rules which govern the state's administration of the income tax regime. This requirement could be particularly relevant in a nascent petroleum economy, where the principles and processes of tax incidence and administration may be basic or opaque at the outset, and may be open to evolution as the economy matures.
(3) An investor's liability could be accompanied by a stabilization provision in the concession. This is addressed further below.

Where an investor is taxed on the profits which it generates from petroleum production, it is axiomatic that increased production leads to increased revenues and so to increased state take in the form of taxation. This could in turn support the desire of a state to see maximized economic recovery provisions (8.4) becoming part of its concession

[20] The Uganda 1999 PSC provides (at 11) that: 'All central, local district administrative, municipal or other taxes, duties, levies or other lawful impositions applicable to Licensee shall be paid by the Licensee in accordance with the laws of Uganda in a timely fashion.'

[21] See the Liberia 2013 PSC (at 17.4).

terms. Such provisions could have the twin ambitions of reducing costs and increasing production levels, thereby increasing an investor's profit element which could be subject to tax.

An investor may be reluctant to be exposed to the incidence of income tax for several reasons. The rates at which the tax is levied by a state could change over time to the detriment of an investor, and so could the definitions of the taxable activities, and also the exemptions and allowances which could benefit an investor. The administrative procedures by which income tax is levied could also change over time to the detriment of an investor. These variables could expose an investor to unpredictable levels of taxation and to uncertain projections of investor take over the lifetime of the concession.[22]

The alternative basis for addressing income tax as part of the fiscal terms is for a concession to say that an investor is absolved from exposure to its incidence. This could be effected in a number of ways (sometimes described collectively as a 'tax paid provision'). Before a new concession is entered into, the presence of a tax paid provision could attract prospective investors in a licensing round, where being competitive with the fiscal terms which are being offered by other states could be important. A tax paid provision will create a key part of the economic bargain between a grantor and an investor and an investor may have an expectation that the bargain will remain in place for the concession's duration. A tax paid provision could be represented by several devices:

(1) *Exemption from liability to tax*—a concession may declare that an investor has no liability to pay income tax. This exemption could apply to present and future forms of taxation.[23] In practical terms (at least as far as an investor is concerned, although this level of detail might not be set out in a concession) this could mean that a grantor will procure that no income tax claims are made against an investor, that a grantor will procure that any income tax claim which is made against an investor is withdrawn, and that ultimately a grantor will reimburse an investor for any liability which the investor has in respect of income tax.

[22] The risk of the imposition of a so-called 'windfall tax' by the state could be a particular issue for the investor. Such an imposition could arise where the investor is perceived to have enjoyed unexpectedly large profits during a period of high petroleum prices, or where the investor has made a particularly significant (and unexpected) discovery. The Tanzania 2013 PSA provides (at 17) for what it calls an 'Additional Profits Tax', as does the Zanzibar 2024 PSA (at 34). The Kenya 2012 PSC provides (at 27) for what it calls a 'Windfall Tax', and the Gambia 2022 licence provides (at 8.14.1) for the payment of an Additional Profits Payment. See also the Pakistan 2000 PSA (at 6.9). Despite the nomenclature used, these are at least predictable tax incidences, and they offer more certainty than has been experienced by investors in the United Kingdom where, in 2022, the Energy Profits Levy was introduced as an additional layer of taxation on profits made from UK oil and gas production (initially set at 25 per cent, and increased to 35 per cent in 2023). The Energy Profits Levy was described as a temporary measure, intended to extract an increased level of rent for the state from the increased revenues from oil and gas sales which investors experienced in 2022 primarily as a result of the Russian invasion of Ukraine. In 2024, the Energy Profits Levy percentage was increased to 38 per cent, certain allowances were removed, and the measure is to remain in place until 2030. UK petroleum production licences do not include a stabilization provision.

[23] The Tajikistan 2008 PSC provides (at 17.2) that: 'Each Contractor Party, Foreign Subcontractor, Foreign Employee and Operator shall be entitled to full and complete exemption from Taxes according to the Tax Code of the Republic of Tajikistan prior to or after the Effective Date of this Agreement except as otherwise provided for in this Contract.' The Bangladesh 1997 PSC provides (at 18.1) that: 'In respect of Petroleum Operations undertaken by Contractor as envisaged hereunder Government except as provided herein, will hold and keep Contractor harmless from all present and future Bangladesh taxes including ...'

(2) *Assumption of the tax liability*—a concession may reflect a grantor's assumption of the income tax liability which might otherwise be borne by an investor,[24] which could include provision that the incidence of income tax to which an investor would otherwise be exposed will be applied as an offset to state take under a concession. In practical terms this could mean that the share of the revenues due to a grantor under a concession will include the amounts which would otherwise be due for payment as tax by an investor, such that no further payment is due from the investor.[25] Alternatively a grantor could assume direct responsibility for paying an investor's assessed tax liability.[26]

(3) *Reimbursement of the tax liability*—a concession may provide that where an investor has made a payment in respect of income tax then a grantor will reimburse that payment.[27] This reimbursement provision might seem incongruous if a concession otherwise exempts an investor from the incidence of income tax, but it addresses the practical situation of where an investor has paid a tax liability because it is expedient to do so, even though the investor is not legally obliged to do so. A state's national tax authority is ordinarily not a party to a concession, and it could have its own revenue-raising agenda to pursue against an investor, which could result in an investor deciding to make a tax payment in a particular circumstance.

(4) *Tax liability disapplication*—a grantor could offer some form of temporary tax holiday to an investor, to apply for a number of years during the production period (6.5) as an incentive to an investor to enter into a concession. This is sometimes offered by a grantor on a project-specific basis, rather than as a matter of course in concession terms.[28]

[24] The Qatar 2002 DPSA provides (at 22.5) that: 'The GOVERNMENT shall assume, pay and discharge or cause to be discharged on behalf of CONTRACTOR all Qatar income tax of the CONTRACTOR (including for greater certainty, Qatar income tax payable on payments made on behalf of the CONTRACTOR pursuant to this Article 22.5). QP, acting on behalf of the GOVERNMENT shall perform these duties.'

[25] The Trinidad and Tobago 2023 PSC provides (at 21.5) that: 'The Minister shall pay on behalf of the Contractor, out of the Government's share of Profit Petroleum referred to in Article 18.14, the Contractor's liability under applicable law for royalty petroleum impost, petroleum profits tax, supplemental petroleum tax, petroleum production levy, green fund levy, unemployment levy and any other taxes or impositions whatsoever measured upon income or profits arising directly from the Petroleum Operations under this Contract.' The Cyprus 2007 PSC provides (at 9.2) that: '[U]nder the provisions of this Production Sharing Contract, the applicable corporate tax shall be deemed to be included in the Republic's share of Profit Oil. Therefore the portion of Available Oil which the Contractor is entitled to, pursuant to the provisions of Article 8, shall be net of corporate tax.'

[26] The Qatar 2002 DPSA provides (at 22.5) that: 'The GOVERNMENT shall assume, pay and discharge or cause to be discharged on behalf of CONTRACTOR all Qatar income tax of the CONTRACTOR (including for greater certainty, Qatar income tax payable on payments made on behalf of the CONTRACTOR pursuant to this Article 22.5).'

[27] The Bangladesh 2023 PSC provides (at 19.7) that: 'In the event, whether for the purpose of expediency or otherwise, Contractor or any other person on behalf of Contractor pays any amount on account of any of the aforementioned taxes or duties that Government has agreed to hold Contractor harmless from, Petrobangla shall arrange reimbursement to Contractor'.

[28] In 2009, the New Exploration Licensing Policy (NELP) in India offered a seven-year tax holiday for investors in respect of profits accruing from oil production, in an attempt to boost indigenous production and to reduce national reliance on crude oil imports.

Each of the above elements serves the same final purpose, which is to protect an investor from the incidence of income tax (and also to give the comfort of that protection to an investor's current or prospective lenders). However, the elements are different in nature and they achieve that final purpose in different ways.

The exemption of an investor from income tax, a grantor's assumption of the income tax liability as part of state take under the concession, and the provision of a period of tax liability disapplication, are each primary protections. This means that an investor does not have the financial burden of funding the payment of an income tax liability from the outset. Because a grantor has the primary responsibility to discharge an income tax liability which might otherwise be borne by an investor, there is perhaps a reduced likelihood that an income tax claim will be made against an investor in the first place.

A mechanism for the grantor's reimbursement to the investor of a liability to tax which the investor has paid is a secondary protection for an investor. This means that although an investor should be reimbursed by a grantor for payments made by the investor in respect of income tax, an investor is exposed initially to the working capital impact of a payment which is made. This element might also result in an investor having to take proceedings to enforce its right to be reimbursed by a grantor, with all of the costs, timings, and uncertainty of outcome issues which might be associated with such enforcement proceedings.

A concession may recite certain obligations of an investor to comply with various tax administration requirements, including the preparation and filing of income tax returns and the maintenance of records. This approach makes sense where the incidence of income tax is borne by an investor, and this approach could apply also where an investor has the benefit of a tax paid provision. A grantor may desire revenue transparency in respect of an investor, which is served by an investor's compliance with certain tax administration requirements, and a state's national tax authority (which will not be a party to a concession) could have its own tax administration machinery which it could require a grantor to ensure that an investor complies with.[29]

Where an investor is required to accept the incidence of income tax, a stabilization provision—which (in broad terms) might operate to rebase the economic terms of the grantor–investor relationship if there are circumstances which would adversely affect the parameters of the original relationship (B7.6)—could be included in a concession to protect the investor.

The stabilization provision may be written in general terms, or it may be made tax-specific and may relate to matters such as changes in tax bases, exemptions and allowances, and administration.[30] Whether a stabilization provision will be sufficient to

[29] The Bangladesh 2023 PSC provides (at 19.3) that: 'Contractor shall ... comply with the requirements of such laws with respect to the filing of returns, the assessment of tax and the keeping for review by authorized persons of books and records.'

[30] The Afghanistan 2013 EPSC provides (at 16.4) that: 'If, at any time after the Effective Date, (a) any new tax, levy or other fee is introduced in Afghanistan that (i) is targeted at Hydrocarbons Operations or (ii) is in the nature or the equivalent of a value added tax or provincial, local, municipal tax or windfall tax (the taxes referred to

guarantee protection to an investor against the adverse economic impact of changes to the tax regime as it applies to a concession will depend on the wording of the particular provision.

A tax paid provision shares some of the characteristics of a stabilization provision, in that it is intended to demonstrate predictability in respect of the economic bargain which the concession creates in favour of an investor, but it is not a stabilization provision in its own right (and for that reason a tax paid provision may be supplemented by a stabilization provision in the concession).

in this clause (ii) being ("Designated Taxes")) or (b) there is any change in Afghanistan Law (or the interpretation thereof) that (i) is targeted at Hydrocarbons Operations or (ii) discriminates or has the effect of discriminating against the Contractor or any Contractor Entity (including but not limited to a Progressive Tax Rate) and (c) as a result of the circumstances described in (a) or (b), the Contractor or any Contractor Entity suffers an adverse effect of a material nature on the economic benefits it derives from Hydrocarbons Operations or the Contract, the Contractor will notify the Ministry in writing and the Parties will, as soon as possible thereafter, meet to verify such effect and, within ninety (90) Days of such meeting, agree on such changes to this Contract as may be required in order to restore, as closely as possible, the economic benefits that the Contractor and each Contractor Entity would have derived from the Hydrocarbons Operations or the Contract in the absence of such new tax, levy or other fee or such change of Afghanistan Law (or the interpretation thereof).' Also see the Suriname 2015 PSC (at 19.4).

10
Other Grantor Benefits

10.1 Introduction

State take is the principal vehicle by which benefits accrue to a grantor from the award of a concession, but a concession may be engineered so that a grantor (and a state) can benefit in a number of other ways.

Activities under the broad heading of capacity building (which could include offering training, secondment and temporary or permanent employment opportunities to state nationals, or funding the costs of training and development activities) could bring significant intangible benefits to a grantor (and a state).

Local content provisions in a concession are intended to give preference to the use of locally sourced goods and services in the performance of the petroleum operations for the benefit of a state's wider economy.

A concession may provide for the transfer to a grantor of assets used in the performance of the petroleum operations, and for a grantor to assume ownership of data which is generated from the performance of those operations.

A concession may secure certain quantities of produced petroleum for priority use by a grantor, through a domestic market obligation which applies to an investor.

A concession may give a grantor certain rights to conduct petroleum operations in its own name and for its own benefit in a concession area, and also the right to participate in a concession as an investor party (either from the outset or by subsequent accession).

10.2 Capacity Building

'Capacity building' describes the commitment of an investor to enhance the petroleum sector know-how of a grantor (and of a state), which could be represented through several provisions. A concession's capacity- building provisions may also be helpful in managing objections to a grantor's award of concessions for the exploitation of the state's patrimony to external investors by demonstrating the wider value of a concession.

An investor could be required by a concession to commit to the education and the empowerment of the personnel of a grantor (or of a state), through offering opportunities for on-the-job training, secondments, and temporary and permanent employment. This commitment may be written in a generalized manner or it may be represented by more specific arrangements which identify the placement of defined numbers of grantor/state personnel into the businesses of certain of the investor parties.[1]

These training, secondment, and employment provisions represent a form of technology transfer which could enable personnel from a grantor (or from another state entity) to understand and operate a concession's underlying petroleum project, leading eventually to the removal of the assistance which is provided by the expatriate personnel of an investor. This is part of a process which is sometimes called 'localization'.

As an addition or as an alternative to the foregoing activities, an investor could be required by a concession to commit a defined sum of money to be spent (typically annually) on training the personnel of a grantor (or of another state entity) on technical, legal, commercial, and financial aspects of the petroleum industry. The extent of an investor's funding obligation could also be reset to a higher rate when petroleum production commences, as an investor earns revenues from the production of petroleum from a concession.[2] This requirement for funding could also be applied to facilitate the acquisition of hardware (such as books, computers, access to databases, and seismic analysis equipment).[3]

A grantor may wish to ensure that the training payments it receives can be spent on service providers of its choosing. This would enable the grantor to select what it believes is the most appropriate form of training, and for that training to come from service providers which a grantor does not regard as being unduly connected with an investor.

An investor's concern in relation to making such training payments could relate to handing over cash to a grantor which is intended to fund training activities and not knowing where the cash goes after that. This could be addressed in a concession by a provision that an investor will procure (and will directly pay for) the provision of training courses which are agreed with a grantor.

[1] The Afghanistan 2013 exploration and production sharing contract (EPSC) provides (at 20.1) that: 'The Contractor undertakes to give priority to Afghan nationals with equivalent qualifications and experience and actively search for Afghan nationals in order to meet the training and employment obligations established in the prevailing legislation and to gradually replace its expatriate staff with qualified Afghan nationals as they become available' and (at 20.1) that: 'The Contractor agrees to as far as possible train and employ qualified Afghan nationals in the Hydrocarbons Operations and after Initial Commercial Production will undertake the schooling and training of Afghan nationals for staff positions, including administrative and executive management positions. The Contractor will require its major contractors and subcontractors to do the same'.

[2] The Bangladesh 2023 production sharing contract (PSC) provides (at 25.2) that: 'During the Exploration and Development Period, Contractor shall expend a minimum of fifty thousand Dollars ($50,000) each Calendar Year for training pursuant to Article 25.2(a). Following the Date of Commencement of Commercial Production, the minimum expenditure for training pursuant to Article 25.2(a) in each Calendar Year during the term hereof shall be one hundred thousand Dollars ($100,000).' The Gambia 2022 licence provides (at 15.5.1) that: 'In order to establish programmes to train Gambian personnel for work in Petroleum Operations, to ensure the transfer of management, financial, technical and other skills required for the efficient conduct of Petroleum Operations, and to acquire resources needed for the development of institutions working in the Petroleum sector, the Licensee shall pay the Government: (a) Five hundred thousand United States Dollars (USD 500,000) during each year of the Exploration Period (whether or not it runs concurrently with one or more Development and Production Periods); and (b) One million United States Dollars (USD 1,000,000) during each year of each Development and Production Period in respect of each Development and Production Area and each Satellite Development.'

[3] The Guyana 2023 production sharing agreement (PSA) provides (at 33.1) that training payments made can be used 'to purchase for the Government of Guyana data management systems and infrastructure as well as technical software tools and subscription services necessary for performance of its role in administering the oil and gas resources.'

Where a grantor cannot spend the entirety of the training payment budget in a particular year, the monetary amounts due as the training payments could be deposited by an investor into a separate bank account, to be drawn down as the grantor's training needs evolve over time.[4]

Training payments made by an investor are typically cost recoverable under a production-sharing contract (PSC) (9.3) but there could be variations on this theme. Training payments could be cost recoverable where they are paid during the exploration period, but not so when they are incurred during the production period (to reflect the improved economic circumstances of the concession for the investor).

An investor might also be required to make payments to certain development funds specified by a grantor, which could relate to the promotion of the wider petroleum industry (and to the promotion of diversified (non-petroleum) industries) in the state and for environmental reparations.[5]

10.3 Local Content

A concession may contain a local content provision, by which an investor is obliged to procure goods and/or services which are needed for the performance of the petroleum operations from within the state rather than from the international market. The purpose of such a provision is to stimulate the local economy of the state, but an investor may have a concern that the goods and/or services on offer locally (if they even exist) do not match the standards required for the performance of the petroleum operations, or that locally sourced goods and services (if they do exist) are available only at costs which exceed the comparable costs of internationally sourced goods and services. Even so, a concession may provide for a certain degree of cost overrun in the provision of locally sourced goods and services as a permissible measure of costs which are

[4] The Guyana 2023 PSA provides (at 33.2) that: 'Payments for training under Article 33.1 shall be paid directly into bank accounts held and controlled by the Government', and (at 33.3) that: 'To facilitate the Contractor's right to an accounting of spending of the funds deposited under Articles 33.1. and 33.2 the Minister shall provide quarterly statements of the respective bank account, accompanied by invoices and other proper documentation supporting the withdrawal and usage of the funds.'

[5] The Guyana 2023 PSA provides (at 44.7) that: 'The Minister and the Contractor shall establish a programme of financial support for environmental and social projects to be funded by the Contractor. The Contractor shall directly fund the amount of one million United States Dollars (US$1,000,000.00) per Calendar Year with any funded but unspent portion be carried over into the ensuing Calendar Years of the Agreement.' The Trinidad and Tobago 2023 PSC requires (at 21.1 (b)) the contractor to fund '[a] training contribution to the University of Trinidad and Tobago and/or the University of the West Indies and/or such institution as the Minister may direct for the financing of training of nationals of the Republic of Trinidad and Tobago in appropriate fields of study in accordance with the priority needs of Trinidad and Tobago.' The Pakistan 2000 PSA provides (at 31.4) that: 'Contractor shall pay to the Government the following minimum amounts during the term of this Agreement for the purposes of marine research.' The Liberia 2013 PSC provides (at 19.3.1) that: 'To stimulate research in the field of hydrocarbon, most especially in continental areas, and to assist the Government in its overall goal of achieving energy sustainability, a Hydrocarbon Development Fund, to be managed by NOCAL, has been established. Within thirty (30) days of the Effective Date of this Agreement, the Contractor shall make a contribution of________________ ______________ to this Fund.'

'comparable' with prices for internationally sourced goods and services (meaning, in reality, that the local content's costs are not really comparable).[6]

'Hard local content' describes the situation where a grantor specifies a minimum value or percentage requirement for local content provision in the concession.[7] Correspondingly, 'soft local content' describes the situation where an investor is required to do whatever it reasonably can to promote local content in the performance of the petroleum operations but without the imposition of a fixed target.[8]

As a state's petroleum economy matures over time, and the necessary goods and/or services on offer locally are increasingly able to meet the requisite standard for the performance of the petroleum operations, there could be movement from soft local content to hard local content. A measure of hard local content could also be secured by provision in a concession that goods and services valued below a certain monetary threshold must be procured locally.

A concession may also provide for varying levels of expenditure to be made by an investor in order to satisfy local content requirements.[9]

Allied to local content requirements are tendering and procurement provisions in a concession which regulate the procurement by an investor of goods and services necessary to perform the petroleum operations (including the hire of drilling rigs from, and the provision of drilling services by, independent contractors). This could entail the involvement of a grantor in any of the management of contract awards, the selection of the contractors, and the terms of the contracts which are awarded by an investor.

Under a PSC, the cost recovery mechanism means that the incidence of the associated petroleum operations costs will ultimately be borne by the state (9.3). Consequently, the grantor could have an interest in controlling the nature and the quantum of those costs, and also in determining the identity of the suppliers of goods and services to the investor. This control element could be manifested through provisions relating to

[6] The Angola 2008 PSC provides (at 14) that: 'Contractor Group, through the Operator, and its subcontractors shall ... contract local contractors, as long as their services are similar in quality and availability to those available on the international market and the prices of their services, when subject to the same tax charges, are no more than ten percent (10%) higher compared to the prices charged by foreign contractors for identical services'.

[7] The Pakistan 2000 PSA provides (at 13.12) that: 'At least ten percent (10%) of the computer software contracts shall be awarded by the Contractor to use the local software capabilities, subject to such software capabilities being available at a competitive price.' The Brazil 2017 PSA provides (at Annex IX) detailed local content percentage requirements for all aspects of the petroleum operations.

[8] The Suriname 2015 PSC provides (at 32.1) that: 'In the acquisition of plant, equipment, supplies and services for Petroleum Operations, Contractor shall give preference for materials, services and products produced in Suriname if these materials, services and products can be supplied at prices, grades, qualities, delivery dates and other commercial terms equivalent to or more favorable than those at which similar materials, services and products can be supplied from elsewhere.'

[9] The Gambia 2022 licence provides (at 14.3) that: 'The Licensee shall use all reasonable endeavours to meet the following minimum amounts to be spent by the Licensee on the use of domestic goods and services: (a) no less than an amount equal to three percent (3%) of the costs associated with Exploration within the annual Work Programme and Budget; and (b) no less than an amount equal to two percent (2%) of the costs associated with Development within the annual Work Programme and Budget; and (c) no less than an amount equal to: (i) until the fifth (5th) anniversary of the date of commencement of Production, five percent (5%) of the costs associated with Production within the annual Work Programme and Budget; (ii) thereafter until the tenth (10th) anniversary of the date of commencement of Production, seven and half percent (7.5%) of the costs associated with Production within the annual Work Programme and Budget; and (iii) thereafter, ten percent (10%) of the costs associated with Production within the annual Work Programme and Budget.'

tendering and procurement and local content. Where, however, a concession takes the form of a licence or a PSC with a revenue-sharing mechanism (2.2) a grantor may be less insistent on the control element because the incidence of those costs should ultimately be borne by the investor.

10.4 Ownership of Assets

Under a PSC, the costs of acquiring or developing assets or equipment which are used in the performance of the petroleum operations will ultimately be borne by the state, through the cost recovery mechanism (9.3)). A PSC will provide a mechanism for how title to items acquired or developed by an investor and used in the performance of the petroleum operations will pass to a grantor at some point in time. Paradoxically, although title to such items passes to the grantor, a PSC will provide that an investor has the responsibility for the decommissioning of those items (8.5), except where a grantor has an interest in doing something with certain of the items which would not otherwise be decommissioned.

Provisions in a PSC relating to the transfer of items to a grantor apply principally in respect of items which have been acquired or developed by an investor during the development period (6.5) for the production of petroleum. The concession may also describe certain items which reflect a grantor's interest in acquiring particular items which are to be transferred to the grantor.[10]

The PSC may provide for title to an item which has been purchased by an investor to transfer to a grantor at any of the following times: when the item is purchased by the investor; when the item is first imported into the state; when the item is first used for the performance of the petroleum operations; when the costs associated with the item have been fully cost recovered by the investor; when the tax depreciation of the item has concluded; or when the concession expires or is earlier terminated.

When title to an item has transferred from an investor to a grantor but the petroleum operations are still continuing, a concession may give an investor a continuing right to use the item for the petroleum operations, and an obligation to maintain the item for the benefit of a grantor.

Because of a grantor's interest in items where title is due to transfer to the grantor, the PSC may provide that an investor will not sell or otherwise dispose of an item without the grantor's consent, and that if an item is disposed of by an investor then the proceeds of sale will either be accounted for to the grantor or will be applied to reduce the cost recovery pool (9.3). This could be relevant to certain items which are no longer needed

[10] The Equatorial Guinea 2006 PSC provides (at 6.22) that: 'Upon the first Commercial Discovery, the Contractor shall, to the extent that it has not already done so, construct a prestigious building for its offices in Equatorial Guinea using modern and permanent materials and of an appropriate size and design as shall be approved by the Ministry. All costs related to such construction shall be recoverable as Petroleum Operation Costs in accordance with this Contract. Once such construction costs have been recovered by the Contractor, such property shall be owned solely by the State and the Contractor shall pay rent to the State at a price and on terms to be negotiated and such rent shall be considered recoverable Petroleum Operations Costs.'

for the performance of the petroleum operations, and may be a particular issue where an investor wishes to sell an item and then lease the same item back for its continued use, to improve the overall economics of the petroleum project.

A concession may also provide that an investor will insure an item in a manner which reflects the grantor's prospective interest.

An investor might wish to retain in a concession the right to create a security interest over any items which have not yet transferred to a grantor in favour of any lenders who have financed the investor's project costs, but a grantor could be reluctant to allow the creation of such an encumbrance over items which it regards as its own (albeit prospectively).

The title transfer provision in the PSC will not apply to items which are leased by an investor for the performance of the petroleum operations and which belong to another person (notwithstanding that the leasing costs could be cost recovered by an investor). This provision applies principally in respect of drilling rigs and survey ships which are hired by an investor for performing activities during the exploration period (8.2), and it would apply also to items which have been hired for petroleum production operations (such as a floating production and storage offshore (FPSO) unit or a floating liquefied natural gas (LNG) production facility). An investor could also use the leasing route to prevent the risk of confusion where the investor itself owns an item which it wishes to use in the performance of the petroleum operations, but does not want to take the risk that a grantor will assume an entitlement to own that item. In this situation an affiliate of an investor could own the item and could lease it to the investor.

A concession may provide that, wherever an investor has an option to purchase or to lease an item for use in the petroleum operations, then (to prefer a grantor's interests) preference would be given by an investor to the exercise of the purchase option wherever possible.[11]

10.5 Title to Data

A licensing round (in whatever form it takes (2.5)) which offers little geological and geophysical data to prospective investors could struggle to attract interest. To overcome this a state could commission the performance of a seismic survey at its own expense (often called a 'multi-client survey'), as a precursor to launching a licensing round. The grantor could then seek to recoup a share of the multi-client survey costs by requiring a prospective investor to purchase access to the data as part of its licensing round application, or later under the terms of a concession once the concession has been awarded,

[11] The Gabon 1995 PSC provides (at 10.3) that: 'Under equivalent economic conditions, Contractor commits itself to give priority to buying goods instead of leasing or renting.' On the other hand, the Somalia 2023 PSA recognizes (at 18.2) that: 'The Contractor's approach to acquisition of the (movable or immovable) assets shall be cost-driven, so, to the extent it is financially more beneficial, the Contractor shall rent or lease assets rather than acquire ownership thereof.'

in each case on the basis that title to the data remains with the grantor, and the prospective investor has only a right to access and use the data.

The requirement for such a data purchase raises cash for a grantor which could cover the costs of running a licensing round, and it could be useful in weeding out pure speculators from bidders with more serious intent. The data purchase costs incurred by an investor might not be cost recoverable under a PSC (9.3), although the data purchase costs could be credited towards satisfaction of the associated costs of an investor's exploration period obligations (8.2).

Alternatively, once an investor is in place under a concession, such data could be provided to the investor as part of the grantor's obligations under the concession (6.2).

Further data will be generated under a concession through the investor's performance of its exploration period obligations. Such data could take the form of seismic survey results and processed seismic data, drilling reports, cuttings, and core samples (all of which could be required to be kept at a location within the state at which they can be accessed by or on behalf of a grantor). A concession will usually provide that the data will belong to a grantor[12] (and in turn that data could be something which a grantor is able to further licence to third parties for a fee).

A grantor may also want to own such data because it enables a grantor to build a better picture of the state's patrimony, as a part of wider, cumulative exercise across all of a grantor's concessions. From an investor's perspective, the data's relevance is ostensibly limited to the boundaries of a concession area, and is useful principally in helping the investor to make more informed decisions regarding relinquishment or development (unless an investor has, or is interested in having, contiguous acreage interests across a number of concessions).

A concession's provisions relating to ownership of the data will also need to be reconciled with the corresponding provisions of the joint venture arrangement (5.3), which could regard such data as an entitlement of the parties to that arrangement.

10.6 The Domestic Market Obligation

An investor may require the freedom to export the entirety of its produced petroleum entitlements from the state (assuming the existence of the necessary export infrastructure), or it could be content to sell the entirety of those entitlements within the state if the terms for doing so are acceptable.

As a partial exception to the principle of an investor's freedom to do as it wishes, a concession may contain a form of domestic market obligation provision, which is

[12] The Uganda 1999 PSC provides (at 8.5) that: '[A]ll original data resulting from Petroleum Operations are the property of the Republic of Uganda, including, but not limited to, geological, geophysical, petrophysical, engineering, well logs, magnetic tapes, cuts of core and cutting samples, production data and completion status reports and any other data which the Licensee may compile during the term hereof, including all reports, analyses, interpretations, maps and evaluations thereof prepared by the Licensee and any sub-licensees or consultants to the Licensee or by Affiliated Companies, and cuttings of all samples that have been obtained or compiled during the term hereof'.

intended to give the grantor a competitive advantage in respect of at least some of the petroleum which is produced from the concession area. This provision could have a particular appeal to a grantor where the state wishes to keep produced petroleum in-country to meet local demand (whether for domestic or industrial consumption).

A concession may set out the terms of a domestic market obligation, by reference to the quantity of petroleum to which such an obligation would apply and the price which is payable by a grantor to an investor for that petroleum.[13]

In the interests of fairness, an investor could require that the incidence of a domestic market obligation is applied rateably to all investors holding concessions but this might not always be the case where the state utilizes different forms of concession over time, or where a grantor applies a domestic market obligation inconsistently between different investors and their concessions.

A concession might also provide that domestic market obligation provisions will apply only until the state has achieved a defined measure of self-sufficiency with respect to its petroleum production and consumption.[14]

10.7 Exclusive Operations

Although the principal expectation of a concession is that an investor will be responsible for undertaking the petroleum operations within a concession area, a concession may also reserve a right for a grantor to undertake petroleum operations in its own name and for its own account in some circumstances. This right, which is generally known as an 'exclusive operation', is akin to a sole risk provision in a joint operating agreement.[15]

A grantor could seek to apply its exclusive operation right in parts of the concession area which have not been relinquished by an investor (7.6) but which are not the subject of ongoing exploration and/or development activities, or as a reaction to a proposed petroleum operation which was instigated by an investor but which was not approved

[13] The Suriname 2015 PSC provides (at 20.2) that: 'Contractor shall supply at the Delivery Point from the Contractor's entitlement, that portion of the Domestic Supply Requirement ... on a pro rata basis with other crude oil producers except Staatsolie, in Suriname, but not exceeding twenty-five percent (25%) of Contractor's entitlement, which portion the Contractor shall be paid at the Crude Oil Basket Price.' The Somalia 2023 PSA provides (at 21.3) that: 'The maximum amount of Crude Oil and/or Natural Gas that the Federal Government may require from the Contractor's share of Production of Petroleum shall be calculated each Calendar Quarter, and shall be equal to the excess of the total Crude Oil and/or Natural Gas domestic consumption in Somalia multiplied by a fraction, the numerator of which is the average Crude Oil and/or Natural Gas Production from the Contract Area and the denominator of which is the total Crude Oil and/or Natural Gas Production from all producers in Somalia, over the amount of Crude Oil and/or Natural Gas available to the Federal Government from the Contract Area as in the form of Federal Government's share of Production of Petroleum (under clause 10.3) and in the form of the Federal Government's participation share (under clause 17).'

[14] The India 2010 PSC provides (at 18.2) that: 'If, during any Year, India attains Self-sufficiency, the Government shall promptly thereafter, but in no event later than the end of the first Quarter of the following Year, so advise the Company(ies) by written notice. In such event ... domestic sale obligation shall be suspended and the Company shall have the right to lift and export its Participating Interest share of Crude Oil and Condensate until such time, if any, as Self-sufficiency shall have ceased to exist.'

[15] The Ghana 2000 petroleum agreement sets out an extensive exclusive operation provision for the grantor (at 9), as does the Angola 2008 PSC (at 30).

by a management committee (5.5) for continuation, or in respect of a discovery which has not been declared as commercial, or which has been declared as marginal, by the investor (8.3).[16]

A discovery which is made as the result of an exclusive operation would belong to a grantor, but a concession might give an investor an option to buy back into the exclusive operation, whereupon it would effectively be reconstituted as a petroleum operation in the ordinary course of the concession.

In recognition of the operational reality that, despite having reserved an exclusive operation right for itself, a grantor might not be able to carry out such an operation, a concession may provide for how such an operation could be conducted. The investor would be the obvious candidate to perform the operation for the grantor.[17]

An exclusive operation right in favour of a grantor in a concession could be written less prescriptively than the corresponding terms might appear in a joint operating agreement. Whether a grantor should also be obliged to indemnify an investor for losses or liabilities which were caused by the conduct of the exclusive operation, in the manner of a joint operating agreement's sole risk right, will be an issue to consider, as will the issue of whether the promise of such an indemnity would, in practical terms, be worth anything to an investor.

10.8 State Participation

A grantor is the visible embodiment of the state on one side of a concession. The state, acting through a nominated representative such as a grantor (or possibly the national oil company (14.1), or some other state entity), could seek to participate on the other side of a concession too, as one of the investor parties. This is the essence of state participation.

Where a grantor (as the state representative) becomes an investor party under a concession then the grantor would also become party to the joint venture arrangement (5.3), with a defined percentage participating interest (and also in the concession, if the concession adopts such an interest formulation). That interest would be contributed by the existing parties to the joint venture arrangement, pro rata to their respective existing interests. Such a participating interest is typically set at 10 per cent but the figure

[16] The Egypt 2021 concession agreement provides (at III (c) (iv)) that: 'If Crude Oil or Gas is discovered but is not deemed by CONTRACTOR to be a Commercial Discovery of Oil or Gas under the above provisions of this paragraph (c), EGAS shall one (1) month after the expiration of the period specified above within which CONTRACTOR can give notice of a Commercial Discovery of Oil or Gas, or thirteen (13) months after the completion of a well not considered to be a Commercial Oil Well or twenty five (25) months after the completion of a well not considered to be a Commercial Gas Well, have the right, following sixty (60) days written notice to CONTRACTOR, at its sole cost, risk and expense, to develop, produce and dispose of all Crude Oil or Gas from the geological feature on which the well has been drilled.'

[17] The Angola 2008 PSC provides (at 30) that: 'Sonangol shall elect to have the operations carried out at Sonangol's sole risk and expense referred to in paragraphs 1(e) and 1(f) carried out either by itself, by Contractor Group for a mutually agreed fee or by any third party entity contracted to that effect by Sonangol, provided that such operations may be carried out only if they will not conflict with or cause hindrance to Contractor Group's obligations or any Petroleum Operation, or delay existing work plans.'

varies between different concessions.[18] State participation could apply in respect of the concession as a whole or in respect of discrete development projects, and also at different levels which are reflective of participation by a federal government and by a federal member state as part of a wider resource benefits-sharing agreement (1.2).[19]

State participation takes place ostensibly to enable a state (via a grantor) to secure a direct share of petroleum production as an investor party, but state participation could also have certain other advantages as far as a state is concerned. It enables the grantor to secure direct access to current operational data as an investor party with a position in a concession and the joint venture arrangement. It also offers a form of on-the-job engagement for a grantor's personnel, and it creates a saleable interest in a concession and the joint venture arrangement for a grantor. State participation can also be a politically popular device, since it shows the state's population how the state is becoming directly involved in developing the state's patrimony.

There are several options for a grantor to participate in a concession (and the joint venture arrangement), in either the exploration period (6.2) or the production period (6.5). These options may be indicated in the terms of a concession. The question for an investor (as it exists before a state participation right is exercised) is whether the various ambitions of a grantor could be addressed by means other than the application of a state participation right.

To facilitate state participation, a concession may append a pro forma agreement (often called a 'participation agreement') which regulates the completion of the participation process between an investor (as it exists before a state participation right is exercised) and a grantor.[20]

A grantor could be an investor party from the outset of the concession, and on that basis the grantor could participate in the exploration period as a fully paying party. The grantor would also be party to the joint venture arrangement from the outset, with a defined percentage participating interest.[21]

[18] The Gabon 1995 PSC provides (at 19.1) for 7.5 per cent; the Somalia 2019 PSA provides (at 16.1) for up to 10 per cent (and the Somalia 2023 PSA provides (at 17.1) for up to 20 per cent); the Ghana 2000 petroleum agreement provides (at 2.4) for 10 per cent; the Zanzibar 2024 PSA provides (at 9 (b)) for 15 per cent; the Uganda 1999 PSC provides (at 9.4) for up to 20 per cent; the Kenya 2012 PSC provides (at 28) for 20 per cent.

[19] This formulation is suggested by the Somalia 2023 PSA (at 17.1 and 17.4).

[20] The Kenya 2012 PSC provides (at 28) that: 'If the Government exercises its right to participate in a Development Area, the Government and the Contractor shall enter into either a Participation Agreement of an amendment and novation of the Joint Operating Agreement, to add the Government or its Appointee as a party to the Joint Operating Agreement within three (3) months after notice to the Contractor under subclause 28(1)', and it provides (at 1B) that: '"Participation Agreement" means that model agreement as set out in Appendix C between the Government and Contractor that sets guidelines with respect to the relationship between the Government and Contractor in connection with their respective activities, obligations and responsibilities and which shall only come into force after negotiation of a mutually acceptable form and on signature by the Parties upon the election of the Government to acquire, hold and execute a fully paying working Participating Interest in one (1) or more Development Areas in accordance with Clause 28 of this Contract.' The Kenya 2014 PSC provides (at 41(3) that: 'If the Government exercises its right to participate in a development area, the Government and the contractor shall execute the Participation Agreement, in a format as prescribed in Appendix "C" and made a part hereof.'

[21] The Equatorial Guinea 2006 PSC provides (at 1.3) that: 'On the Effective Date the Participation Interests of the Parties comprising the Contractor are as follows: [The Company] [insert number]%; The National Company [insert number]%; Total 100%.'

This approach exposes a grantor to the risks of wasted expenditure on unsuccessful exploration, which a grantor may be unable to afford. Alternatively, a grantor could be an investor party from the outset of a concession and could participate in the exploration period but with the benefit of being fully carried for its share of the exploration period costs for which it would otherwise be liable by the other investor parties. This carry arrangement could be converted into a paying interest for the grantor when the production of petroleum from a development begins.[22]

Such a carry arrangement may be 'hard' (ie the amount of the carry which has accrued in favour of a grantor during the carry period is not repayable to the other investor parties when production begins) or it may be 'soft' (ie the amount of the carry is repayable to the other investor parties when production begins). Repayment by a grantor is typically made from a grantor's petroleum entitlements as they accrue, rather than in cash. Where the carry is repayable, the amount of the carry could be repayable by a grantor at par or with the application of a premium.[23] The latter case could be akin to the repayment of a loan, and the arrangement may even be expressed as such.[24]

Participation by a grantor as an investor party from the outset of a concession (whether as a fully paying party or as a carried party) would give a grantor direct access to exploration data under the terms of the joint venture arrangement (to which it would also be a party), in addition to whatever data a grantor is already entitled to receive under the concession.

An alternative formulation by which state participation in a concession could be effected is one whereby a grantor becomes an investor party from the outset, but the

[22] The Equatorial Guinea 2006 PSC provides (at 8.2) that: 'The National Company's Participation Interest will be carried and paid for in full by the other Parties comprising the Contractor (other than the National Company) in proportion to their respective Participation Interests (other than the National Company's) until such time as the National Company elects to convert its carried Participation Interest into a full working Participation Interest in accordance with the Hydrocarbons Law. From that point on, the National Company shall be responsible for all its costs in respect of the area covered by the approved Development and Production Plan. For the avoidance of doubt, the National Company's Participation Interest in respect of the remainder of the Contract Area shall continue to be carried and paid for by the Parties comprising the Contractor (other than the National Company) in proportion to their respective Participation Interests (not including the National Company's) until such time as the National Company elects to convert its carried interest into a full working interest.'

[23] The Mauritania 2012 PSC provides (at 21.6) that: 'The State will transfer and will continue to give the Contractor forty five percent (45%) of the production share accruing to it in respect of its participation and in respect of its recovery of Petroleum Costs in accordance with article 10.2 above and the Accounting Procedure set out in Appendix 2, until the sum of these transfers or payments, valued at the provisions of articles 14 and 15 above is equal to one hundred and twelve percent (112%) of the Petroleum Costs referred to in the second paragraph of article 21.5 above'.

[24] The Ethiopia 2011 PSC provides (at 6.1.3) that: 'The Government may, upon reasonable written notice, require the Contractor to lend to the Government up to______ per cent (____ %) of the funds required to pay the Government's pro-rata share of expenditure. The loan shall bear interest at ______ per cent (____ %).' The Gambia 2022 licence provides (at 20.5.1) that: 'Upon acquiring a participating interest, the Government may send notice to the other Licensee(s), requesting that the other Licensee(s) pay, in proportion to their respective participating interests, the Government's participating share (up to an aggregate participating share of fifteen percent (15%)) of all expenses incurred by the Licensee(s), Government, and/or the Appointee (and in case of the Government and/or the Appointee on behalf of the Licensee(s)) in relation to Petroleum Operations in the Development and Production Area after the approval of the Approved Development and Production Plan, which shall take the form of a Development Loan', and also (at 20.6.3) that: 'The rate of interest shall be negotiated between the Parties based on comparable resource projects being funded at that time but, in any event, shall not be in excess of LIBOR plus 2%.'

grantor has the right to elect to withdraw from a particular development project, whilst remaining as an investor party under the concession.[25]

A grantor could elect not to be an investor party from the outset of a concession, but could elect to 'back in' to a concession as a paying party at a later stage in the lifetime of the concession. This election could be made when a commercial discovery has been made and has been approved for development, so that a grantor pays its share of the development costs only as they then accrue going forward.[26] Alternatively a grantor could assume an interest under a concession later, but prior to the start of the production period (6.5), so that the grantor does not pay its share of the development costs as they accrue.

The back in right, in either of the above situations, could be free to a grantor or it could be subject to payment by a grantor of a share of the historic exploration and/or development costs (as appropriate) which have been incurred by the other investor parties.

A question may arise as to how to deal with a grantor's failure to fund its share of the costs of petroleum operations after a state participation right has been exercised. A concession may provide a remedy for such a default.[27]

Even where a grantor does not participate in the exploration period (or in a later development project) a grantor could still require ongoing access to exploration and development data under a concession and the joint venture arrangement so that a grantor can make a more informed decision about the possibility of exercising a right to participate as an investor party later in time. This information right would be necessary particularly if a grantor has to make payment to the other investor parties as a condition of an election to participate.

[25] The Tanzania 2013 PSA provides (at 10) that: 'TPDC may at any time, by notice in writing to Contractor, elect to contribute its Participating Interest of not less than twenty five percent (25%) of Contract Expenses other than Exploration Expenses (such Exploration Expenses to include expenses in respect of Appraisal Programme) incurred in the first and every subsequent Development Area from the date such notice is rendered.'

[26] The Kenya 2012 PSC provides (at 28) that: 'The Government may elect to participate in the petroleum operations in any development area and acquire an interest of up twenty per cent (20%) (hereinafter referred to as "Participating Interest") of the total interest in that development area. The Government may participate either directly or through an appointee', that the government shall '[a]ssume its share of Petroleum Costs incurred in respect of that Development Area, from the Effective Date of its participation as defined in sub-clause 28(3), pro-rata to its Participating Interest', and also that the Government shall: 'reimburse the Contractor, without interest, pro-rata to the Government Participating Interest, its share of all costs, expenses and expenditure incurred in respect of the Development Area from the date the Development Plan for that Development Area has been adopted to the date the Government serves notice pursuant to sub-clause 28(3) exercises its right to participate in that Development Area.' The Somalia 2023 PSA provides (at 17.1) that: 'The Federal Government may elect to participate in the Petroleum Operations in any [Development Area] and acquire an interest of up to twenty percent [20 per cent] ("Participating Interest") of the total interest in that Development Area.'

[27] The Gambia 2022 licence provides (at 20.5.4) that the remedy will be forfeiture of the grantor's interests: 'In the event that the Government is not able to fund its participating share of all expenses to be incurred in relation to Petroleum Operations in the Development and Production Area, the Government and/or Appointee will be required to relinquish its participating share in the Licence and its share shall be shared equally between the other Licensees pro rata to their current interest.' The Tanzania 2013 PSC provides (at 10 (b) (iii)) that the remedy will be the reclassification of the grantor's default to an interest-bearing loan: 'If TPDC fails to pay its share of Contract Expenses and such failure is not rectified within a period of thirty (30) days after receipt of a written notice of such failure from the Contractor, the Contractor shall advance by way of loan up to 100% of unpaid amount of TPDC's share of Contract Expenses. Such Contract Expenses shall bear interest at a rate of LIBOR plus one percent (1%) for the period that such amount remained unpaid and will be recovered from TPDC's Cost Oil[and/or Cost Gas] as defined in Article 12.'

The model for state participation which is suggested above is one whereby a grantor holds a defined percentage participating interest as an investor party and with a position under a concession and the joint venture arrangement, but this is not the only option to consider. A grantor could require that operatorship of the petroleum operations is vested in a state representative (which could be the grantor, or which could be the national oil company (14.1)). This possibility could be provided for in a concession, or in the terms of the joint venture arrangement.[28] As a further refinement of this approach, the national oil company and the investor parties could elect to incorporate a company (in which they would all be shareholders) which could act as the operator during the production period.[29]

An investor's natural inclination may be to not encourage state participation in a concession because it adds another layer of complexity to the conduct of the petroleum operations, and because it represents a form of joint venture with a grantor (or its nominee) as a state-owned entity whose objectives might be less obviously aligned with those of an investor (1.3). A state participation right could also create a working capital impact for an investor which is disproportionate to the investor's equity interest (where a grantor participates in a concession at the outset and requires to be carried by the other investor parties for its share of the necessary exploration and development costs), and it could be particularly unattractive where the amount of the carry is not repayable when petroleum production begins.

A further issue for an investor to be aware of is where a state participation right which exists in a concession is traded for value to another person by a grantor before or after its exercise. A grantor could reserve in a concession a right to transfer this interest to another person, or to allow another person to exercise the right directly, which might not be subject to certain conditions in favour of an investor.[30] Alternatively, the state participation right in a concession could be exercised by a grantor for the benefit of an (unnamed) nominee. In either of these instances, if a grantor effects such a transfer or exercises the state participation right in favour of a nominee, the investor parties are faced with the prospect of an unknown or unapproved other person becoming party to the concession and the joint venture arrangement as a fellow investor party.

[28] In Brazil the Pre-Salt Law of 2010 (12351/2010) provided that the state oil and gas company Petrobras would be appointed as the operator of all approved projects (and would also have a mandatory 30 per cent participating interest). Amendments to the law two years later transformed Petrobras's mandatory right of operatorship into a preference right for Petrobras (partly in response to criticisms that Petrobras's right was stifling inward investment).

[29] The Egypt 2021 concession agreement provides (at VI (a)) that: 'Upon the approval of the first Development Lease, EGAS and CONTRACTOR should form in the A.R.E. a company to carry out operations pursuant to this Article VI and Annex "D" (hereinafter referred to as the "Joint Venture Company") … Said company shall be a private sector joint stock company, subject to the laws and regulations in force in the A.R.E. to the extent such laws and regulations are not inconsistent with the provisions of this Agreement or the Charter of the Joint Venture Company.'

[30] The Kurdistan Iraq 2007 PSC provides (at 4.8) that: 'The GOVERNMENT shall have the option of nominating a third party, in respect of the Contract Area, as a CONTRACTOR Entity, with an undivided interest in the Petroleum Operations in respect of the entire Contract Area and all the other rights, duties, obligations and liabilities of the CONTRACTOR (save as provided in and subject to this Article 4), under this Contract.'

11

Constitutional Provisions

11.1 Introduction

A number of provisions make up the constitutional basis of a concession and will further define the relationship between a grantor and an investor.

These provisions include selection of the governing law of a concession, establishing the agreed allocation of liability between a grantor and an investor, and identifying a means of resolving disputes which arise between a grantor and an investor.

A concession may contain a force majeure provision which could relieve the liability of a party for a failure to perform its obligations under the concession.

A concession may also include a stabilization provision (which is intended to offer some comfort to an investor (and its lenders) regarding the long-term stability of the concession) and provisions relating to the making of amendments to the concession and to ensuring the confidentiality of the concession.

A concession may also append an accounting procedure which is intended to apply between the parties.

11.2 Governing Law

A concession will ordinarily recite the governing law which is intended to apply to it. This governing law could import certain provisions into the relationship between a grantor and an investor which the concession creates, and it may be applied to interpretation of the wording of the concession in the event of a dispute between the parties.

A grantor could say that because a concession is the contractual vehicle by which the state's mineral wealth is exploited, the governing law of the concession ought to be the law of the state. This suggestion is ordinarily almost impossible for an investor to resist.[1]

The selection of the law of the state to apply to a concession will expose an investor to the need to comply with all of the laws of the state (unless exceptions are made), which in the context of a concession could include a petroleum law, health, safety, and environmental regulations, procurement laws, civil and criminal law compliance, taxation

[1] Although for a contrary view, the Kurdistan Iraq 2007 production sharing contract (PSC) provides (at 43.1) that: 'This Contract, including any dispute arising therefrom, thereunder or in relation thereto and the agreement to arbitrate in Article 42, shall be governed by English law (except any rule of English law which would refer the matter to another jurisdiction), together with any relevant rules, customs and practices of international law, as well as by principles and practice generally accepted in petroleum producing countries and in the international petroleum industry.'

provisions, and any other legislation to which the concession may be subject. Such a selection would also expose a concession (and an investor) to any subsequent changes in the law of the state[2] and also to any other changes which might have a quasi-legal effect.[3]

A counter-argument that the law of the state lacks the commercial sophistication which is necessary to enable a concession to function properly (particularly in a nascent petroleum economy) could be met by a particular solution—the governing law provision could also include a reference to another body of law[4] or to international law (which is not easy to define)[5] as supporting codes which could apply to address any deficiencies which become apparent in the law of the state.

Such a construction may give comfort to an investor (and to its lenders) that a more comprehensive body of law could be made to apply to a concession, but it could also lead to some confusion of interpretation as to where one body of law ends and another one begins. More confusion could be generated where the supporting reference in a concession is not to another body of law but, rather, to some variant of good and prudent oil and gas field practice (8.7).[6]

[2] The Ghana Petroleum (Exploration and Production) (General) Regulations 2018 (L.I. 2359) changed several aspects of the standard Ghana petroleum agreement (including those relating to conditions regarding transfers of interests and changes in control and the approval of joint venture agreements). These changes would ostensibly have been applicable to existing petroleum agreements governed by the laws of Ghana.

[3] The Brazil 2017 production sharing agreement (PSA) provides in the governing law provision (at 36.1.2) that: 'ANP may issue general instructions, with no regulatory nature, on the performance of the agreement through its website.'

[4] The Bangladesh 2023 PSC provides (at 29) that: '29.1 The validity, interpretation and implementation of this Contract shall be governed by the law of the People's Republic of Bangladesh. 29.2 Notwithstanding Article 29.1, in the event of a dispute amongst the Parties where there is any lacuna in Bangladesh law, the laws of England and Wales will have persuasive value to that extent.' The Qatar 2002 DPSA provides (at 33) that: 'This Agreement shall be governed by and interpreted in accordance with the laws of the State of Qatar. In the event that the substantive laws of the State of Qatar do not address a particular issue or point that is in dispute between the Parties, or they expressly refer to the laws of jurisdictions other than the State of Qatar, the laws of England and Wales shall be used to resolve the issue. In all cases of conflict between the laws of the State of Qatar and the laws of England and Wales, however, the laws of the State of Qatar shall prevail.' The Azerbaijan 1996 PSA provides (at 23.1) that: 'This Agreement shall be governed and interpreted in accordance with principles of law common to the law of the Azerbaijan Republic and English law, and to the extent that no common principles exist in relation to any matter then in accordance with the principles of the common law of Alberta, Canada (except for laws regarding conflicts of laws). This Agreement shall also be subject to the international legal principle of pacta sunt servanda (agreements must be observed).'

[5] The Liberia 2013 PSC provides (at 23) that: 'The laws and regulations in force in the Republic of Liberia and the provisions of international law as may be applicable to international oil and gas activities shall apply to the Contractor, to this Contract and to the Operations which are the purpose thereof, unless otherwise provided by the Contract.' The Turkmenistan 1997 PSA provides (at 29.1) that: 'This Agreement shall be governed by, interpreted and construed in accordance with the laws of Turkmenistan and, as applicable, the principles of international law and the decisions of international tribunals and international treaties to which Turkmenistan is a Party.'

[6] The Guyana 2023 PSA provides (at 43) that: 'This Agreement shall be governed by, interpreted, and construed in accordance with the Laws of the Cooperative Republic of Guyana, and, consistent with such rules of international law as may be applicable or appropriate, including the Best International Industry Standards and Practice.' In turn, 'Best International Industry Standards and Practice' is defined (by reference to the applicable petroleum law) as 'all those uses and practices that are, at the time in question, in accordance with the most up to date international standards that are generally accepted in the oil and gas industry as being state-of-the-art or otherwise appropriate to the operations in question, safe, economical, environmentally sound and efficient in exploring for, developing, producing, processing and transporting petroleum'.

11.3 Allocation of Liability

The allocation of liability between a grantor and an investor for losses and liabilities which they are each exposed to as a consequence of the performance of a concession could be left to be determined by the governing law of a concession (11.2).

Alternatively, and more typically, a concession may specify an express regime for the allocation of liability between the parties. Such a liability allocation regime will usually reflect the following elements:

(1) *Third party claims*—a concession may require an investor to indemnify a grantor (and possibly also a wider class of state entities) against claims made by third parties who allege to have suffered loss or damage arising from the performance of the concession. There could be an exception to an investor's liability where the damage complained of could be attributable to the grantor or to the wider state.[7] As a *quid pro quo* for this exposure, a concession may provide that an investor (or, more typically, the operator (5.5)) will have the right and the responsibility to manage the defence of claims made by third parties.[8]

(2) *Investor default*—a concession may identify a number of circumstances which constitute an investor's default under the concession. These circumstances could relate to an investor's mis-performance or non-performance of a concession or to a breach of a law of the state by an investor (where the investor's failure is not relieved by force majeure (11.5)). The concession might also apply a test of materiality for such a default.

    An investor default (whether it is a default which is capable of being remedied and has not been remedied within a defined cure period, or whether it is a default which is incapable of being remedied) could also lead to grounds for the termination of a concession by a grantor (or, more likely, to the termination of a concession in respect of the investor party in default (6.6)). It could also be an event which entitles a grantor to make a claim under the collateral support which has been provided by an investor in respect of its commitments (5.4) in order to compel the proper performance of the concession.

    An investor default could also (depending on the governing law of the concession) generate a liability of an investor to pay damages to a grantor for breach of

[7] The Egypt 2021 concession agreement provides (at XV) that: 'CONTRACTOR shall entirely and solely be responsible in law toward third parties for any damage caused by CONTRACTOR's Exploration operations and shall indemnify the GOVERNMENT and/or EGAS against all damages for which they may be held liable on account of any such operations. However, in the event that any damage results as a consequence of the issuance of any order, regulation or direction of the GOVERNMENT of the A.R.E. whether promulgated in the form of a law or otherwise, then EGAS and/or CONTRACTOR shall be exempted from the responsibility resulting from the non-performance or delay in performance of any obligation under this Agreement as long as such non-performance or delay in performance is arising out of the issuance of such laws, regulations or orders within the limits imposed by such laws, regulations or orders.'

[8] The Nigeria 2021 PSC provides (at 8.1.1) that the contractor shall 'conduct litigation and settlement of claims ln connection with the Contract Area or Petroleum Operations for and on behalf of the Parties pursuant to the direction of the Management Committee'.

contract. The quantum of these damages will be determined by the loss which the grantor has suffered, and this might not always be an easy amount to assess. A concession may also apply a liquidated damages formulation to certain aspects of a concession. This could apply to an investor's failure to perform an exploration period obligation (8.2).

An investor's liability to a grantor for a breach of contract, and the circumstances in which an investor is obliged to compensate a grantor, could apply as a consequence of any standard of behaviour by an investor, or it could be expressed to apply only where an investor's behaviour falls into a particularly egregious category such as gross negligence or wilful misconduct (as those terms might be specifically defined in a concession).[9] A concession may also provide that where a state participation right has been exercised (10.8), the state's nominee will not be liable to contribute a share of the recompense which might otherwise be due from the investor to the grantor.[10]

(3) *Consequential loss*—whether or not an investor's liability to a grantor for a breach of the concession should include a liability of an investor to recompense a grantor's consequential losses (as that term might be specifically defined in a concession,[11] or as it might be determined by a concession's governing law) should be considered.[12] A broad exclusion of liability for consequential losses in the concession might not be effective under the governing law of a concession, and should be careful not to limit the right of an investor to recover the

[9] The Nigeria 2021 PSC provides (at 22.2) that: '[T]he CONTRACTOR shall indemnify and hold the CORPORATION harmless ... against all losses, damages, injuries, expenses, actions of whatever kind and nature ... as long as they are attributable to the Wilful Misconduct of the CONTRACTOR in the conduct of Petroleum Operations' and (at 1.1) that: '"Wilful Misconduct" means any act or failure to act of a Party (whether sole, joint, or concurrent), which was intended to cause or which was in reckless disregard of or wanton indifference to the harmful consequences that such Party so acting knew or should have known, such act or failure to act would have on (a) the safety of personnel or property; or (b) Petroleum Operations, but shall hot include an intentional, reckless disregard, or wanton indifference of either (a) or (b) if the same is in compliance with the instruction of any Government authority, pursuant to a decision of the Management Committee, or any act or omission reasonably required to meet emergency conditions including the safeguarding of life, property, or Petroleum Operations.'

[10] The Gambia 2022 licence provides (at 20.4.1) that: '[T]he Government shall be liable for its participating interest share of all expenses incurred by the Licensee in relation to Petroleum Operations ... provided that the Government shall not be liable for its participating interest share of any claims, losses, costs, liabilities or expenses arising out of in connection with the negligence, gross negligence or wilful misconduct of the Licensee' and that (at 20.4.2): '"[N]egligence, gross negligence or wilful misconduct" means the failure by a person to exercise the standard of care that a reasonably prudent person would have exercised in the same or similar circumstances, and any act or failure to act (whether sole, joint or concurrent) by any person which was intended to cause, or which was in reckless disregard of or wanton indifference to, harmful consequences such person knew, or should have known, such act or failure to act would have on the safety or property of another person.'

[11] The Azerbaijan 1996 PSA provides (at 20.7) that: 'For the purposes of this Article 20.7 the expression "indirect or consequential loss" shall mean any indirect or consequential loss or damage including but not limited to inability to produce Petroleum, loss of or delay in production of Petroleum or loss of profits.'

[12] The Afghanistan 2013 exploration and production sharing contract (EPSC) provides (at 27.3) that: 'Notwithstanding any other provision of this Contact, no Party shall be liable to any other Party (and for the benefit of the Contractor, the Ministry agrees that no Contractor Entity, its Shareholders or their respective Affiliated Entities, or any subcontractor of the Contractor shall be liable to the Ministry) for loss of profits, punitive damages, exemplary or indirect damages, business interruption damages or loss of goodwill arising out of a failure to comply with an obligation (including in respect of Hydrocarbons Operations) under this Contract.' The Somalia 2023 PSA provides (at 36.1) that: 'Except as specifically provided herein, neither Party shall be liable to the other Party for the other Party's consequential losses', but without providing a definition of what those consequential losses might be.

full value of compensation which might otherwise be due under a stabilization provision (11.6).

(4) *Joint and several liability*—a concession will usually prescribe that any liability of the investor parties to a grantor is joint and several, although this might not be entirely so.[13] Joint and several liability means that a claim which can be made by a grantor against an investor may be brought against any one, or some, or all of the investor parties, at the discretion of the grantor. This will be a particular issue where a state participation right has been exercised in respect of a concession (10.8), on the basis that a grantor is unlikely to make an indemnity claim against the state's representative.

Such a claim would then become a matter to be reallocated between the investor parties under their joint venture arrangement, which could be according to the several interests created by their percentage participating interests (5.3) (unless another basis for allocation has been agreed between them).

(5) *Insurance protection*—a concession may require an investor to arrange and maintain certain policies of insurance for the lifetime of the concession. These insurances (in respect of which the insured person would be the investor, but also with the possibility of the grantor (and/or other state entities) being named as a co-insured person) could relate to protecting the value of the assets or equipment which are required for the performance of the petroleum operations from loss or damage, protection of the grantor (and other state entities) and the investor from the incidence of third party claims, and coverage of the costs of cleaning up instances of pollution.

The choice of the insurer may be left to an investor, or a grantor may have a say in the selection of the insurer. As an alternative to placing the insurance with commercial insurers, a concession may provide that an investor can self-insure,[14] or that an investor can effect the insurances through an affiliated captive insurer.[15] A concession may also rule out these possibilities,[16] or introduce other requirements.[17]

13 The Kurdistan Iraq 2007 PSC provides (at 4.3) that: '[T]he Public Company will be individually and separately liable (and not jointly and severally liable with the other CONTRACTOR Entities) to the GOVERNMENT for its obligations, duties and liabilities under this Contract as a CONTRACTOR Entity'. The Mauritania 2012 PSC provides (at 21.10) that: 'The National Company on the one hand and other entities constituting the Contractor on the other hand, will not be jointly and severally liable for obligations under this Contract. The National Company shall be individually responsible vis-à-vis the State for its obligations as provided in this Contract. Any failure by the National Company to perform any of its obligations shall not constitute a failure of the other entities constituting the Contractor and shall, in no case, be invoked by the State to terminate this Contract.'

14 The Brazil 2017 PSA provides (at 27.2) that: 'At ANP's sole discretion and provided that previously authorized by it, self-insurance may be accepted.'

15 The Liberia 2013 PSC provides (at 27.4) that: '[T]he Contractor will be provided the opportunity to self-insure or underwrite any or all of the insurance required by this Article 28.4 through one or more insurance Affiliates of Persons participating in the Contractor or, if such direct insurance is not permitted, through reinsurance policies to such Affiliate insurance companies provided that the security and creditworthiness of such self-insurance or insurance arrangements have been disclosed to and are reasonably satisfactory to NOCAL.' The Suriname 2015 PSC provides (at 26.1) that: 'Contractor shall not self-insure or insure through Affiliates without the specific prior approval of Staatsolie.'

16 The Zanzibar 2024 PSA provides (at 20 (m)) that: 'Contractor shall not self-insure or insure through Affiliates.'

17 The Qatar 2002 development and production sharing agreement (DPSA) provides (at 12.4) that: 'All insurance required to be carried for Petroleum Operations shall be placed through a GOVERNMENT authorised

Insurance which is taken out by an investor to cover an investor's own liability to a grantor (or to other state entities) which arises under a concession, or to give protection to an investor for business interruption, the expropriation of its interests, or the occurrence of defined political risks, would less typically be countenanced by a concession (although such insurance could still be effected by an investor at its own election, and its own cost).

It is also possible that a grantor may be liable to an investor for a failure to perform its obligations under the concession (and in some circumstances an unremedied breach of a concession by a grantor could give a termination right in favour of an investor (6.6)), but in practical terms, an action for enforcement by an investor against a grantor for an alleged breach of contract is rare, given the political sensitivities which might be associated with taking such a step.

11.4 Dispute Resolution

A concession will ordinarily contain a mechanism for the resolution of disputes which arise between a grantor and an investor relating to the content or the effect of a concession.

As a starting point a concession may require the parties to make efforts to resolve a dispute amicably, through informal consultation.[18] If such consultation fails then a next step towards formal dispute resolution could apply.

A concession may prescribe the courts of the state as the venue for dispute resolution[19] but an investor (and its lenders) could have concerns relating variously to securing impartiality, managing confidentiality, providing for swift and effective resolution, being comfortable that the courts have the necessary capacity to adjudicate the dispute, and enforcing a court judgment against a grantor outside the state.

The principal alternative to recourse to the courts is for a concession to provide for disputes to be resolved by binding arbitration between the parties, ideally (from an investor's perspective) with that arbitration hearing to be held in a neutral venue and

Qatari national insurance company, if required by and in accordance with applicable GOVERNMENT rules and regulations.' The Somalia 2023 PSA provides (at 35.3) that: 'The Contractor shall give preference to Somali insurance companies, if such companies offer insurance policies that are comparable to those generally acceptable by international financing institutions in the same or similar circumstances.' The Afghanistan 2013 EPSC requires (at 27.1) that insurance is placed 'through an internationally recognized insurance company'.

[18] The Cyprus 2007 PSC provides (at 22) that: 'In the event of any dispute between the Republic and the Contractor regarding the interpretation or performance of any provisions of this Contract, the Parties shall make their best efforts to settle such dispute amicably through consultation.' The Qatar 2002 DPSA provides (at 34.1) that: 'The Parties shall in good faith and with a spirit of cooperation use all reasonable efforts to settle amicably any dispute that arises out of or relates to this Agreement or the breach, termination or validity thereof through constructive discussions and negotiations.'

[19] The Egypt 2021 concession agreement provides (at XXIV (a)) that: 'Any dispute, controversy or claim arising out of or relating to this Agreement or the breach, termination or invalidity thereof, between the GOVERNMENT and the parties shall be referred to the appropriate courts in A.R.E. and shall be finally settled by such courts.'

to be conducted according to the rules of a recognized independent arbitral institution. The governing law of a concession (11.2) could be selected to apply as the procedural governing law of the arbitration, unless an alternative is specified.

The particular attractions of arbitration as a means of dispute resolution are that it is private between the parties (which could be important to a grantor, which might not want the fact of a dispute with its investors to be made public), and that recognition and enforcement of an arbitral award could be made by the courts of a state if the terms of the United Nations Convention on the Recognition and Enforcement of Arbitral Awards (New York, 1958) are applicable. On the other hand, the often stated attractions of arbitration, namely the speed of the process and its cost effectiveness, can be less apparent in certain cases, and (despite what the arbitration provisions in the concession say), there is always a risk that an arbitrator could seek to exercise its functions *ex aequo et bono* (ie according to what seems fair and just given the particular circumstances, rather than strictly according to the rule of law).

A particular feature to note is the possibility that a dispute may qualify to be arbitrated under the auspices of the World Bank's International Centre for the Settlement of Investment Disputes (ICSID). For this to happen, an investor has to be a national of an ICSID contracting state, the state has to have acceded to the ICSID arbitration of disputes under the concession, and in a concession, the parties must have consented to submit the dispute to an ICSID arbitration for resolution.[20]

As a further option, a concession may provide for the appointment of an independent expert to determine certain agreed financial and technical issues (such as the recoverability of costs under a production-sharing contract (PSC) (9.3), the terms of a field development plan (8.4), the calculation of royalty amounts (9.4), or the valuation of petroleum (9.3)).[21] In contrast to a court decision or an arbitral award, an expert determination is not readily enforceable in its own right.

A concession may also include a waiver of sovereign immunity, ostensibly given by a grantor but such a provision would apply also in respect of any parastatal entity which constitutes an investor party (whether from the outset of a concession or by subsequent accession). A waiver of sovereign immunity, which represents a partial abrogation by a state of its sovereign rights, reflects a release of certain rights of immunity against the

[20] The Afghanistan 2013 EPSC provides (at 24.1) for such an approach, as does the Somalia 2023 PSA (at 48.3.1).

[21] The Somalia 2023 PSA provides (at 48.2) that: 'Each Party, may refer any dispute or disagreement (which includes inaction by a Party, the SPA or, where applicable, any other Person) concerning: 48.2.1 singular issues that, in the reasonable opinion of the referring Party, can be resolved by expert determination; or 48.2.2 technical/operational issues (including, without limitation, those related to the valuation of Crude Oil and approvals by the Federal Government, the SPA, or any other Somali Government Authority of various work programmes, budgets and plans) for determination by an internationally recognised sole expert to be appointed by agreement of the parties ... In such case, the Parties shall agree on the terms of reference for the expert determination, schedule and other procedural matters.' The Guyana 2023 PSA provides (at 46.3) that: 'Any Dispute arising out of or in connection with this Agreement may be referred to a sole expert, by a Party giving notice to such effect. The sole expert shall be requested to issue an opinion for use by the Parties in an effort to settle any such Dispute', and (at 46.4) that: 'The sole expert shall be appointed by agreement between the Parties, and in the event the Parties fail to agree on the sole expert within forty-five (45) days after receipt of the written notice from any Party proposing the appointment of a sale expert, such expert shall be appointed by the International Chamber of Commerce ("ICC") in accordance with its Rules for the Appointment of Experts and Neutrals. A sole expert shall be an independent and impartial person of international standing with relevant qualifications and experience.'

enforcement of a court decision or an arbitral award which a sovereign person might otherwise enjoy.[22]

A concession might provide that the costs which are incurred by a grantor in respect of a dispute with an investor must be borne by the investor, with such a provision being intended to apply before any share of the revenues which are associated with the production of petroleum have begun to accrue to the grantor under the concession, on the basis that a grantor in a nascent petroleum economy could simply lack the funds to finance an expensive dispute resolution process.[23]

11.5 Force Majeure

Force majeure is a mechanism which (in certain circumstances) gives relief to a party to a contract from a liability which that party would otherwise have for a failure to perform a contractual obligation. Broadly, the performance failure (which could be evidenced as non-performance or a delay in performance) must have been caused by a supervening event which was beyond the control (or the reasonable control) of the affected party.

A popular misconception is that force majeure relief absolves the affected party from the obligation to continue to perform the affected contractual obligation (or even the contract). This is not so (unless the contract says so). The affected party could still be obliged to perform as much of the contract as possible, and the availability of force majeure relief to the affected party is usually conditional upon the affected party taking reasonable steps to overcome the force majeure event and to resume normal contractual performance as soon as possible.

As examples, an investor could require a force majeure provision to protect against liability to a grantor for a failure to perform an exploration period obligation (8.2) or a work programme obligation (8.6) (in either case where, eg, the failure could have been caused by unforeseen subsurface conditions which were encountered during the drilling of a well (although the drilling obligations in the concession may be absolute requirements, in the sense that they may be capable of being satisfied in the alternative

[22] The Suriname 2015 PSC provides (at 43.1) that: 'The Parties agree that the activities contemplated in this Contract are an investment and are commercial in nature. Each Party irrevocably waives, to the fullest extent permitted by the laws of applicable jurisdiction, any defense of or right of immunity (including sovereign immunity) (a) in respect of arbitration proceedings or the enforcement of any award, including (without limitation) immunity from service of process or from the jurisdiction of any court or tribunal, or (b) as to it or its property in respect of the enforcement and execution of any arbitration award rendered under this Contract, and expressly consents to any legal action or proceeding (including pre-judgment attachment) in relation to the enforcement and execution of such arbitration award including in respect of any property held by such Party, whether for commercial purposes or otherwise.'

[23] The Gambia 2022 licence provides (at 31.8.1) that: 'If there is a Dispute prior to the first payment by the Licensee of a royalty pursuant to Article 8.2, the Government may by written notice to the Licensee require that the Licensee promptly reimburse the Government for out-of-pocket costs reasonably incurred by the Government in relation to the conduct of that Dispute, including in relation to the retention by the Government of international and domestic legal counsel and one or more experts' and also (at 38.1.2) that: 'The aggregate amount of costs for which the Government may be reimbursed pursuant to Article 31.8.1 during the Term shall be limited to four million United States Dollars (USD 4,000,000).'

by the obligation of an investor to drill a substitute well or to make a compensatory payment to a grantor), or where an investor's intended performance of a concession would be inhibited by the imposition of sanctions.

A concession is less likely to create a liability of a grantor for a failure to perform its obligations for which the grantor would require force majeure relief, although this is a possibility and the force majeure provisions in a concession may equally countenance the ability of a grantor to claim force majeure relief for itself.

What constitutes 'force majeure' may be defined specifically within a concession (and ideally should be, to avoid imprecision and the risk of later disputes). This approach could include a list (which could be exhaustive or illustrative) of the intended force majeure events. The definition of force majeure may also be derived from a law of the state to which the concession is subject,[24] or by reference to other provisions.[25] The definition of force majeure protection under a concession must also be read in light of the governing law of a concession (11.2), which might colour a contractually agreed definition.

A force majeure provision may also include an indication of certain events which will not be eligible for force majeure relief.[26] It is customary that a force majeure provision will not excuse the liability which a party has to make a monetary payment which is due under a contract. In the context of a concession, this exclusion would principally impact the investor, as the party which is responsible for making various monetary payments to a grantor.[27]

Force majeure relief may also be expressed not to apply to a failure which is attributable to an act or an omission of the affected party (which, in respect of a force majeure claim which is made by a grantor, may be extended to include other state entities, such that a grantor could be precluded from claiming force majeure relief in respect of certain acts of the state).[28]

Force majeure relief may also be expressed not to apply to economic hardship or to a change in market circumstances which adversely affects the returns which the affected party expects to make from the concession. This could apply where an investor is required to continue to produce petroleum during a sustained period of low petroleum

24 See Guyana Petroleum Activities Act 2023, s 42(1).

25 The Cyprus 2007 PSC provides (at 21.2) that: 'The intent of the Parties is that the term Force Majeure shall be interpreted in accordance with the principles and practice of international law.' The Kurdistan Iraq 2007 PSC provides (at 40.3) that: 'The intention of the Parties is that Force Majeure shall receive the interpretation that complies most with prudent international petroleum industry practice.'

26 The Trinidad and Tobago 2023 PSC provides (at 34.2) that: 'Notwithstanding anything in Article 34.1 (and without prejudice to the generality thereof) the following events or circumstances shall not be treated as being Force Majeure or caused thereby: (a) failure by either Party to pay money when due or fulfil any financial obligation under this Contract; (b) the insolvency of Contractor or any entity constituting Contractor.'

27 Although even this exclusion from relief may be qualified in some circumstances. The Somalia 2023 PSA provides (at 38.3) that: 'In the event of Force Majeure the Contractor will continue to pay the surface fees pursuant to clause 33.2 provided that the Contractor will not be obligated to pay any further amounts pursuant to clause 28 (Training Fund), clause 33 (Fees and Bonuses) or otherwise under the Agreement.'

28 The Qatar 2002 DPSA provides (at 32.5) that: 'The GOVERNMENT and QP shall not be relieved of any obligations hereunder as a result of any Government Order of the State of Qatar.' The Guyana 2023 PSA provides (at 42.6) that: 'The Government shall not invoke Force Majeure due to any order, regulation or written directive of the Government which affects the Government's performance of its obligations under this Agreement.'

prices. A renegotiation of the requirements of a concession between a grantor and an investor might be possible in such circumstances[29] but a concession will not necessarily guarantee this relief to the investor.

Periods of time when force majeure is claimed and which impact the performance of a concession could be added to give an extension to the term of a concession (6.3).[30] A concession may also be subject to possible termination because of a prolonged event of force majeure (11.5), whether automatically, by the election of one of the parties or by agreement between the parties.

11.6 Investment Protection and Stabilization

A concession may contain certain provisions which are intended to protect an investor's bargain, but the concession is not the exclusive source of such protection. An investor could also benefit from some form of state-level accord which gives protection against the risks of interference by the grantor (or the wider state) with the bargain which a concession creates. This accord could take the form of a multilateral investment treaty to which a number of states are signatory (such as the Energy Charter Treaty[31]) or a bilateral investment treaty between two states.[32]

What is sometimes called a 'host government agreement' could be entered into, as a specific agreement between a grantor (or another state entity) and an investor which governs the rights and obligations of them both in relation to the development and operation of a particular project by the investor.[33] A host government agreement could be used in the development of a project which does not afford protection to an investor through a bilateral investment treaty. Most host government agreements are essentially founded around a stabilization provision which is intended to protect the investor. A host government agreement is not a concession in its own right, but it is sometimes equated with a concession because of the protection which it affords to an investor.

A concession is a long-term commitment which requires a significant amount of investment by an investor, and which supposes the assumption of a significant number of risks by the investor. The most obvious of those risks is that the exploration for

[29] See note 20, Chapter 12.

[30] The Cyprus 2007 PSC provides (at 21.4) that: 'If the performance of any of the obligations of the Contract is delayed due to a case of Force Majeure, the duration of the resulting delay together with such time period as may be required for the repair of any damage caused by the case of Force Majeure, shall be added to the term of this Contract.' The Bangladesh 2023 PSC provides (at 27.3) that: 'If the Petroleum Operations in the Contract Area are partially or entirely suspended as a result of the Force Majeure referred to in article 27.1 herein, the period of the Petroleum Operations shall be extended by a period not exceeding the corresponding period of such suspension.'

[31] <www.energycharter.org/process/energy-charter-treaty-1994/energy-charter-treaty/> accessed 3 April 2025. The Energy Charter Treaty is facing its own uncertainties—see Andrei Belyi, 'The Energy Charter Process in the Face of Uncertainties' [2021] JWELB 363.

[32] A summary of investment treaties can be found at <www.icsid.worldbank.org/node/20271> accessed 3 April 2025.

[33] A model form host government agreement has been published by the Energy Charter Secretariat—see <www.energycharter.org/what-we-do/trade-and-transit/model-agreements> accessed 3 April 2025.

petroleum is unsuccessful, but the success of a petroleum production project could bring its own risks too.

A concession which has moved into the production period (8.4) could have a long prospective duration. An investor may be concerned by the possibility that a grantor will try to modify the terms of the concession in the grantor's favour over time, through unilaterally reinterpreting and applying the concession's fiscal or other terms (whether directly or indirectly).[34] The level of state take which a concession creates (9.2) could (in a grantor's opinion) become inadequate (which might be the case particularly if a concession's fiscal terms are not progressive (9.2)), and as a reaction a grantor could make (or could procure the making of) changes to the terms of a concession, changes to the governing law of a concession (11.2), or changes to the taxation regime of a concession insofar as it affects an investor (9.5), any of which could adversely affect the investor's interests under a concession. Such changes could in themselves be, or they could accumulate to the point where in the aggregate they could be, regarded by an investor (or its lenders) as a form of expropriation of the investor's interests.

The risk of this possibility is ordinarily not accepted by an investor as a necessary consequence of doing business in a state, and to this end a concession might contain what is called a 'stabilization' provision, which is intended to protect an investor (and possibly also an investor's contractors – see *Maersk Drillship JV Singapore Pte Ltd v The Commissioner General Ghana Revenue Authority* SC (Civil Appeal 14/59/2024)) against the risk of direct or indirect adverse interference by a grantor (or by other state entities) with the concession.

An investor's demand for a stabilization provision tends to be resisted by a grantor in a well-developed petroleum economy, and particularly so in respect of an economy which has a demonstrable commitment to upholding the rule of law and recognizing the sanctity of contract. But a grantor in a nascent petroleum economy could accede to an investor's request for the inclusion of a stabilization provision in the concession in order to encourage inward investment. Over time, a grantor could take the view that it has evolved sufficiently to no longer need to offer a stabilization provision in the terms of its forthcoming concessions where previously it had felt the need to do so.[35]

[34] This possibility is sometimes described as the 'obsolescing bargain model', in recognition of a behavioural proposition for how states could react to long-term investments made by foreign investors (initially in general, but over time reviewed to apply in the context of concession) which was advanced in the early 1970s by the US economist Raymond Vernon: 'There may have been a time in international affairs when foreign producers of raw materials anticipated that a bargain with the government, once made, would not come unstuck. Today the opposite is generally assumed. And the assumption derives in part from an increasing appreciation of the process that leads governments repeatedly—almost predictably—to reopen the issues involved in the exploitation of raw materials ... almost from the moment that the signatures have dried on the document, powerful forces go to work that quickly render the agreements obsolete in the eyes of the government ... a pronounced changing outlook can be expected to occur, however, after the initial exploration has been completed ... the returns to the foreign company no longer seem appropriate to the risk, and the government feels justified in demanding more out of the project ... foreign investors must resign themselves to the fact that the national goals and preferences to which they were responsive at the time they entered any country are likely to undergo periodic metamorphoses' [Raymond Vernon, *Sovereignty at Bay* (Penguin, 1971)].

[35] The Tanzania 2004 PSA provided that: 'If at any time or from time to time there should be a change in legislation or regulations which materially affects the commercial and fiscal benefits afforded by the Contractor under this Contract, the Parties will consult each other and shall agree to such amendments to this Contract as are necessary to restore as near as practicable such commercial benefits which existed under the Contract as of the Effective Date.' Such a provision did not make an appearance in successive Tanzania model PSAs in 2008 and 2013.

But, because the economic and political circumstances associated with the petroleum sector are in constant evolution, an investor may be reluctant to dispense with this form of protection.

A stabilization provision may be entered into by a grantor as a term of a concession. From an investor's perspective, the protection of a stabilization provision should ideally be given directly by a duly authorized state representative (as a superior entity to a grantor), rather than solely by a grantor. Where this is possible, the stabilization provision could be set out within a concession (with the state's representative as an additional signatory to the concession[36] or with the grantor expressed to act as the authorized agent of the state) or it could be set out in a separate host government agreement.

There is no standard form for a stabilization provision, and whether a provision which is offered up as such actually constitutes stabilization (in the generally accepted meaning of the term) will be a matter of opinion. Broadly, a stabilization provision may be represented as the promise of a grantor (and/or of the state, represented by a state entity) to undertake any (or any combination) of the following commitments during the lifetime of a concession:

(1) To protect the sanctity of an investor's position by enacting a concession as a law of the state in its own right (sometimes called a 'force-of-law' provision). This then creates a presumption that the concession would thereafter only be capable of being changed by a new law (which always remains a possibility).[37]
(2) To offer equal treatment to all investors in the state (sometimes called a 'non-discrimination' provision).[38]
(3) To offer a broad guarantee of protection of an investor's interests.[39] Also, a tax paid provision in a concession could be seen as a form of stabilization provision in its own right, and this could be supported by a tax-specific stabilization provision in a concession (9.5).
(4) To consolidate the legal and taxation basis which applies to an investor to that which applied in relation to a concession at the date when the concession came

[36] See the Egypt 2021 concession agreement.

[37] The Egypt 2021 concession agreement provides (at XXIX) that: 'This Agreement shall not be binding upon any of the parties hereto unless and until a law is issued by the competent authorities of the A.R.E. authorizing the Minister of Petroleum to sign this Agreement and giving this Agreement full force and effect of law notwithstanding any countervailing governmental enactment, and the Agreement is signed by the GOVERNMENT, EGAS and CONTRACTOR.'

[38] The Afghanistan 2013 EPSC provides (at 19) that: 'The treatment accorded to the Contractor, each Contractor Entity, its Affiliated Entities and Shareholders by Afghanistan in relation to the Contract shall not be less favorable than the treatment required to be accorded to foreign investors under Afghanistan Law.'

[39] The Ghana 2000 petroleum agreement provides (at 26.2) that: 'The State, its departments and agencies, shall support this Agreement and shall take no action which prevents or impedes the due exercise and performance of rights and obligations of the Parties hereunder. As of the Effective Date of this Agreement and throughout its Term, the State guarantees Contractor the stability of the terms and conditions of this Agreement as well as the fiscal and contractual framework hereof specifically including those terms and conditions and that framework that are based upon or subject to the provisions of the laws and regulations of Ghana . . . any legislative or administrative act of the State or any of its agencies or subdivisions which purports to vary any such right or obligation shall, to the extent sought to be applied to this Agreement, constitute a breach of this Agreement by the State.'

into force. This could be realized through a statement that a grantor will guarantee the stability of a concession for its duration, or a grantor's undertaking that the state will not (directly or indirectly) vary the terms of a concession (at least, not without the investor's consent).[40] Commitments of a grantor along these lines are sometimes described as a 'freezing' provision, or as an 'intangibility' provision.[41]

(5) To commit to modify a concession so as to restore the original benefits which were enjoyed by an investor in the event of adverse changes which relate to a concession (sometimes called an 'economic equilibrium' provision).[42]

(6) To commit to give fair compensation to an investor (which might be left as an undefined amount, or which might be the subject of a specified compensatory formula) in the event of adverse changes which relate to a concession and/or an investor's position.[43]

The manner in which concessions have reflected stabilization provisions has changed over time, and in particular, in the drafting of such provisions, there has been a move away from precluding the grantor's ability to effect what might be seen as an

[40] The Kurdistan Iraq 2007 PSC provides (at 43.2) that: 'The obligations of the CONTRACTOR in respect of this Contract shall not be changed by the GOVERNMENT and the general and overall equilibrium between the Parties under this Contract shall not be affected in a substantial and lasting manner.'

[41] The Afghanistan 2013 EPSC provides (at 16.6) an interesting variation to this form of stabilization: '[T]he Contractor shall be entitled to the benefit of any future changes to Afghanistan Law; provided that this Section 16.6 shall not apply to any benefit arising from any changes in Afghanistan Law that relate to financial or fiscal matters agreed in this Contract, including in respect of royalty, cost recovery, production sharing and surface rental fees (other than any change in the Income Tax rate).'

[42] The Bangladesh 2023 PSC provides (at 37.2) that: 'If any change (including changes in interpretation or application) in Bangladesh law, regulation, Government decision or other legally enforceable governmental instrument (including those on taxes) negatively impacts the economic benefits of the Contractor, the Government/Petrobangla will expeditiously implement measures so as to restore and maintain those economic benefits of the Contractor as they were as at the Effective Date.'

[43] The Bangladesh 2023 PSC provides (at 37.1) that: '[T]he Contractor's interest in this Contract, and assets and rights in Bangladesh held by the Contractor hereunder, shall not be expropriated or nationalized or be subject to any measures having effect of expropriation or nationalization except for a public purpose against adequate compensation which shall be paid expeditiously and be freely transferable. Adequate compensation for the purpose of this Article 37.1 shall be an amount equivalent to the market value of investment expropriated or nationalized immediately before the expropriation or nationalization.' The Somalia 2023 PSA provides (at 39.3.4) for the payment of a defined amount of compensation in favour of an investor: 'Following the commencement of Commercial Production, in the event the Contractor terminates the Agreement as a result of the Federal Government's default then the Contractor has the option to require that the Federal Government (or its designee) shall purchase the Termination Transfer Assets for the Federal Government Default Termination Amount' (with the amount of compensation to be set according to a defined formula), and also provides (at 45.4) a monetary threshold for the trigger of the requirement to pay compensation to the investor: 'No obligation to compensate the Contractor shall arise under clause 45.2 unless the Stabilization Events cause a cumulative Material Adverse Effect in excess of fifteen million (15) USD ("Threshold Amount") per Calendar Year. If the Threshold Amount is exceeded only the portion of the economic impact in excess of the Threshold Amount shall be compensated.' The Azerbaijan 1996 PSA provides (at 23.3) that: 'If any of Contractor's rights, interests or property are expropriated, nationalised or otherwise taken by reason of any act or failure to act of any Governmental Authority, then the arbitrators shall apply the principle of indemnification (including prompt, full and effective compensation in Dollars) at the full market value, on the basis of an on-going concern utilising the discounted cash flow method, assuming a willing buyer and seller in a non-hostile environment, and disregarding the unfavourable circumstances under which or following which Contractor shall be deprived of its rights, interest (including its interest in undeveloped reserves) or property. The arbitrators shall select an investment bank of good international reputation for purpose of appraising the full market value of said rights, interest (including its interest in undeveloped reserves) or property of Contractor.'

expropriatory action (on the grounds that a concession should not be permitted to fetter a state's sovereign discretion)[44] and instead towards addressing the consequences of an expropriatory action from an investor's perspective.

The initial reaction to an event or circumstance which, in the opinion of an investor, necessitates a claim for protection under a stabilization provision is that the grantor and the investor would meet and seek to agree a solution to restore the investor's position. If agreement cannot be reached then an investor could have recourse to the dispute resolution mechanisms of a concession (11.4) to settle the issue—but it should be noted that the adverse events complained of by an investor might not be something which a grantor can obviously be blamed for, and consequently a concession's dispute resolution provisions might not offer a ready solution to an investor if the wider state is not caught by the commitments made in the concession.

11.7 Amendments

A concession may include a provision that its terms can only be amended by agreement between the parties[45] (which reinforces the notion of a concession as a contract rather than a regulatory instrument[46]), although such a provision could also seek to recognize the sovereign rights of a state.[47]

A concession may also suggest that its terms could be improved by agreement between the parties where a case can be made for doing so.[48]

The application of the governing law of a concession (11.2) could also result in changes being made indirectly to the terms of a concession. The impact of such indirect changes may need to be considered in light of the protection which might be afforded by a stabilization provision in a concession.

44 The Bangladesh 2023 PSC provides (at 38.2) that: 'Without prejudice to the Government's prerogative of Sovereign powers to act in the public interest, this Contract shall not be amended or modified except by mutual agreement in writing of the Government, Petrobangla and Contractor.' The Mozambique 2006 EPC provides (at 27.12 (a)) that: 'The Government, its political subdivisions, agencies and instrumentalities, to the extent that they have or may acquire the power to do so, will not expropriate, nationalise or intervene in the assets, rights, interests or any other property of any kind of the Concessionaire held for the purpose of Petroleum Operations including the rights held by the Concessionaire hereunder.'

45 The Ethiopia 2011 PSC provides (at 17.4.2) that: 'This Agreement shall not be amended, modified or supplemented except by an instrument in writing signed by the Parties.'

46 See note 8, Chapter 2.

47 See note 1, Chapter 12.

48 The Tajikistan 2008 PSC provides (at 2.6) that: 'The Contractor and the Ministry may as between themselves, agree in writing to amend any provision of this Contract where to do so would, in the opinion of both the Contractor and the Ministry improve the day to day operations contemplated hereunder, but not so as to vary any fundamental provision of this Contract.' The Angola 2008 PSC provides (at 37.1) that: 'In order to avoid the international double taxation of Contractor Group's income, Sonangol shall favorably consider any amendments or revisions to this Agreement that Contractor Group may propose as long as those amendments or revisions do not impact on Sonangol or Angola's economic benefits and other benefits resulting from the Agreement.' The Azerbaijan 1996 PSA provides (at 22.1) that: 'The Parties acknowledge the necessity of continuing to work in good faith to resolve any matters not presently covered by this Agreement.'

11.8 Confidentiality

A concession will usually contain a confidentiality provision, whereby confidential information is defined by a concession and the parties are obliged to keep that information confidential and are only permitted to disclose it under a limited number of circumstances.

The principal purpose of the confidentiality provision is to protect the value of the operational information (and any unregistered intellectual property) which is generated through the performance of the petroleum operations. This information will ordinarily belong to a grantor, and could be released to third parties by the grantor for a fee. The obligation of confidentiality would also apply to the contents of a concession, and to the outcome of any dispute between the parties regarding a concession which is not in the public domain.

The confidentiality obligation will apply in respect of each investor party, and will apply not only for as long as the investor party is party to a concession but also after it has ceased to be party to the concession (and typically for a defined time thereafter).

An investor party might be obliged to publish a (possibly redacted) version of a concession to comply with the requirements of a stock exchange upon which it is listed, and could reserve a specific disclosure right for this in the confidentiality provision. A grantor might also reserve a similar right.[49]

A grantor or an investor party might also wish to reserve a specific right to publish the terms of a concession as part of a commitment to certain extractive industries transparency initiatives.[50]

11.9 The Accounting Procedure

A procedure will ordinarily be appended to the concession which sets out the accounting elements that will exist between the parties as a consequence of the performance of the petroleum operations, where the procedure is intended to be administered by the concession's appointed operator (5.5). In the event of a conflict between the

[49] The Afghanistan 2013 EPSC provides (at 33.1) that: 'Within ten (10) Days following the Effective Date, the Ministry shall (i) register this Contract in the Hydrocarbons Register and (ii) publish in at least three (3) newspapers of national circulation in Afghanistan and on the Ministry's website an announcement summarizing the material terms of the Contract.'

[50] The Afghanistan 2013 EPSC provides (at 33.1) that: 'The Ministry shall have the right to keep a copy of this Contract in the Hydrocarbons Register, publish and keep publicly available and distribute to provincial offices such information and reports on the Contract, related documents and the Contractor as is required pursuant to the Hydrocarbons Law and any regulations issued thereunder or pursuant to any transparency principles or policies adopted by the Government, including the EITI ... The foregoing shall not preclude the Ministry from disclosing the Contract or any information relating to Hydrocarbons Operations if the Ministry concludes that such disclosure is in the national interest or complies with the EITI or other internationally accepted norms relating to transparency in the extractive industries.' The Somalia 2023 PSA provides (at 44.4) that: 'The Federal Government may publish such information concerning the Agreement as may be required by Law, including for purposes of obtaining ratification of the Agreement or in accordance with internationally accepted standards and norms concerning transparency in the extractive industries.'

accounting procedure and the main body of the concession, the usual resolution is that the main body of the concession will take precedence.

Although the content of accounting procedures will vary between different concessions, as a general observation the concession's accounting procedure will typically include the following elements:

(1) The periodic reporting (usually monthly, and also with provision for an annual statement) by the operator to the grantor of the movements on a number of items over a defined period of time, such as: incurred petroleum operations costs; received petroleum production revenues; quantities and grades of produced petroleum; petroleum valuation and realized petroleum sales prices; payments of rental payments, royalties, and other amounts due to the grantor; and decommissioning fund movements.
(2) The definition of recoverable and irrecoverable petroleum costs where the concession is a PSC.
(3) The operator's maintenance of accounts, records, and reports (and the preservation of physical samples) relating to the petroleum operations, to be held at a defined location and to be made available for the grantor's inspection.
(4) The maintenance of bank accounts by the operator and the specification of the investor and grantor bank accounts to which payments due under the concession are to be made.
(5) The valuation of materials which have been purchased and disposed of by the operator in the performance of the petroleum operations.
(6) The conduct of periodic inventories by the operator, the valuation of assets or equipment, and the maintenance of asset records.
(7) The preparation of periodic budgets and forecasts by the operator.

The accounting procedure will describe the accounting standards and conventions, the languages, the currencies (and the currency conversion protocols), and the units of measurement which will apply variously to its contents. The accounting procedure will also describe whether the cash basis or the accruals basis (or even both) will apply to the operator's accounting.

The accounting procedure may also reserve rights for the grantor to inspect the various accounts, records, and reports, and also to commission an independent audit of the same if it so chooses.

PART C

EVOLVING CONCESSIONS AND SECTOR DEVELOPMENTS

12

Modifying Concessions and Concession Awards

12.1 Introduction

A state might wish to modify (or terminate) existing concessions, to reflect its perception of the energy transition. A state's ability to unilaterally effect modification or termination will typically be constrained by the terms of a concession, and there could be consequences where a state (also acting through a grantor) nevertheless purports to do so.

A state might also wish to modify the terms of its future concessions, to reflect its perception of the energy transition and also to reflect a number of initiatives which are intended to be favourable to the state. It could be easier for a state to realize this ambition.

12.2 Modifying or Terminating Existing Concessions

A concession typically provides that its terms can only be modified by agreement between the parties (11.7), such that unilateral modification is not an option.[1] Consequently, the customary assumption is that the direct modification of the terms of an existing concession can only be done by agreement between a grantor and an investor.[2]

A grantor might wish for a unilateral right to terminate a concession, to bring the concession to an end or to award a fresh concession to another person on terms which reflect the state's energy transition ambitions. However, a grantor ordinarily has the right to terminate a concession only if an investor (or an investor party) is in breach of the concession's terms or another specified termination event arises (6.6), and a right of termination for the grantor's convenience is not common. In practical terms, it could be difficult for a grantor to terminate a concession for convenience whilst at the same

[1] As an example of this standard approach, the Guyana 2023 production sharing agreement (PSA) provides (at 48.4) that: 'This Agreement may not be altered, amended, or modified except by a written instrument signed by the duly authorized representatives of each of the Parties.' As a variation to this approach, the 2023 Bangladesh model production sharing contract (PSC) provides (at 38.2) that: 'Without prejudice to the Government's prerogative of Sovereign powers to act in the public interest, this Contract shall not be amended or modified except by mutual agreement in writing of the Government, Petrobangla and Contractor.' This provision suggests that the PSC is a contract which can only be amended with the mutual consent of the contracting parties, but it also appears to reserve a sovereign right of the state to act in the public interest (which arguably could include making unilateral modifications to the PSC).

[2] Although a concession could reserve certain rights for a party which, if exercised, could modify the concession's application (such as an investor's voluntary relinquishment right or surrender right, or a grantor's right to modify an investor's exploration period obligations or their timings).

time requiring an investor to effect a harmonious handover (6.6) or continue to be responsible for managing any required decommissioning works (8.5).

Any putative modification to, or termination of, a concession which is effected by a grantor without a contractual basis for doing so under the concession could create an actionable breach of contract in favour of an investor.

Where (as is usually the case) a concession is governed by the laws of the state (11.2), the state could pass a law which purports to modify the terms of the concession.[3] There could be a temptation for a state to make small but frequent changes to the terms of a concession by this route which could, when viewed in the aggregate, represent significant overall modification to the concession.[4] Alternatively, the state could pass a law which purports to terminate a concession.

Any putative modification to, or termination of, a concession which is effected unilaterally by a grantor, or which is engineered by a state by a wider change in the governing law of the concession, would also need to be considered in light of the protections which might be afforded to an investor by investment protection provisions to which the concession is subject, such as an investment protection accord or a stabilization provision (11.6), (unless the protection which is otherwise afforded to an investor is expressed not to apply in certain circumstances).[5]

In the case of states which have declared an intention to withdraw from the future licensing of petroleum exploration activities (4.1), the concessions for petroleum exploration and/or production which had already been granted by those states were allowed to expire in accordance with their terms. The concessions were not terminated prematurely, nor were they amended to reflect any new aspirations of the relevant states for the remainder of their terms.

The obsolescing bargain model (11.6) presumes that a change in the balance of a commercial relationship which is created by a concession is a one-way process which works only in favour of a grantor and against the interests of an investor, and it casts a concession as something which an investor would do anything to keep hold of. The obverse could be true, however, since in some circumstances an investor could be equally keen to change the terms of (or to withdraw from) a concession.

12.3 Modifying Future Concessions

Assuming that a state intends to have continuing involvement with the exploration and/or production of petroleum (and so also with the award and the performance of

[3] See note 2, Chapter 11.

[4] This represents what the social scientist Charles Lindblom called 'disjointed incrementalism', as the achievement of a radical position by the implementation of a series of small steps where an attempt to take a single large step would likely have failed.

[5] The Guyana 2023 PSA provides (at 49.7) that: 'The stabilization provisions of Articles 49.3–49.4 do not apply to enactments, amendments, modifications, or other change to acts or regulations that govern the industrial and environmental safety of petroleum operations, social and environmental protection, occupational health and safety, labour relations, and climate change.'

concessions) as part of the state's energy transition ambitions, future concessions could be modified to reflect the perceived requirements of the energy transition and to reflect certain state-focused initiatives. These modifications could be intended to meet the following objectives (which in some cases might conflict):

(1) The continued exploration for and/or production (and processing and transportation) of petroleum within the state will at all times be conducted in the most environmentally friendly manner, and with the realization of the lowest possible associated carbon intensity (3.3).
(2) The continued exploration for and/or production of petroleum will generate the greatest level of return for the state (recognizing also that petroleum production revenues accruing to the state could be deployed to develop and sustain non-petroleum related activities in the state).
(3) A concession will reflect (and could be capable of further modification to reflect) the requirements of the energy transition (including, in due course, a transition away from petroleum exploration and/or production if the state decides to make such a transition).
(4) The continued exploration for and/or production of petroleum in a manner which increases the state's capability to better manage its own patrimony (including a greater involvement of a national oil company (14.1)), with greater participation by the state and consequently less participation by investors, could give the state more flexibility and greater freedom to further implement the requirements of the energy transition in respect of its concessions
(5) Investors should be encouraged to assume the risk and expense which is associated with exploiting a state's patrimony, concession terms should be made attractive to investors to continue to secure and maintain inward investment, and other incentives could apply to drive down production costs.[6]

Potential modifications to future concessions which could be made in pursuit of the above objectives are suggested below under several thematic headings:

(1) *The concession's scope*—a concession's scope is ordinarily focused on the business of commercializing petroleum, through the activities of exploration and appraisal, development and production (and possibly also processing, transportation, and storage), and decommissioning (6.2). That said, a concession may also reference a number of activities which could be seen as part of an investor's commitment to assist the state in realizing its energy transition objectives. In the Guyana 2023 PSA, the preamble introduces the

[6] In Nigeria the Upstream Petroleum Operations (Cost Efficiency Incentives) Order 2025 introduced a performance-based tax credit for contractors whereby the realisation of lower production costs leads to a 50% tax credit on the incremental revenue which is thereby generated (up to a cap of 20% of the contractor's annual tax liability).

notion of sustainable exploitation,[7] the section of the PSA which addresses the contractor's rights and obligations introduces a greenhouse gas abatement obligation,[8] and the PSA provides that a field development plan which is to be submitted by an investor could also be required to include elements relating to carbon capture and storage.[9]

Notwithstanding that an investor might have an interest in undertaking non-petroleum-related activities as part of its own commitment to realizing the energy transition (including where the investor's commitment to such activities may have resulted from additional requirements in the terms of a licensing round (12.4)), a concession's scope provision is not the place in which the terms of the investor's commitment and the detail of those activities should be recorded. Rather, the investor's commitment and the activities should be set out in a separate but ancillary accord between the investor and the grantor (or another state entity).

An ancillary arrangement, rather than an expansion of the scope of the concession, would also be a better fit with an underlying joint venture arrangement, the scope of which customarily does not extend to include activities beyond petroleum exploration and/or production. On the other hand, if a concession is chosen as the vehicle to record these activities, then the concession's exploration period obligations (8.2) could still be written to address customary exploration-focused activities but also with the expectation that further works relating to the performance of these activities could be compelled as a condition of the later approval of a development plan in respect of a commercial discovery (8.3).

(2) *The concession's duration*—the timings which define a concession's exploration period (6.4) and production period (6.5) could be modified in several ways.

A grantor will benefit from a concession which requires early assessments of the prospectivity of the concession area to be made, to accelerate the timings for mandatory relinquishment by an investor (7.6) and to allow the grantor to re-award parts of the concession area (whether to other prospective investors or for the benefit of a national oil company (14.1)) which have not been explored or sanctioned for development by the investor.

Consequently, a concession may define an overall exploration period which is shorter than that which an investor ideally requires. Provisions in a concession which give an investor any of a unilateral right to defer the performance of an exploration period obligation for its convenience, a lengthy period of time to

[7] Preamble to the Guyana 2023 PSA: 'WHEREAS, the Cooperative Republic of Guyana wishes to ensure the sustainable exploitation of these 'non-renewable resources' in a prudent and environmentally sound manner in accordance with Best International Industry Standards and Practices.'

[8] Guyana 2023 PSA 3.1 (c): 'The Contractor must take reasonable practical steps to ensure that its activities have the lowest commercially and technically possible Greenhouse Gas (GHG) operational emissions'.

[9] Guyana 2023 PSA (at 16.5): 'The Development Plan shall include but not be limited to: ... (o) Carbon Capture and Storage (CCS) technologies: information on technologies and measures to be taken to capture GHG emissions associated with Petroleum Operations; (p) Carbon storage: analysis of suitability of Petroleum Reservoirs for carbon storage and potential storage capacity'.

appraise a discovery, or a right to defer a declaration of commerciality pending the outcome of other exploration period activities, could be disapplied. A right in a concession for an investor to compel an extension of a production period or the extension or the renewal of a concession in its favour could also be disapplied.

A unilateral right for a grantor to terminate a concession could have some value where the state decides that it does not wish to continue with the business of petroleum exploration or production for energy transition reasons, or where the state wants a grantor (or the state's nominee) to take over the performance of the concession. The inclusion of such a right in a concession would, from an investor's perspective, have to be accompanied by provision for the payment of compensation to the investor which covers the investor's sunk costs and recompenses the investor for its loss of bargain. This compensation formula could be derived from similar provisions already found in some stabilization provisions (11.6).

(3) *Reshaping the exploration activity*—a grantor could seek to sequence the performance of the exploration period obligations in a concession (8.2) in proximate geographical areas and over consecutive time periods to promote greater operational efficiency and to reduce environmental impacts by reference to the activities which are required to be performed under other concessions.

Where the totality of the exploration period obligations which are owed to a grantor take the form of drilling wells across a number of concessions, those obligations could be structured with a requirement that a well which is required to be drilled under one concession is drilled within a particular exploration phase, and a well which is required to be drilled under another proximate concession is drilled shortly thereafter. The closer sequencing of the drilling of the two wells would allow a drilling rig to drill consecutively, without the need for its intervening demobilization and remobilization.[10] This would reduce the overall costs of performance of the exploration period obligations (which should be welcomed by whichever of an investor or a grantor is ultimately required to bear those costs).

A right in a concession for an investor to defer the performance of an exploration period obligation in favour of paying a monetary sum to a grantor (8.2) could be less valuable to a grantor than actual performance of the obligation and the generation of data, and might, therefore, be resisted by a grantor.

The exploration perspective which has historically been adopted by investors (and recognized by grantors) has been that continued exploration is the lifeblood of the petroleum industry, maintaining high reserves replacement ratios (2.4) and creating new value. This hypothesis has supported greenfield, deepwater, and frontier exploration activities. Against this perspective must be

[10] Such an arrangement could also be reflected in a rig-sharing agreement which is entered into between different groups of investors to optimize their efforts and expenditures.

weighed the reality that, in the last decade, the volume of exploration activities being conducted has plummeted worldwide on economic grounds, and exploration suffers from a perception problem on environmental grounds.

In contrast to the historical exploration hypothesis, a zero exploration hypothesis assumes that historical drilling activities have already revealed abundant undeveloped petroleum reserves which could be sufficient to meet continued petroleum demand for the foreseeable future. On this basis, the expense and environmental impact of more exploration drilling is not justified, and industry investment should instead be focused on developing existing discoveries and extending the life of existing production projects.

As something of a mid-point, a focused exploration hypothesis recognizes a continued demand for petroleum and the necessity for certain amounts of exploration to take place, but suggests that any exploration which does take place could be limited to identified 'high impact' locations (where major discoveries are targeted which could support new infrastructure hubs and satellite field tiebacks) or to infrastructure-led exploration (where discoveries will be developed if they can be tied back to existing infrastructure in the interests of more cost effective developments). In this hypothesis, new discoveries could benefit from more efficient facilities and decarbonization initiatives during the development period, and could have better emissions profiles compared to reworked existing production projects.[11] This could result in the production of what is sometimes called 'advantaged petroleum'. A preference amongst investors for developing new discoveries could also explain why a state might choose to offer improved fiscal terms to investors for the reworking of existing production projects,[12] in order to encourage the maximum exploitation of the state's patrimony.

High-impact exploration and infrastructure-led exploration could also focus more on gas discoveries, allowing increased gas production to displace the combustion of other higher carbon-intensity fuels in the power sector. An emphasis on gas in the focused exploration hypothesis suggests that continued oil production could be underpinned by the zero exploration hypothesis. High-impact exploration and focused petroleum production could still be relevant even if there is a retreat from reliance on petroleum as part of the energy transition.

The realization of petroleum though exploration by an investor could also be more cost effective than acquiring such petroleum through an asset acquisition

[11] Wood Mackenzie has estimated that new petroleum production developments due to commence production in the period 2025–30 could, on average, have combined Scope 1 and Scope 2 emissions of 17kgCO^{2}e/boe—this compares with a figure of 28 kgCO^{2}e/boe for the production of petroleum from existing mature fields <www.woodmac.com/lens/upstream/> accessed 3 April 2025.

[12] Brazil Resolution 749 of 2018 offers a reduction to conventional royalty rates in respect of incremental petroleum production from mature fields (further defined as small mature fields (onshore: production <5000 boe/d, offshore: production <20,000 boe/d) and large mature fields (onshore: production >5000 boe/d, offshore: production >20,000 boe/d).

(assuming also that such an asset is even available for purchase by an investor on the open market). Exploration success by an investor could also lead to a partial divestment of a discovery, as a means of generating more value for an investor party.

(4) *Reshaping the development and production activity*—the terms of a field development plan (8.4) could require the inclusion of a number of steps which are intended to decarbonize planned petroleum production, including active methane leakage management, the elimination of unwarranted gas flaring and gas venting, provision for carbon capture, utilization, and storage, and the use of (preferably renewable source-generated) electricity to power the petroleum operations.

A grantor could require the concentration of planned petroleum development and production activities in contiguous acreage areas through the installation of common facilities for petroleum processing, storage, and transportation, and with compellable third-party access rights (7.7), to promote greater operational efficiencies and reduced environmental impacts. Those common facilities could even be developed and owned by a grantor (or another state entity), with investors paying an appropriate tariff for usage rights. The creation of common facilities as part of an integrated plan for the development of discoveries could also mitigate the risks of domino decommissioning (3.4) which might be more apparent in respect of facilities which have been developed and interconnected on a piecemeal basis.

An investor should still be required to comply with defined environmental protection standards during the performance of the development and production activities (8.7), but more could be required by a grantor. An investor may be obliged to conduct rigorous emissions measurement, verification and reporting activities, with those activities in turn demonstrating an investor's compliance with any emissions management targets which are set by a concession. The definition of maximized economic recovery (8.4), which is set as a performance obligation of an investor, could also be expanded to include a requirement that petroleum production is effected in a manner which meets defined carbon intensity limits.

(5) *Options for state participation*—in a concession, a number of provisions are intended to create options for state participation (whether by a grantor or through another state entity) in the concession, and these provisions could be invaluable in realizing greater levels of state involvement in the exploitation of the state's patrimony.

Notable amongst these provisions (not all of which will exist in every concession) are: the state participation right (10.8); a grantor's rights in respect of approval and oversight of the investor parties' joint venture arrangements (5.3) (which could also be represented by the creation of a management committee for control of the business of the concession (5.5)); the pre-emptive right of a grantor (or another state entity) to take over the interests of a transferring investor party or where an investor party undergoes a change in control (5.6); the right of a grantor to take over a producing interest at the time of expiry of the concession (6.6); the right of a grantor to conduct a petroleum operation as an exclusive operation (10.7); and the right of a grantor to take over a declared marginal discovery (8.3).

Allied to these provisions within a concession could be the promotion of a national oil company as a national champion which is properly resourced and incentivized to be the state's representative in managing the national petroleum sector (14.1), with the additional possibility that the extent of the national oil company's presence as an investor party in the state's concessions could grow as levels of private-sector investment recedes over time. The ability of the national oil company to step up in this manner would be encouraged by the enhancement of various provisions in a concession relating to capacity building and localization (10.2).

A state needs to have more inherent familiarity with, and a better understanding of the risks (and their mitigants) which are associated with, petroleum exploration. Improved knowledge within the state could make a grantor more comfortable to offer increased flexibility to prospective investors in the design of exploration period obligations, and could even make the state more willing to consider undertaking exploration in its own right. Such familiarity and understanding could be generated by a state exercising a participation right in respect of the exploration period, and not just at the point of development and production.

Greater state participation in the production of petroleum from within the state offers a number of perspectives which might not be so readily realized through the exploitation of the state's patrimony by external investors:

(a) With a state entity as an investor party the corresponding amount of investor take (9.1) which is recovered by that investor party stays within the state, effectively as a closed loop.
(b) A state entity as an investor party could have different perspectives on issues such as the definition of marginality in respect of a discovery (8.3), which could improve the prospects for the exploitation of the state's patrimony.
(c) A state's preferred view of issues such as maximized economic recovery (8.4) and the decommissioning (or not (8.5)) of assets and equipment on a state-wide rather than a project-wide basis could improve the prospects for the exploitation of the state's patrimony.

States could also work together on certain capacity-building initiatives for their mutual benefit, moving away from a siloed state-specific approach which could be less efficient overall.

(6) *More efficient management of the state's patrimony*—a number of provisions in a concession are intended to promote a grantor's ability to manage the state's patrimony in a manner which protects the state's interests. Notable amongst these provisions are: the mandatory relinquishment by an investor of parts of the concession area (7.6); the right of a grantor to mandate the common use of facilities; and (at the behest of a grantor) the unitization of common discoveries or the joint development of proximate discoveries (7.7).

The provisions in a concession which relate to the initial sizing of the concession area (7.2) are ordinarily unexceptional, but they could also be a candidate for modification in order to improve the position of a grantor (and a state).

In Nigeria, a series of reforms to the upstream concessions regime were implemented by the Petroleum Industry Act (PIA) 2021. Notable amongst these reforms was the resizing of standard concession areas, to increase the quantity of acreage (by reference to individual concession areas) which could be made available for the award of individual concessions.

Under the regime which preceded the PIA, an investor could hold an oil prospecting licence (OPL) or an oil mining licence (OML), where the maximum permissible surface area sizes were 2950 km^2 for the OPL and 1295 km^2 for the OML. Under the PIA, the OPL and the OML were replaced by the petroleum prospecting licence (PPL) and the petroleum mining licence (PML), respectively, where the maximum permissible surface areas were reduced in the PPL to 350 km^2 for onshore areas and shallow waters, 1,000 km^2 for deepwater areas, and 1,500 km^2 for frontier areas, and to the size of a commercial discovery area for the PML. The holder of an OPL or an OML could elect to convert its interest to a PPL or a PML (to access the revised fiscal terms and taxation regime which were on offer in the PML or the PPL under the PIA) subject to relinquishing part of the original OPL or OML concession area to come within the dimensional requirements of the new regime.

The process of relinquishment (7.6) facilitates the return to a grantor of undeveloped parts of the concession area. Voluntary relinquishment is within an investor's gift, whereas mandatory relinquishment gives a grantor more certainty of outcome. In either case, relinquishment is important to a grantor because the relinquished areas could be awarded by a grantor to another investor under a separate concession, or they could be made available to a national oil company for consolidated development (14.1). A grantor could be interested to enhance the opportunities for growth and more efficient acreage management which relinquishment could present.

Mandatory relinquishment provisions could be written to ensure that the maximum amount of the concession area is always relinquished to a grantor at the earliest opportunity (so reducing the optionality for an investor to defer relinquishment). A faster timetable for mandatory relinquishment could allow the grantor to recycle the state's acreage more efficiently, with relinquished acreage being consolidated by the grantor for further award.

Provision in a concession which gives an investor the ability to defer relinquishment in respect of discoveries made which an investor regards as marginal, and possibly also for an investor to consolidate those marginal discoveries within a later development plan (8.3), could create a lengthy and inexact timetable from which only an investor will benefit. This could come at the expense of a grantor's ability to recycle its acreage according to its preferences (which could include assisting a national oil company to consolidate its portfolio position (14.1)). There could be a move away from this investor-friendly position, to afford to a grantor the priority right to take over a marginal discovery which has been declared as such and which must then be promptly relinquished by an investor if it is not taken forward for commercial development. This suggestion might be particularly relevant to the discovery, development, and production of gas, which might not appeal to every investor because of the challenges associated with commercializing a gas discovery (13.3). The prospect of such gas could be consolidated within a national oil company and used to develop a domestic gas economy.

This approach could also be accompanied by ensuring that provisions in a concession which afford quiet enjoyment to an investor in respect of the concession area (7.4) do not unduly hamper the ability of a grantor (or another state entity) to enter into the concession area for the further appraisal or the development of a marginal discovery.

It is important not to lose sight of the objectives which underlie the activities of unitization and joint development (7.7). Both of these activities are intended to eliminate competitive drilling, the suboptimal exploitation of a common discovery, and the associated costs and emissions which could otherwise ensue. The pursuit of these activities should be encouraged, with continued emphasis on their application wherever subsurface and operational circumstances permit.

(7) *Fiscal terms generally*—where a state has determined to continue with petroleum exploration and/or production, modification of the fiscal terms (9.1) which could apply in respect of a concession is an obvious tool which can be applied by a grantor to attract and retain greater investment interest. Certain fiscal terms could be modified in concessions in a way which gives more encouragement to prospective investors to take the award of a concession but without reducing the prospective levels of state take, and without suggesting some weakness in a grantor's bargaining position. Lowering the bar to secure the participation of what could be a dwindling pool of potential investors (and particularly so where there is increased competition between states to attract continued levels of external investment) could be engineered by a grantor in a number of ways.

The following are examples of what a grantor might do with the fiscal terms: the requirements for the provision of collateral support in respect of the performance of an investor's obligations under a concession (5.4) could be relaxed; the liability of an investor party to pay some form of capital gains tax or transfer tax consequent upon a transfer of its interests in a concession (5.6) could be disapplied; and, in a PSC, more attractive profit-share ratios could be accompanied by a relaxation of the ring-fencing of costs (9.3) to promote cross block exploration and development activities. The relaxation of a state's insistence on the payment of a signature bonus by an investor (9.4) could also increase the uptake of concessions.

As an alternative to consolidating marginal discoveries within a grantor (see point (6) above), the right of an investor to consolidate marginal discoveries in order to make one commercial development project could be emphasized (possibly also with the introduction of more attractive fiscal terms for the development of marginal discoveries), where the alternative to petroleum production which is at least undertaken by an investor on this basis is that the marginal discoveries are otherwise never taken forward for development.

(8) *The role of taxation*—the taxation of investors by the state needs careful consideration. A perceived expectation that state take should be applied equally to all energy sector investors in the interests of fairness (9.2), could be undermined where a subsidy is granted to one set of investors (such as in the form of a tax paid provision (9.5) which applies to non-petroleum sector project developers) and not to another set of investors (such as petroleum project developers, who could find themselves indirectly subsidizing other investors). From the state's perspective (in hindsight), a tax paid provision could also become an economic impossibility to sustain later in a concession's lifetime.

Perhaps a better route for the state to take in allocating the incidence of income tax would be to make all investors (in respect of all forms of energy projects) liable to pay income tax from the outset but on the basis of flexible and progressive rates of taxation which respond to changes in the level of profits enjoyed over time (including additional tranches to cater for perceived additional profits or windfalls, on a clear and prescriptive basis).

Alternatively, the basis of an investor's tax liability could be set not by reference to an investor's profits (where the measure of profit will, in its calculation, be subject to the determination of allowable costs and expenses in an investor's favour and could be subject to manipulation) but rather by reference to measures such as revenues from the sale of petroleum (or other forms of energy) earned by an investor, or the internal rate of return which an investor's project enjoys.

(9) *Dispute resolution*—a concession will contain a mechanism for the resolution of disputes between the parties (11.4). Some commentators have observed that a concession's dispute resolution mechanism can operate to protect the interests of an investor at the expense of a grantor, and that the presence of an arbitration agreement could expose a grantor to becoming embroiled in the expense

and effort of a dispute and to the risk of losing that dispute.[13] Other commentators have observed that the risk of the outcome of such an arbitration could be unfavourable to a grantor's ambitions,[14] and they have suggested, as alternative provision for the resolution of disputes between a grantor and an investor, that recourse could be had to the state's courts.[15] This is a proposition which has also found some support in the European Union (EU), in respect of the determination of investment protection disputes brought against member states.[16]

It is naïve to suggest that a mechanism for dispute resolution which has been agreed in a concession should, in respect of modifications to a concession which are made by a grantor (and which are disputed by an investor) to reflect the terms of the energy transition (which could have significant economic consequences for an investor), be disapplied in favour of a form of local dispute resolution within the state. To accept this proposition would be likely to result in a form of concession which would be unacceptable to an investor (and its lenders). This conclusion could be unsatisfactory to a state, but attributing the blame for unpalatable arbitral outcomes to the proper performance of an arbitration process is misplaced.

(10) *Stabilization*—stabilization provisions in a concession (11.6) are also seen by some commentators as impediments to a state's ability to procure direct or indirect modifications to the terms of the concession.[17] This should not come as a surprise since that is the essential purpose of a stabilization provision. There has been some recognition that a state may wish to modify its laws and regulations (appreciating also that this could translate to a modification of concession terms) to reflect evolving best practices in relation to health, safety, and environmental change.[18] This principle could be amplified to reflect the requirements of the energy transition.

[13] 'Combined with stabilization clauses, arbitration clauses could have a chilling effect on government regulation to reduce emissions in existing petroleum projects. The mere cost of defending an arbitration suit may deter some governments from applying new climate regulations to existing projects.' (Nicola Woodroffe, *Tying Their Hands? How Petroleum Contract Terms May Limit Governments' Climate Policy Flexibility* (Natural Resource Governance Institute, Briefing September 2021)).

[14] '[A]rbitration can have unintended and undesirable consequences like undermining state sovereignty, regulatory space and the rule of law. Arbitrator discretion over interpretation and application of the law of the host state has resulted in overriding the public interest-focused determinations of regulatory and administrative agencies.' (Victoria R Nalule, Raphael J Heffron, and Damilola S Olawuyi, *Renegotiating Contracts for the Energy Transition in the Extractives Industry* (Palgrave Macmillan 2023)).

[15] '[P]etroleum agreements ... should be amended to provide for expedited national dispute resolution as the first alternative for energy transition and environmental disputes. This will enable Host counties and the related stakeholders address the underlying disputes with the national context fully aligned with the nation's pathway and aspirations' (ibid).

[16] Note the decisions of the Court of Justice of the European Union (CJEU) in: *Slovak Republic v Achmea BV* (Case C-284/16) (in respect of arbitration under a bilateral investment treaty involving member states); *Republic of Moldova v Komstroy* (Case C-741/19) (in respect of arbitration under a multilateral investment treaty involving member states); and *Poland v PL Holdings Sarl* (Case C-109/20) (in respect of ad hoc arbitration between European Union (EU) investors and member states).

[17] See note 13 above.

[18] The Uganda 2015 PSA provides (at 30.5) that the stabilization protections effected in favour of the contractor 'shall not apply to changes in the laws of Uganda regarding health, safety and environmental standards'.

(11) *Transfer and surrender*—a concession ordinarily reserves rights for an investor party to transfer its interests in a concession to another person (5.6), or to surrender a concession and for the investor party's interests to be redistributed between the remaining investor parties (6.6).

From an investor's perspective, surrender rights in a concession which have the least amount of associated restriction or conditionality could be more attractive so that an investor can surrender its position in the concession where it perceives a need to do so to meet its own energy transition commitments. As a corollary of this, a concession could require an investor to do more to effect a proper handover to a grantor, including creating a period of transitional operatorship (6.6).

It may be thought that a transfer or a surrender is an option for an investor party to reflect the requirements of the energy transition. An investor party could decide to no longer participate in a petroleum project (or in petroleum projects generally within a state), and particularly so where the project or the state ranks comparatively highly in respect of its carbon intensity.[19] The notion that a transfer of, or the surrender of, a concession by an investor party will represent an automatic reduction in the carbon intensity which is associated with the performance of a concession is illusory (notwithstanding that the departing investor party could also be planning to redirect its investment towards non-petroleum sector activities).

Such a transfer or surrender will lead to a reduction in the carbon intensity which is associated with the performance of that concession in respect of the transferring or the surrendering investor party because it is no longer party to the concession, but the overall carbon intensity position which is associated with the performance of the concession will not be reduced (if petroleum production levels from the concession, and the demand for petroleum, remain unchanged) where the concession continues to be held by the remaining parties (and possibly also with the increased participation of the state). In such a case the associated carbon intensity which existed prior to the transfer or surrender has been redistributed, rather than reduced.

(12) *Amendments*—a concession could provide that its terms can be modified by agreement between the parties specifically to reflect the requirements of the energy transition. This possibility would require some control over its application however, so that proposing and making such modifications does not become an activity devoid of rules. A mechanism to achieve this outcome could be based on concession provisions which seek to address and allocate the occurrence of hardship under the concession between the parties.[20]

[19] In 2021, Shell announced a decarbonization strategy in which it said it would aim for an expected gradual reduction in oil production of around 1–2 per cent each year, to be achieved through divestments and natural decline. In the same year, Shell announced a sale of oil production interests in the Permian Basin in Texas to ConocoPhillips. This reduced Shell's daily level of oil production, leading a Shell spokesperson to observe that 'our target of a reduction in oil production by 2030 has not changed. We've just met it eight years early.'

[20] The Liberia 2013 PSC provides (at 36.3) that: 'In the event of changes in circumstances from those existing at the Effective Date, that have a material effect on the terms of this Agreement, either NOCAL or the Contractor

Although this mechanism does not depart from the basic requirement that modifications to a concession will require the agreement of a grantor and an investor (11.7), it does have the advantage that it sets out the expectations for the possible engagement of the parties in a good faith negotiations about prospective changes.

(13) *Force majeure*—it was previously recognized that a force majeure provision typically does not extend to afford relief to purely economic hardship (11.5). Some commentators have queried whether force majeure provisions might be revised so that petroleum buyers and sellers could obtain relief from their contractual obligations following collapses in market prices for petroleum which could result from the introduction of low-carbon regulation.[21]

(14) *The form of the concession*—the potential preferences of grantors and investors in respect of the form of a concession has previously been considered (2.2). Although the form of a concession could influence the ability of an investor to book the associated reserves (2.4), this is an issue which is relevant only to certain investors. The special needs of a group of investors in this regard should not be allowed to dictate the preferred form of concession for a state.

The form which a concession takes could also come to reflect a less adversarial regime between the parties, with a move towards a more collaborative arrangement which has a greater sense of operational and fiscal alignment between them, with more balanced risk and reward sharing and improved transparency and knowledge sharing. The lessons learned from more enlightened forms of service contracts (2.2) which reflect certain gainsharing principles between the employer and the contractor may have a relevance which could be applied to the wider family of concessions.

shall at the request of the other consult together. If it is established that such Profound Changes in Circumstances have occurred, then the Parties shall effect such changes in or clarifications to this Agreement that they agree are necessary. The Parties shall meet in good faith to make the necessary revisions and adjustments to the Agreement in order to maintain such expected economic benefits to each of the Parties, provided that the economic benefits to the Parties shall not be reduced as a result of exercising the terms of this article. For the purposes of this Agreement the term "Profound Changes in Circumstances" shall mean such changes in the economic conditions of the petroleum industry world wide or in Liberia or such changes that result in such a material and fundamental alteration of the conditions and assumptions relied upon by the Parties at the Effective Date of this Agreement (or the time after any subsequent review under this Article) to the effect that the overall balance of equities and benefits reasonably anticipated by the Parties will no longer be achievable.' The Ghana 2000 petroleum agreement provides (at 26.3) that: 'Where a party considers that a significant change in the circumstances prevailing at the time the Agreement was entered into, has occurred affecting the economic balance of the Agreement, the Party affected hereby shall notify the other Parties in writing of the claimed change with a statement of how the claimed change has affected the relations between the Parties.'

[21] Anatole Boute, 'Environmental Force Majeure: Relief From Fossil Energy Contracts in the Decarbonisation Era' [2021] JEL. 339. The author observes that: '[W]ith the rare exception of contracts that specifically include economic hardship in the definition of force majeure, force majeure clauses do not provide relief in cases where energy prices and demand for energy collapse. instead, oil, gas and coal contracts usually require the parties to continue to perform their obligations', and argues that this 'incentivises irrational energy use, and is thus incompatible with decarbonisation'. The author makes a plea for force majeure provisions to include economic hardship as a relevant event, based on the need to 'weaken the irrational incentive to continue to supply and take delivery of energy even when there is no longer any reasonable demand'.

A particular form of concession could also be developed to facilitate gas project developments (13.5), which combines the requirements of upstream and midstream project development.

12.4 Managing Concession Awards

The terms of a licensing round (in whatever form it takes (2.5)) could be structured to reflect certain elements of the energy transition which might be required by a state,[22] and be more attractive to investors.

A common feature of a licensing round is that it will set out certain parameters which a prospective investor is obliged to demonstrate to a grantor, as part of the prospective investor's bid documentation. As a starting point, these parameters could relate to the following matters, as standards which are required for the investor's performance of the petroleum operations:

(1) *Health, safety and environment (HSE) and environment, social and governance (ESG) methodology*—a statement of the prospective investor's proposed methodologies to ensure that the petroleum operations will be carried out safely and in a manner which ensures protection of the environment in which they are carried out (including provisions for preventing and addressing pollution, minimizing gas flaring, managing waste products, and minimizing greenhouse gas emissions).
(2) *Decarbonization methodology*—a statement of the prospective investor's proposed methodologies to ensure emissions reduction and abatement, and for the measurement, reporting, and verification of emissions. The terms of recent licensing rounds in Colombia[23] have included a carbon management bidding parameter whereby an investor is required to reduce Scope 1 emissions (3.3) against a baseline measure of 25 kgCO^{2}e/boe (failing which an investor would be required to compensate for its failure by the purchase of carbon offsets).

There are several options for a grantor in dealing with the responses of a prospective investor which are made in relation to the above matters. The responses could be noted by the grantor, but they may have no bearing on the award of a concession. Alternatively, the responses could be weighed against certain minimum standards which the grantor

[22] The Nigeria 2024 licensing round guidelines (see note 20, Chapter 2) offer a very limited acknowledgement of the energy transition, with the inclusion of the following objective in the list of nine objectives for the 2024 licensing round: 'To expand opportunities for gas utilisation and development in Nigeria, in view of energy transition.' This is the only occasion on which the phrase 'energy transition' makes an appearance in the guidelines, and it does not feature in either of the model form concessions referenced in the guidelines. The licensing round guidelines for the 2024 Suriname shallow offshore 2 bid round made no particular reference to energy transition initiatives, nor did the licensing round guidelines for the 2025 Trinidad and Tobago deepwater bid round <www.energy.gov.tt/wp-content/uploads/2025/02/Legal_Notice_No._20_of_2025.pdf> accessed 3 April 2025.

[23] Reflected in the Agencia Nacional de Hidrocarburos (ANH) Acuerdo (Agreement) No 003 of 2022.

has established, with the responses to be assessed as contestable items. This will in turn require that a weighting is ascribed to the responses, relative to the other contestable items which form part of the prospective investor's bid. If the responses fall short of those standards then the prospective investor might not qualify for the award of a concession. Finally, the responses could be recited in the concession (if the prospective investor's bid is successful), as baseline standards which an investor will be required to meet in the performance of the petroleum operations.

The terms of a licensing round could also be written so that they further require a prospective investor to submit proposals and commitments for the undertaking of specific non-petroleum related activities, and these proposals could be assessed by a grantor as contestable items in deciding the award of a concession.

These proposals, which, if they are selected to go forward, would more likely be governed by an ancillary arrangement rather than by an amendment to the scope of a concession (12.3) to encompass them, would reflect an investor's undertaking to assist in realizing the state's energy transition objectives. This notion has already been seen in part with the introduction of plans to promote projects for carbon capture, storage, and utilization as part of licensing round requirements in certain jurisdictions.[24]

From an investor's perspective a commitment to engage in such activities could be the price it has to pay for being awarded a concession which has high petroleum prospectivity. The investor could also be an international energy company which has already become involved in various non-petroleum related activities elsewhere, and that investor could apply its experience in these areas for the benefit of the grantor or the wider state.

For prospective concession areas, a lack of existing geological and geophysical data could give prospective investors limited incentive to assume the expense and uncertainty associated with the exploration risk by seeking the award of a concession. Alternatively, prospective investors might be persuaded to sign up for a concession but only on the basis of reduced exploration period obligations. The result to the state is that no, or only limited, additional data will thereby be generated. This perpetuates the lack of existing geological and geophysical data and creates a vicious circle. To break this continuum a state could choose to fund a multi-client survey (10.5) in order to increase the availability of data to prospective investors.

An open door policy (2.5) could also be more conducive to attracting interest from prospective investors because it does not set parameters around when investors can (and, so, cannot) investigate the possibility of securing the award of a concession.

[24] In September 2023, the United Kingdom's North Sea Transition Authority awarded a number of licences purely for carbon storage <www.nstauthority.co.uk/news-publications/net-zero-boost-as-carbon-storage-licences-accepted/> accessed 3 April 2025. In January 2024, the Indonesian government enacted Regulation 14/2024 for implementing carbon capture and storage activities as part of petroleum operations under a concession (including provision for amending an existing concession which does not already make provision for such activities), with proposals to be submitted as part of a plan of development.

13
Promoting Gas Production

13.1 Introduction

A concession is ostensibly intended to regulate the exploration for and the discovery, development, and production of all forms of petroleum. A concession could, however, be inclined more towards making a success of an oil discovery, and could say comparatively less about the mechanics for the effective monetization of a gas discovery.

Gas has a major role to play in the realization of the energy transition (through displacing the combustion of other forms of fossil fuels, and through the production of clean gas and hydrogen).

The form of a concession could be modified to do more to promote the discovery, development, and production of gas, recognizing the growing importance of gas to states and investors alike. A particular form of concession which is focused on gas developments could also be promoted.

13.2 The Attraction of Gas

The classic gas advocacy narrative suggests that gas is versatile and adaptable because it has a role to play in the energy transition both as a destination fuel (meaning that an economy will grow its dependence on gas as a primary fuel for combustion in its own right because the combustion characteristics of gas are superior to those resulting from the combustion of other fuels such as biomass, coal, or oil) and as a transition fuel (to support an economy's increased reliance on renewable energy, where gas could become essential to make good the inherent intermittency of renewable energy production). Gas can also be produced and/or consumed on a localized basis (including through the development of small-scale liquefied natural gas (LNG) facilities), which gives gas the flexibility to meet local and regional energy needs.

This narrative positions gas as an essential part of the low carbon landscape, as a plentiful and widely distributed feedstock which offers energy security and a sustainable basis for economic growth and social progress. Such a narrative can be contrasted with a more extreme interpretation of the energy transition which suggests the need for a complete exit from reliance on all fossil fuels, and which applies no distinction between gas and oil.

Gas is increasingly being recognized as a valuable commodity in its own right (and perhaps with a prospective value greater than oil), with a major role to play in the energy transition including through the production of clean gas and hydrogen.

There is no standard definition of 'clean gas'[1] but as a term it is intended to connote gas to which various greenhouse gas abatement processes and/or carbon offsets have been applied to reduce the Scope 1 and Scope 2 emissions (3.3) which are associated with its production and processing. This could result in clean gas in a gaseous form, or clean gas which has been liquefied to give 'clean LNG'.

The production of clean gas could be desirable to an investor for several reasons: to facilitate the opportunity to supply gas to a buyer which itself is required to comply with jurisdictional decarbonization regulatory obligations; as a response to sociopolitical pressures and to meet corporate scorecard requirements to which the investor is subject; to meet the requirements of the investor's project lenders; and to realize a premium-priced commodity, where the investor can find a buyer which is willing to pay a higher price for clean gas.

Gas production which benefits from demonstrable reductions in carbon intensity in the production process (which could be effected by any of curbing flaring, reducing methane emissions, using e-drive and renewable power sources for associated industrial activities, and applying carbon capture, utilization, and storage techniques to the associated carbon production) could result in the production of what could be certified as clean gas. Issues associated with the reliable measurement, reporting, and verification of the carbon intensity of gas production could, in practical terms, make it difficult to assess the achievement of this ambition.

Clean gas could also result from applying carbon offsets to gas production. A carbon offset is a tradeable instrument which represents a quantified reduction in carbon intensity in a particular place or in connection with a particular activity, which can be bought from an issuing registry and then applied to offset emissions. The best-known carbon offset registry is the UN Clean Development Mechanism (CDM) which was originally established under the Kyoto Protocol (3.2). There are also several independent carbon offset registries which issue carbon offsets. Some countries also operate their own carbon offset registries. Qualifying carbon offset activities include afforestation, reforestation, and avoided deforestation, biomethane production, carbon capture, utilization, and storage, other forms of greenhouse gas capture, and solar farming.

Increasing efforts by an investor over time to achieve net zero carbon targets associated with gas production should correspondingly reduce the quantities of carbon offsets which need to be acquired to prove clean gas, but achieving a figure of zero for the carbon intensity associated with gas production is likely to be a practical impossibility and so carbon offsets will continue to play a role.

The production of clean gas through reducing the associated carbon intensity will inevitably have a cost to it. The price of carbon offsets bought by an investor could

[1] Clean gas is also variously referred to variously as 'advantaged gas', 'carbon neutral gas', 'decarbonized gas', and 'lower carbon gas'. These terms are used interchangeably and inexactly.

increase the production cost of gas on a unit basis. Reducing carbon intensity will be more appealing to an investor where the costs of doing so are less than the costs of purchasing carbon offsets. Whether any of these costs will be borne exclusively by an investor, or could be passed on to a buyer through an increase in the price which is payable for clean gas, will be a matter for negotiation.

Hydrogen is perceived to be a clean fuel because it emits water when combusted, although the manner in which hydrogen is produced will inevitably have some carbon intensity associated with it. To displace gas consumption, hydrogen could be combusted to generate electricity (particularly on a standby basis to make good the inherent intermittency of renewable energy power generation), it could be used as a feedstock for energy-intensive industrial processes such as steel, cement, and paper manufacture, and it could be used as a source of energy for domestic and industrial heating. Hydrogen could also be used (in a fuel cell) as a motive power fuel for application in trains, motor vehicles, ships, and (eventually) aircraft.

Hydrogen is the most abundant element on earth but it generally does not occur naturally and so it must be manufactured by extraction from other compounds (such as water or methane) if it is to be produced on a scalable basis. In the context of gas production, what is sometimes called 'turquoise hydrogen' is produced by the pyrolysis[2] of methane, releasing hydrogen and separating the carbon element. 'Blue hydrogen' is produced by the reformation[3] of methane, with capture of the resultant carbon emissions (although, that said, approximately 15 per cent of the resultant carbon is not captured and so blue hydrogen is really low carbon hydrogen production, rather than carbon-free hydrogen production). 'Grey hydrogen' is produced by the reformation of methane, but (in contrast to blue hydrogen) without the capture of the resultant carbon emissions.

Grey hydrogen is the source of approximately 95 per cent of commercial hydrogen production today. The carbon capture technology required for the industrial-scale production of blue hydrogen production is in its relative infancy, and the scalable production of turquoise hydrogen has yet to commence. Principally as grey hydrogen or as blue hydrogen, gas has a key role to play as a feedstock in the major-scale production of hydrogen, and there are other aspects of the gas/hydrogen relationship which could be exploited. Hydrogen could (subject to certain metallurgical constraints) be transported (or blended with gas) in a pipeline and a gas grid. Blending hydrogen for transportation in an existing gas pipeline network could facilitate the carriage of significant volumes of hydrogen, and could connect hydrogen producers and their customers without the need for additional investment in implementing purpose-built hydrogen pipeline infrastructure. Hydrogen could also be stored in a depleted gas field.

[2] Pyrolysis is a process by which methane is thermally decomposed to release hydrogen (in a gas form) and carbon dioxide (as a solid).

[3] The principal process forms of reformation are steam methane reforming (SMR), where methane is combusted with air to create steam, and autothermal reforming (AFR), where methane is combusted with purified oxygen. SMR is the most widely used reformation process.

The role of ammonia is also relevant. Conventional ammonia (sometimes called 'grey ammonia') results from the synthesis of grey hydrogen and nitrogen, and 'blue ammonia' results from the synthesis of blue hydrogen and nitrogen. Ammonia exists as a gas which is easily compressed to give a liquid under pressure for transportation, can be used as a low-carbon fuel across a wide range of industrial applications, and is a useful transportation vector for the inherent hydrogen which can then be liberated for separate use.

13.3 Dealing With Gas

Aside from flaring or reinjection, the principal options for the disposal of produced gas are through domestic consumption (for consumer and/or industrial purposes) and export (as pipeline gas and/or as LNG or as compressed natural gas), which in either case depends on access to markets and the presence of the necessary production, processing, and transportation infrastructure. The availability (or not) of a commercially viable option for the disposal of gas could be a major influence on an investor's willingness to invest in gas exploration and production in the first place.

A concession could oblige an investor to offer its share of any produced gas to a grantor on a priority basis (for a grantor to do what it will with that gas, although the presumption could be that the gas would then be consumed or commercialized domestically):

> Contractor shall first offer its share of Cost Recovery Gas and Profit Gas to Petrobangla, and Petrobangla shall undertake that it or its Affiliates will purchase the gas . . . the contractual terms of purchase and sale of such marketable Natural Gas shall be negotiated with Petrobangla or its Affiliate prior to approval of the Development Plan . . . [4]

Alternatively (or if a grantor does not take up an investor's offer) an investor could be free to sell its share of the produced gas to other persons domestically:

> Contractor has the option to sell Contractor's share of Natural Gas in the domestic market to a third party, at a price and on such other contractual terms as the Contractor may negotiate and agree, subject to Petrobangla's right of first refusal.[5]

Furthermore, thereafter, an investor could be free to export its share of the produced gas from the state:

[4] Bangladesh 2023 production sharing contract (PSC) (at 15.6 (a)). The India 2010 PSC provides (at 21.1) that: 'Until such time as the total availability of Natural Gas from all Petroleum production activities in India meets the total national demand as determined by the Government, each Company comprising the Contractor, shall sell in the domestic market in India all of the Company's entitlement to Natural Gas from the Contract Area.'

[5] Bangladesh 2023 PSC (at 15.6 (c)).

> Contractor shall have the right to export any Marketable Natural Gas, as defined in Article 15.5, produced from the Contract Area ...[6]

although a concession could also apply certain restrictions to an investor's ability to do so:

> Contractor shall not enter into any agreement for export unless the price or the pricing formula and the agreement itself are previously approved by Petrobangla. Such approval shall not be withheld where Contractor can demonstrate that the price received or pricing formula established represents the fair market value at the point of export for gas taking into account the volumes of gas export to be sold and the nature and geographical location of the markets to be served, as well as the transport and distribution costs of gas from the point of export to the market are acceptable to Petrobangla.[7]

An issue for a state to consider is whether the state's primary focus is intended to be on domestic gas market development with any overspill being made available for export, or whether gas export is the state's primary ambition and the revenues thereby earned can be applied towards developing a domestic gas market.[8] The distinction may seem fine but it becomes relevant where a curtailment of gas production makes it impossible to meet the entirety of domestic and export requirements, and some order of priority needs to be applied by a state.[9] It is also possible that a state could pursue both ambitions. In recent years, Indonesia and Malaysia, both significant LNG exporters, have each developed LNG import facilities so that they are also able to import LNG to meet local gas demands.

A concession will typically distinguish associated gas (ie gas which is produced in conjunction with oil production) and non-associated gas (ie gas which is produced independently of oil production) through the application of certain commercial terms. Both forms of gas discovery might be open to the creation of a separate development plan by an investor.

A concession may provide that associated gas can be used by an investor as fuel for operational purposes and to maintain capillary pressure for continued oil production and thereafter the associated gas is to be offered to the grantor if the investor does not wish to develop such gas in its own right:

[6] ibid 15.7.

[7] ibid 15.9.

[8] The Guyana 2023 PSA provides (at 23.2) a definition of the domestic market: 'For the purpose of this Agreement, Natural Gas Domestic Demand shall consist of those quantities of Natural Gas used for domestic residential, commercial and industrial consumption, including fuel used for domestic power generation. Natural Gas liquefied or compressed in Guyana for export or used as feedstock for other exports, such as methanol and fertilizer, shall not be considered part of Natural Gas Domestic Demand.'

[9] In Australia, concerns over the paucity of gas on the country's east coast led to the agreement (in 2022, replacing an original version which dated from 2021) of a protocol made between the Australian government and Australia's east coast LNG exporters, which was intended to give priority in gas production to meeting the needs of local gas market demands: 'The Australian East Coast Domestic Gas Supply Commitment', Domestic gas supply | Department of Industry Science and Resources – see <www.industry.gov.au/sites/default/files/2021-01/australian-east-coast-domestic-gas-supply-commitment-heads-of-agreement.pdf> accessed 3 April 2025.

15.1 Contractor shall use with priority any Natural Gas in the Contract Area for the purpose of increasing the recovery of Oil, where good international reservoir practices indicate that the use of Natural Gas for this purpose is required.

15.2 Contractor may use free of charge any Natural Gas in the Contract Area for Petroleum Operations.

15.3 Any Associated Natural Gas as is not used under Article 15.1 or Article 15.2 and which Contractor does not consider possible to recover economically shall be offered to Petrobangla without any payment to Contractor but at Petrobangla's cost at the well-head or field facilities in the Production Area.[10]

A concession may also provide that any part of the concession area (7.2) which contains a gas discovery which an investor does not develop will be relinquished to a grantor, or could otherwise be taken on by a grantor in its own right as an exclusive operation. This could relate to non-associated gas:

> [I]f after completion of the Appraisal work, the Contractor considers that the Unassociated Natural Gas Discovery is not commercial, the Ministry may, with ninety (90) days' advance notice, require the Contractor to relinquish all of its rights over the Appraisal Area encompassing such Discovery[11]

or to associated gas:

> In the event the Contractor does not consider the exploitation of the excess Associated Natural Gas is justified and if the State at any time wishes to utilize it, the Ministry shall notify the Contractor of the State's wish, in which event:
>
> (a) the Contractor shall put at the disposal of the State free of charge the Crude Oil and Associated Natural Gas separation facilities for all or part of such excess that the State wishes to utilize;
> (b) the State shall be responsible for the gathering, treatment, compression and transportation of such excess Associated Natural Gas from the receiving point at the Contractor's facilities and for bearing any additional costs and liabilities related thereto; and
> (c) the construction of the facilities necessary for the operations referred to in paragraph (b) above, together with the recovery of that excess by the State, shall be carried out in accordance with generally accepted practice of the international petroleum industry.[12]

[10] Bangladesh 2023 PSC (at 15).
[11] Equatorial Guinea 2006 PSC (at 13.1.3).
[12] ibid 13.2.3.

By these devices a grantor could accumulate a number of gas discoveries, to the point where they could be consolidated for the benefit of a national oil company (14.1) in the creation of a specific gas business.

13.4 Modifying Concessions to Promote Gas Developments

A concession is ostensibly intended to regulate the exploration for and the discovery, development, and production of all forms of petroleum[13] but it is not uncommon to find that a concession says comparatively less about dealing with a gas discovery.[14] A concession may even treat gas as a by-product of an oil discovery, with subsidiary status.[15] Whether condensate counts as a light oil or as a heavy gas could be a grey area, which should be addressed in a concession.[16]

Unless a relatively comprehensive gas provision is included in a concession from the start (which might particularly be the case where it is likely that a concession which is being awarded is in respect of acreage which could prove to be gas prone), once a gas discovery has been made it might then be necessary for an investor to develop further gas-specific provisions, through supplementing and/or modifying the terms of an existing concession. This could lead to a lengthy period of negotiations with a grantor. To smooth the process, the investor parties could at least agree certain relevant principles in their joint venture arrangement (5.3) which they could then seek to reflect in modifications to a concession at the appropriate time. The Association of International Energy Negotiators (AIEN) 2023 model joint operating agreement provides that:

> 9.4.B The Parties shall endeavor to include in the Contract, and in any other agreement with the Government Oil & Gas Company concerning the disposition of Natural Gas, the following principles:
>
> 9.4.A.1 assured access to a fair share of the available Natural Gas market, including suitable assurances for Government controlled sales;
>
> 9.4.A.2 the right to market and to export all Natural Gas, including the Government's share, to the highest value outlets (domestic or export);

[13] Except where the concession is tailored to a specific form of petroleum. The Qatar 2002 development and production sharing agreement (DPSA) relates only to the production of gas. Recital 3 observes that: 'The CONTRACTOR will design, develop, construct and operate the Facilities and conduct Petroleum Operations to process natural gas volumes and export (except for Ethane) the associated NGL Products and GTL Products and Sulphur.'

[14] A point noted, eg, in Mohsen Shirazi, *The Commercialization Process in Exploration and Production Agreements* (World Bank, November 1995, IEN Occasional Paper No 5).

[15] The Suriname 2015 PSC provides (at 21.7) that: 'Notwithstanding the foregoing provisions of this Article 21, the Production of Crude Oil shall not be unduly delayed or hindered by any evaluation or indecision with regard to the possible Development of a Discovery of Associated Gas or non Associated Gas.'

[16] The Cyprus 2007 PSC provides (at 13.3) that: 'The Contractor shall have the right to dispose of its share of production of Natural Gas, in accordance with the provisions of this Contract. It shall also have the right to proceed with the separation of liquids from all Natural Gas produced, transport, store as well as sell on the local market or export its share of liquid Hydrocarbons so separated, which will be considered as Crude Oil for purposes of sharing thereof between the Parties.' The Ethiopia 2011 PSC provides (at 13.3.2) that: 'For production sharing purposes, LPG shall be treated as Natural Gas.'

9.4.A.3 a minimum contractual term that provides a reasonable period to develop a Natural Gas market and enables Natural Gas reserves to be produced for their full economic life; and

9.4.A.4 assured access to infrastructure for the purposes of processing and/or transporting Natural Gas at a competitive tariff.

The lack of sophistication in a concession regarding gas matters could be most obvious where a state lacks a developed domestic gas market or has no gas export experience, where a state is unfamiliar with the techniques for commercializing gas compared to an oil discovery, or where, at the time when a concession was entered into, there was no firm plan within the state for whether gas discoveries would be commercialized through exports or through domestic market developments (or at all). This lack of sophistication could offer an investor little encouragement to invest in exploring for and producing gas in its own right.

The perceived reluctance of a concession to legislate for gas in the same amount of detail as it does for oil could also be attributed to certain comparative difficulties which a gas discovery may present. The prospective commerciality of an oil discovery can be evaluated relatively quickly because of oil's ease of transportation and storage (as an inert liquid), and because of the existence of comprehensive global trading terms and published trading prices for the resultant commodity.

A concession may also envisage the agreement between a grantor and an investor of a further addendum which is intended to address various matters relating to the commercialization of gas:

> Within ninety (90) Days of the Contractor determining that there is a market for a non-Associated Gas, which in the written opinion of Contractor may be commercial, the Parties shall initiate negotiations for an addendum to this Contract for non-Associated Gas ('Addendum'), which shall establish the procedures and conditions by which Contractor may Appraise, develop and produce such Discovery ... The Addendum shall include, among others, provisions to:
>
> a) govern the orderly Appraisal, Development and Production of such Discovery;
> b) determine the expected market price for Natural Gas in relation to its location, volume and potential customers;
> c) address Staatsolie's direct participation; and
> d) address cost reimbursement and payment to Contractor and profit sharing between Parties.[17]

[17] Suriname 2015 PSC (at 21.4). The Tanzanian government has issued a pro forma gas addendum which is intended to be entered into between the grantor, the investor, and the Tanzania Petroleum Development Corporation (TPDC) to record the modifications to the terms of the applicable PSC which are necessary to reflect a gas development

Such an addendum usually creates a bespoke set of qualifications to the existing terms of the concession which are intended to apply in respect of a gas commercialization project, leading to the need to review the terms of the concession and the addendum in tandem in order to discover what modifications have been made to the concession for gas.

Modifications to the terms of a concession to better promote the discovery, development, and production of gas could also be effected in a number of areas:

(1) *The duration of the concession*—the duration of a gas commercialization project could exceed the overall duration of a concession (6.3) and also a number of interim timing points within a concession. A concession may recognize the disparity between the respective durations of a concession and the requirements of a gas project:

> The Parties recognise that projects for the Development and Production of Natural Gas are generally long-term in nature for both the project developers and the customers who purchase the Natural Gas. Substantial investments and dedication of facilities require long-term commitments on both sides. This Agreement, being for a specific term of years, may not cover the length of time for which customers in given cases will require commitments on the part of the Parties to this Agreement to deliver their respective shares of the output.[18]

This could lead to the need to extend a number of time periods under the concession. More time could be required within the exploration period (6.4) to allow an investor to explore for gas, and then to appraise a gas discovery which has been made:

> For purposes of assessing the commerciality of the Non-Associated Natural Gas Discovery, the Contractor shall have the right, if it so requests at least two (2) months prior to the expiry of the second renewal of the exploration period ... to be granted the extension of the exploration period with respect to the Appraisal Area related to said Discovery, for a term of two (2) years starting from the expiry of the second renewal of the exploration period.[19]

A concession might also provide for an extended period time for an investor to assess the availability and the economic viability of prospective domestic and export market projects for the produced gas:

> Where the Discovery is a Natural Gas Discovery, the Contactor shall ... prepare a report identifying potential market for Natural Gas, expected volumes for such market, infrastructure potentially required to access such market, expectations of price for the

[18] Ghana 2000 petroleum agreement (at 14.17).
[19] Cyprus 2007 PSC (at 13.1).

> Natural Gas supplied to such market and identify options (including time frames for marketing the Natural Gas within three Calendar Years after the Discovery evaluation is completed).[20]

Such an extension of time could also apply on a wider basis which takes account of multiple discoveries which have been made by an investor:

> If... the Ministry and the Contractor determine that a Discovery of Non-Associated Gas, although substantial, is not then, either alone or in combination with other Discoveries, commercially viable, but is likely to become so within eight (8) years thereafter with appropriate gas marketing operations, feasibility studies and further evaluation, the Ministry and the Contractor shall enter into an agreement for an initial term of five (5) years, extendible for up to three subsequent periods of one (I) year each (the 'Evaluation Agreement') ... to allow for gas marketing operations, feasibility studies and further evaluation, the Ministry shall refrain from exercising its option ... to require the Contractor to relinquish the area corresponding to such Discovery for the term of the Evaluation Agreement.[21]

This could then lead to a defined retention period in favour of an investor:

> Contractor shall subject to the terms of this Agreement and the Rules be entitled to the Retention Period of each Significant Gas Discovery Area of a Significant Gas Discovery for a maximum period of up to ten (10) Years following the Date of a Significant Gas Discovery. The application for the Retention Period in respect of the Significant Gas Discovery Area shall be submitted for approval of DGPC. in accordance with the Rules. If the Contractor does not declare a Significant Gas Discovery as a Commercial Discovery during the Retention Period, the Contractor shall relinquish the significant Gas Discovery Area and the Licence shall terminate automatically upon the termination of the Retention Period. If Contractor declares a Commercial Discovery during the Retention Period, Contractor will select the Development Area out of the Significant Gas Discovery Area ...
>
> 'Significant Gas Discovery' means 'a Discovery of Natural Gas from an Exploration Well in the Contract Area which has tested significant flow rates of Natural Gas (predominantly methane) from one or more reservoirs, and which is estimated to be capable of continuous Production from the said reservoir(s) over a reasonable period and which in the opinion of the Contractor could be declared a Commercial Discovery in the future, provided inter-alia that:
>
> (a) adequate gas pipeline transportation facilities are installed, or

[20] Somalia 2023 PSA (at 40.6). The India 2010 PSC provides (at 21.5.11) that: 'The Contractor will have a two (2) years period, from the date of approval of the Development Plan by the Management Committee or Government, to tie-up the market(s) for sale of Non-associated Natural Gas.'

[21] Afghanistan 2013 PSC (at 15.2).

(b) markets have been sufficiently developed for sale of Natural Gas on a commercial basis, or
(c) the requirements of both (a) and (b) have been met.'[22]

To give an investor an incentive not to delay the assessment and appraisal activities which are associated with a gas discovery, a concession could require an investor to pay a retention fee to a grantor:

> During the market development phase, Contractor shall pay to the Minister at the end of each year of the market development phase or upon earlier termination an annual holding fee of Two Million United States Dollars (US$2,000,000.00), reduced by duly verified amounts that Contractor has expended during such year under specific programmes approved by the Minister on activities or projects directly attributable to the market development area.[23]

The production period under a concession (6.5) could also be extended to accommodate a gas commercialization project:

> In the event of a Commercial Discovery, the term of the Contract shall be twenty-five (25) years from the Effective Date with respect to the Production Area corresponding to such Commercial Discovery; provided, however, if the Commercial Discovery relates to a Natural Gas Field, the term of the Contract shall be twenty-five (25) years from the Effective Date plus the period of any market development phase granted and utilized in accordance with Article 16.1 and any extension granted in accordance with Article 16.6, with respect to the Production Area corresponding to such Natural Gas Field.[24]

(2) *The costs of a gas commercialization project*—specific infrastructure and additional facilities for gas processing and transportation could be provided for in a concession to address gas project requirements, particularly where a gas discovery has been made in a remote area. A concession could reflect the ability of an investor to develop (and, in the case of a production-sharing contract (PSC), to recover the costs (9.3)) of midstream infrastructure necessary to take discovered gas to market, and possibly also of downstream infrastructure to realize the commercial value of the gas, notwithstanding that such infrastructure could be physically located outside of the concession area, and also that the development of such infrastructure could be outside the initial scope of the concession (6.2):

[22] Pakistan 2000 PSA (at 5.9).
[23] Trinidad and Tobago 2023 PSC (at 16.3).
[24] ibid 4.5.

> At any time following the declaration of Commercial Discovery, Contractor shall have the right to construct and to operate one or more Pipeline(s) or alternative transportation facilities within or from the Contract Area to one or more points in Bangladesh for the purpose of transporting Petroleum, from any Production Area to Measurement Point(s) in Bangladesh, at Contractor's option or jointly with other parties. For the purpose of this Contract, a Pipeline shall include related facilities.[25]

(3) *Gas project governance*—a concession may facilitate the establishment of a committee of representatives (representing a grantor and an investor, but also with participation from invited midstream and downstream sector participants and representatives of other state entities) to assess the steps which could be necessary to implement a successful plan for commercializing a gas discovery:

> Where Non-Associated Gas is discovered in the Contract Area and the Contractor has, pursuant to Section 7.I(b), informed the Ministry that the Discovery is of commercial interest, a Natural Gas development committee composed of an equal number of representatives of the Ministry and the Contractor shall be established upon adoption of the Appraisal Program relating to such Discovery pursuant to Section 7.1 (1). The purpose of the development committee is to jointly evaluate the use of such Natural Gas in:
>
> (i) the domestic market and the chain of downstream activities required to bring the Natural Gas to the end consumers in such market; and
> (ii) current or potential export markets.[26]

(4) *Modified fiscal terms*—a concession may apply a different template to assess the commerciality of a gas project. A grantor could offer an investor improved fiscal terms (9.1) in a concession to encourage the exploration for and the development of gas, reflective of the relatively greater uncertainty of undertaking a gas project. Those terms could be set out in the concession from the outset, or they could be agreed later between a grantor and an investor.

In a PSC, gas-specific terms for cost recovery and improved profit shares (9.3) could be agreed to apply:

> The Minister and the Contractor may engage in good faith negotiations to modify the provisions of Section VII on cost recovery and production sharing in respect of

[25] Bangladesh 2023 PSC (at 16.1).

[26] Afghanistan 2013 PSC (at 15.3). The Ethiopia 2011 PSC provides (at 13.3) that: 'For the purpose of expediting the execution of a domestic Gas development project, a Gas development advisory committee shall be established with representatives of the Government and the Contractor to coordinate all upstream and downstream components of the project and facilitate its evaluation and implementation.'

> Natural Gas, if the Minister determines that special circumstances relating to Natural Gas development and production exist which warrant such modification.[27]

A more investor-friendly taxation regime (9.5) may also apply in respect of the profits associated with gas production, and principles of ring-fencing (9.3) might be relaxed for gas production projects in favour of an investor.

Whether improved fiscal terms should apply to associated gas, where an investor might have the benefit of the associated oil production and its revenues, should be considered.

(5) *Gas sales and pricing methodologies*—a concession could outline the terms of a standard contract for the sale of gas to buyers by the designated seller, so that the process of negotiating gas sales arrangements could be accelerated and made more efficient. A concession may also set out a gas pricing methodology for domestic sales (which could come with the expectation that an investor would not sell gas domestically to a person for less than the price which is paid by a state entity, assuming that the state entity is not created as the sole gas purchaser):

> The price for Natural Gas shall be calculated at the wellhead in accordance with the following formula:
>
> $$P_n = Brent_n$$ [28]

That domestic gas price methodology could also set the benchmark for export gas pricing:

> The price for Natural Gas sold to a third party(ies) shall be equal to the price obtained as per Article 15.10 or more.[29]

Export gas prices will be a function of what can be agreed between an investor and its export buyer. The point of the above provision is to ensure that export gas prices are not less than a domestic gas price, so that the accusation cannot be made that payments for gas made by domestic gas buyers are subsidizing lower gas prices for export buyers.

(6) *The declaration of commerciality*—the making of a declaration of commerciality (8.3) in respect of a gas discovery could require the consideration of different issues compared to determining the commerciality of an oil discovery.

The commerciality of a gas discovery might not be capable of being established until the prospects for the discovery's successful marketing (which could involve developing

[27] Ethiopia 2011 PSC (at 13.3).
[28] Bangladesh 2023 PSC (at 15.10).
[29] ibid 15.11.

a comprehensive marketing programme for domestic gas use and/or for gas exports) have been assessed. Often, a firm contract for the sale and transportation of a discovered gas resource will be needed to allow the discovery to be declared as commercial. Essentially, with oil production, the post-discovery sequence is a declaration of commerciality followed by a contract for sale; with gas production the reverse could be true, and this could entail a more time-consuming and less certain route towards monetizing a gas discovery within the terms of a concession.

A grantor could require a declaration of commerciality and the production of gas so that a domestic gas market can be developed but the economic terms for doing so could be insufficiently attractive to an investor (compared to the economics which could apply to an oil project, or to the development of gas for export). Where this becomes an issue between a grantor and an investor, this could be the point at which a national oil company takes over the responsibility for domestic gas production (14.1).

(7) *Gas production limits*—a concession may apply a gas-specific form of a maximized economic recovery provision (8.4) which could influence an investor's thinking about the desirability of commercializing a gas discovery:

> Following good reservoir management practices, Contractor shall have the right to produce annually a total volume of Gas up to seven and a half per cent (7.5%) or a greater percentage as may be agreed by Petrobangla and the Contractor of the Proven plus Probable Recoverable Gas reserves for each Gas Field . . .[30]

A concession could also limit the unwarranted flaring of gas, which could force an investor to do something constructive with any produced gas:

> Flaring of Natural Gas in the course of activities provided for under this Contract, is prohibited except (i) short-term flaring up to twelve (12) Months necessary for testing or other operational reasons in accordance with prudent international petroleum industry practice (which shall include the flaring of Associated Natural Gas to the extent the CONTRACTOR considers that re-injecting Associated Natural Gas is not justified technically and economically and provided the GOVERNMENT decides not to take such Associated Natural Gas), or (ii) with the prior authorisation of the GOVERNMENT, such authorisation not to be unreasonably withheld or delayed.[31]

(8) *Other concession terms*—an investor's relinquishment obligations under a concession (7.6) could be modified to give an investor more latitude in exploration and appraisal (including the development of markets) for gas. A domestic market obligation (10.6) could be disapplied in respect of gas production so that an investor can fully develop a project's export gas potential (and such an

[30] ibid 15.4.
[31] Kurdistan Iraq 2007 PSC (at 14.12).

obligation could be meaningless where the state lacks a developed domestic market for gas which the investor could be obliged to deliver). A stabilization provision in a concession (11.6) could be extended to protect an investor in respect of the consequences of the regulation or development of the domestic gas market in the state.

13.5 The Concession Form for Gas Developments

It is apparent from the preceding section that the manner in which a project for the production of gas (whether that gas is to be sold domestically and/or for export, and whether as pipeline gas and/or as LNG) is undertaken by an investor will need to be reconciled with the terms of the concession to which the investor is party.

In an integrated project model, an investor (assuming that the investor has the necessary competencies to undertake the full range of the required activities) will undertake a gas project's development and production activities and commercial activities under the aegis of the concession. These activities could include developing, owning, and operating the necessary assets or equipment for gas production and processing (and possibly also any infrastructure for onward gas transportation). The investor could also be the seller of gas to buyers (unless the state has reserved a role for itself in this respect). Developing, owning, and operating the assets or equipment which are needed for gas commercialization (which could take place downstream of a delivery point which is identified in the concession (6.2)) and selling gas to buyers are midstream activities, which would be created as extensions to the conventional upstream activities which the concession envisages in order for there to be a single industrial process which runs from gas exploration to gas value realization.

The integrated project model creates ownership and operational alignment between the investor parties in respect of their upstream and midstream activities. Financing of the development costs of all of the investor's activities could be arranged on a single project basis, and taxation of the investor's profits (9.5) could apply in respect of all of the investor's activities, without discrimination between upstream and midstream activities (unless a bespoke tax regime is created to apply in respect of a gas development project).

Effective regulation of an integrated project would require an extension to the scope of the concession (6.2) so that all of the investor's activities are properly authorized. The concession could be modified in a number of respects to apply solely in respect of a gas project, which could lead to the creation of parallel fiscal and non-fiscal terms within the concession, unless the investor and the grantor agree that the gas project terms will be set out in an addendum to the concession for more convenient reference.

In contrast to the integrated project model, a gas project could be undertaken on a disaggregated basis which supposes the existence of a separate form of permit or concession for the gas project's development. The investor parties in the upstream concession would also be party to the midstream concession, in order to create ownership and operational alignment between them across both sets of activities. For the sake of contractual completeness, a formal arrangement could be put in place between the investor (in its upstream capacity, as the gas producer) and the investor (in its midstream capacity, as the gas project developer) for the supply of gas from the former entity to the latter.

The advantages of the disaggregated project model are that it could facilitate different levels of ownership interest between the investor parties in the upstream and the midstream components (which could be applied either at the outset or in the future, through the divestment of interests by an investor party); it could allow the respective investors to be taxed separately in respect of upstream and midstream profits (which in turn could promote greater transparency in respect of the investors' activities); and it could allow financing of the development costs of the upstream and midstream projects to be arranged separately. The disaggregated project model could also enable the investors in the gas development project to acquire gas supplies from third parties to support expansion of their project, if the associated upstream project is unwilling or unable to commit to supply more gas.

The disadvantages of the disaggregated project model are that it will create additional contractual complexity in respect of the gas supply arrangements between the upstream investors group and the midstream investors group, and the pricing terms upon which the gas is supplied could give a state some concerns about transfer pricing between the two investor groups (particularly where different taxation regimes apply between the upstream and midstream activities, which could give the investors an incentive to realize profits in the activity with the more beneficial taxation regime).

The design of a concession which countenances the commercialization of gas in particular does not have to be based on a choice between the integrated project model and the disaggregated project model. A single concession could be created which, in a discrete section, provides all of the legal, commercial, and operational requirements for a gas project's development and long-term management but in a way which embraces the advantages of the disaggregated project model, without the concomitant disadvantages of that model. Such a concession may also embrace the gas project development provisions as a key part of the concession, rather than relegating them to a mere addendum. Future investor parties could accede to the concession with rights and obligations which are relevant only to the part of the overall upstream/midstream project in which they intend to become invested.

The design of such a concession could also be engineered to reflect a better fit with the current and the prospective regulatory shape of the domestic gas market within the state. This could reflect the necessary balance between the state's domestic gas market and gas export aspirations (including making provision for any necessary alteration of those aspirations by the state over time), and allowing also for the evolution of domestic market regulation to include any of the introduction or the discontinuance of gas aggregation or merchant gas market model activities (14.3) as the needs of the domestic market evolve, in each case in a way which does not expose the state to a claim by an investor under the concession's stabilization provisions.

14
Promoting the National Oil Company

14.1 Introduction

A state's national oil company (NOC) could (by reference to a combination of the state's laws, the terms of the concessions awarded in the state, and the manner in which the NOC is resourced, empowered, and promoted) take up positions which enable it to participate on equal terms with external investors in the exploitation of the state's patrimony, and even to assume a position of primacy in that exploitation.

An NOC could also have a critical role to play in assisting the state to realize its ambitions in implementing the energy transition (although much of what an NOC can do will depend on the nature of the NOC).

The key issues to consider are whether an NOC could help the state through widening the NOC's customary activity base to include energy transition-focused activities (recognizing that such a proposition might not suit every NOC, either in terms of ambition or ability) and the position of the NOC as an actor which could be subject to the state's rules in implementing the energy transition.

14.2 Defining the NOC

An NOC is known as such because it is a corporation (or other legal emanation) which is exclusively (or predominantly) owned by the state in the place of the NOC's incorporation and because it has some measure of responsibility for managing the state's interests in respect of petroleum exploitation or procurement.[1]

An NOC's focus will reflect the public policy of the state and its own commercial self-interest, but not all NOCs are the same. They fall into three main groupings:

(1) *The producing NOC*—this is the NOC of a petroleum-producing state, which is involved in the exploitation of the state's indigenous petroleum reserves (for domestic use and possibly also for export). Examples of such NOCs include Petrosen (Senegal), UNOC (Uganda), and PEMEX (Mexico). The producing

[1] It is notable that despite the possible interest of an NOC in gas developments, the customary term for such a corporation has been 'NOC', which is reflective of the petroleum sector's historical focus on oil rather than gas. A more enlightened approach comes from Iran, where the state's interests in petroleum are represented between the National Iranian Oil Company (NIOC), the National Iranian Gas Company (NIGC), and the National Iranian Gas Export Company (NIGEC).

NOC could be vertically integrated, to meet the state's upstream, midstream, and downstream energy needs. A producing NOC could have significant political influence in its home state, and significant economic importance where the state relies on the revenues which are generated from petroleum production as a source of revenue.

(2) *The importing NOC*—this is an NOC which is involved in procuring secure and cost-effective petroleum imports into the state. Examples of such NOCs (which are essentially state-owned petroleum purchasing agencies) include Kogas (Korea), CPC (Taiwan), and Pakistan LNG.

(3) *The international NOC*—this is an entity which started off life as a producing NOC but which has grown to invest in petroleum projects in other states. This development could have occurred because of a natural commercial ambition to expand overseas, or because of an NOC's desire to maintain its relevance despite declining domestic petroleum production by accessing replacement reserves abroad. Examples of such international NOCs include Petronas (Malaysia), Equinor (Norway), and Petrobras (Brazil).

Producing NOCs and international NOCs are the major resource holders, and this allocation is unlikely to change. According to some estimates, such NOCs currently have responsibility for half of all petroleum production worldwide[2] and they hold two thirds of undeveloped petroleum reserves worldwide[3]). These percentages could increase in a state where external investors elect to reduce their presence in petroleum exploration and/or production activities and producing NOCs choose (or are required) to take up the investment slack. Corresponding to the significance of their position, producing NOCs and international NOCs are also responsible for significant carbon creation in their own right, and there is some focus on how they could be incentivized to reduce their emissions as part of the energy transition.

The capacity in which an NOC is acting should be noted. An NOC could have a role to play in formulating its state's energy policy (including concession design), and in some states an NOC could be a grantor of a concession in its own right[4] or in conjunction with the state.[5] An NOC could also be (or could become) an investor party, as the holder (in whole or in part) of a concession, and could act in both capacities of grantor and investor party at the same time.

[2] *Facing The Future: What National Oil Companies Say About The Energy Transition*, National Resource Governance Institute, November 2023 – see www.resourcegovernance.org/publications/facing-future-what-national-oil-companies-say-about-energy-transition accessed 3 April 2025.

[3] *Assessing National Oil Companies Transition Plans: an essential tool for banks, investors and regulators* (World Benchmarking Alliance, November 2023) <- see www.worldbenchmarkingalliance.org/> accessed 3 April 2025.

[4] Examples of this construction include Sonangol (with the Angola production sharing contract (PSC)), Staatsolie (with the Suriname PSC), and NOCAL (with the Liberia PSC).

[5] Examples of this construction include GNPC (in Ghana), Petrobangla (in Bangladesh), and Petrobras (in Brazil).

14.3 Maximizing the Role of the Producing NOC

A number of opportunities could exist to increase the level of a producing NOC's interest as an investor party in a concession, through exclusive operations rights (10.7), pre-emption rights (5.6) and the acquisition of the interests of a surrendering investor (6.6), state participation rights (10.8), and the right of a grantor to take over a relinquished marginal discovery (7.6). When these opportunities are multiplied across the entirety of the concessions which have been granted in a state, then the NOC could become a significant (or even the majority) petroleum producer within the state.

A concession will make some provision for the training (and/or the funding of training) of local personnel, often as part of a wider capacity-building strategy which also includes a requirement for the increased localization of personnel responsible for carrying out petroleum operations (10.2).[6] A concession's training budget provision is effectively a vertical arrangement, whereby an investor pays money to a grantor. A grantor could then advance that money to build capacity within the NOC (unless the NOC is also the grantor and thus already the intended ultimate beneficiary of the training budget).

The NOC's staff could be the beneficiaries of these incentives, and if the training and localization provisions are properly applied, an NOC could get closer to the point where it is capable of running not only ongoing petroleum production and processing operations with reduced levels of external assistance but also of increasing the involvement of the NOC in non-petroleum related activities.

A fully functioning NOC could undertake a variety of tasks, possibly generating a number of benefits for a state:

(1) *The focal point for concession investment*—the principal benefits of having the NOC as an investor party would be enhanced security of supply (if the NOC's share of produced petroleum was kept within the state) and the increased state take (9.2) which could result from being on the investor's side of a concession. Any interest in a concession which was already held by another state entity could also be transferred to the NOC in order to consolidate the state's upstream interests within the NOC.

(2) *Produced petroleum purchases and sales*—the NOC will have its participating interest share of the produced production under a concession in which it is an investor party, and a grantor could also have the benefit of a domestic market obligation under a concession (10.6). Beyond those physical entitlements there may also be an obligation (which could be provided for in a petroleum law

[6] Within a state, the responsibility for managing the local content and capacity-building initiatives across the state's concessions (and for doing so in a transparent manner) could be assumed by a nominated state entity. An example of this, from Suriname, is the role played by the Staatsolie Hydrocarbon Institute <- see www.staatsolie.com/en/staatsolie-hydrocarbon-institute/#ExploreourInvestmentOpportunities> accessed 3 April 2025, which is answerable to the national oil company, Staatsolie.

and/or set out in a concession) for the other investor parties to sell their produced petroleum entitlements to the NOC on a first refusal basis (at prices reflecting the full market value of the petroleum, without a discount in favour of the NOC) if doing so could benefit the national interest (eg to establish and support domestic refinery operations). Paradoxically, the NOC could also require a right to offer its produced petroleum entitlements to the other investor parties for purchase (which could be advantageous to those investor parties with their own refining or processing operations to service).

(3) *Petroleum market evolution*—the state could identify certain roles for the NOC to play in the regulation and development of the state's petroleum sector. In order to promote the development of a domestic gas sector (13.2) the NOC could, for example, be given monopsony rights to purchase all domestic gas production within the state and also monopoly rights to sell that gas to industrial and domestic gas consumers within the state, effectively acting as a state-mandated gas aggregator and establishing the NOC as the price-setter for domestic gas supplies.[7]

(4) *Commercializing marginal developments*—the existence of operatorship capability within the NOC could facilitate the development of otherwise marginal discoveries (8.3) which other investor parties could regard as insufficiently attractive to undertake but which the NOC (with a different perspective on required project returns) could be willing to progress. A consolidation of marginal discoveries (8.3) within the NOC could also create certain economies of scale in favour of the NOC.

(5) *Data development for the state*—exploration activities could be undertaken by the NOC without a principal focus on making (or developing) a discovery, in the interests of building up a repository of exploration and appraisal data for the benefit of the state. Such a data repository could, in due course, enable a grantor to make better-informed decisions about the terms on which it would be prepared to award concessions to investors.

(6) *Managing and promoting national interests*—the NOC, mindful that it is a state-owned agency, could be better placed to undertake petroleum exploration and/or production activities for its own account in sensitive maritime areas where coordination with other national interests (such as fishing, defence, shipping, or the exploitation of other mineral interests) could be beneficial to the state. The NOC, as a state-owned agency, could also have a useful role to play as an intermediary in liaison with other state entities who might have a bearing on the performance of the petroleum operations under a concession, which could benefit the other investor parties.

[7] The notion of gas aggregation (and in particular the contrast of aggregation with a merchant gas market model) is considered in Peter Roberts, 'Gas Aggregation as a Regulatory Model to Promote Improved Security of Domestic Gas Supply' [2018] IRL 293.

(7) *Improved coordination with investors*—the NOC, holding a position as an investor party in the joint venture arrangements which underlie a concession (5.3), could have some influence on the methods and the timing of petroleum operations which the other investor parties wish to undertake so that those operations could be better coordinated with the wider needs of the national interest. The NOC could also seek to apply its influence in circumstances where it might not be possible or appropriate for the state to exercise such influence directly itself in respect of the investor parties.

(8) *Wider national activities*—although the NOC would principally be expected to be involved in petroleum exploration and production within the state, the NOC could also be positioned to expand its interests to encompass other activities (such as petroleum trading and portfolio optimization, refining, distribution, storage and terminaling, and pipeline ownership and operation). A producing NOC could also be interested in developing domestic renewable energy projects in order to free up domestic petroleum production to secure higher export prices.

(9) *International activities*—in due course the NOC could seek to expand its activities overseas (and thus become an international NOC) in relation to petroleum exploration and production (and also in respect of the conduct of the wider activities identified in the preceding point).

(10) *Advisory responsibilities*—operational and commercial information, possibly to a level beyond that which could otherwise be obtained on behalf of the state by a grantor through awarding and managing concessions, could be gained by the NOC through participating as an investor party in the joint venture arrangements which underlie the concessions (and also through the NOC exercising the right which a grantor might have reserved under a concession to attend other joint venture arrangements meetings as an observer). The information which the NOC so accumulates could be shared with the state (subject to a reserved right to do so in a concession's confidentiality provisions (11.8)), with the NOC acting in an advisory capacity, and that information could also be used to monitor the evolution of the state's energy sector policies.

Almost all major petroleum-producing states which vest title to in-ground petroleum reserves in the state (1.2) have some form of NOC in existence (the notable exceptions are Australia and the United Kingdom, although the United Kingdom did experiment with the ill-fated British National Oil Company (BNOC) between 1975 and 1986). Consequently, it would generally not be necessary to create and introduce an NOC to a petroleum-producing state for the first time in order to experience the benefits which such an entity could offer. But in many states much could be done to enhance the capabilities of an NOC which already exists.

14.4 The NOC's Role in the Energy Transition

Private sector investment strategies in response to the energy transition will give signals to a state, but they will not indicate what a state (or its NOC) should do in response. A producing NOC could remain concerned primarily with commercializing domestic petroleum reserves for ensuring domestic security of energy supply, maintaining the employment of the state's citizenry, and generating revenue for the state, and could be less exposed to (or less concerned by) the popular opprobrium which attaches to petroleum exploration and/or production.

An NOC could be cast as an agent of the state with responsibility for applying (and possibly also for assisting with the formulation of) the state's energy policy, and for reflecting that policy through the terms of the concessions which are awarded by a grantor on behalf of a state (remembering also that, in some jurisdictions, a producing NOC could also be the grantor).

If a state adopts a twin track strategy for realizing the energy transition (through greater reliance on developing non-petroleum-related activities whilst simultaneously managing continued petroleum production, in the latter case with the possibility of an increased focus on gas production (13.1) but also with an overall ambition to reduce the emissions associated with petroleum production through decarbonization activities), it is not axiomatic that an NOC is best placed for any of the design, implementation, or management of the entirety of a wider strategy whilst at the same time being required by the state to maintain a focus on petroleum production.

A producing NOC could be the obvious choice to represent the state in the continued development of the state's petroleum reserves (which could be a conscious part of a realization of the state's energy transition ambitions), but whether a producing NOC would also have the necessary aptitude or experience to be responsible additionally for the effective realization of non-petroleum-related activities would need to be considered on a case-by-case basis.[8]

It is not guaranteed that an NOC will be drawn towards expanding its activities to include such activities in the same way that international oil companies have done over recent years, as part of their transition to becoming international energy companies (a step which has as much to do with assuaging the consciences of their shareholders and other stakeholders as it does with adding diversified revenue streams to their bottom lines[9]).

An NOC could be required by a state to embrace such an expansion (since the state may expect the NOC to act according to its energy sector policy) but this might not generate a satisfactory outcome. Many of the skills which may have been learned by a

[8] The Petroleum Corporation of Jamaica was formed in 1977 with exclusive rights to develop Jamaica's petroleum reserves (and the refining, retailing, and distribution of petroleum products). In 1995, its mandate was expanded to include the development of indigenous renewable energy resources <www.mset.gov.jm/2019/07/02/petroleum-corporation-of-jamaica/> accessed 3 April 2025.

[9] See note 9, Chapter 3.

producing NOC in the petroleum sector may not be readily transferrable to the promotion of non-petroleum-related activities, and many of the characteristics of developing petroleum projects (such as long project lead times on single large-scale projects, significant capital intensity expectations, relative cost insensitivity, and the requirement for long-term offtake contracts) might not readily translate into the successful development of non-petroleum-related activities. Much depends on the direction of travel which the state chooses to set for an NOC, but the ambition of the NOC itself and its readiness to be proactive rather than reactive could also play a key part in shaping its future direction. Rather than entrusting responsibility for implementation of the energy transition to what could be an ill-equipped (or unwilling) NOC, responsibility for the design, implementation, and management of renewable energy projects as part of a state's energy transition ambitions could instead reside with a responsible ministry within the state, or with another entity which has been created or designated by the state for that purpose.

A number of producing NOCs have demonstrated their willingness to be involved in developing a wider energy sector,[10] and some NOCs have agreed to collaborate to strengthen their efforts.[11] An international NOC, which has developed a perspective which goes beyond its home state, could also be more comfortable with being part of the implementation of a wider energy transition plan, looking beyond petroleum production alone as the reason for its continued existence.

An importing NOC could have an advantage in how it could assist the state in implementing a wider energy transition strategy because the role of the importing NOC could be recast as part of a wider state-driven technological initiative to diversify from reliance on petroleum imports as a primary source of energy. Import infrastructure which is used for the receipt, processing, storage, and send-out of imported petroleum could become redundant as part of the energy transition but the importing NOC would not need to break old habits to the same extent as would a producing NOC. The state in which the importing NOC resides will also not have the ongoing burden of a petroleum patrimony (and any number of awarded concessions) which it would need to manage as part of a transitional exercise.

A producing NOC could have a major role to play in managing and in growing its involvement in a state's petroleum sector, but it could caught by a particular paradox in the state's implementation of energy transition initiatives through simultaneous

[10] ADNOC (the state oil company of Abu Dhabi) has declared an intention to be carbon net zero in its operations by 2045 and has published plans to reduce the carbon intensity per unit of produced petroleum through decarbonizing its operations, increasing investment in renewable energy and hydrogen and low carbon ammonia production, and applying nature-based offset solutions <www.adnoc.ae/en/sustainability-net-zero> accessed 3 April 2025. Other producing NOCs are engaged in realizing their states' energy transition plans: Malaysia's Petronas <www.petronas.com/sustainability/getting-to-net-zero>; Colombia's EcoPetrol <www.ecopetrol.com.co/wps/portal/Home/en/?1dmy&page=detailNews&urile=wcm:path:/ecopetrol_wcm_library/as_en/news/noticias-2021/emissions-reduction>; Nigeria's NNPCL (Energy Transition Plan <www.energytransition.gov.ng/>; and Saudi Aramco <www.aramco.com/en/sustainability/climate-change> all accessed 3 April 2025.

[11] The Oil and Gas Decarbonization Charter <www.ogdc.org/> (accessed 3 April 2025) was launched at COP28 in 2023, with a large number of NOCs as parties.

engagement in growing, and also being encouraged to retrench from, continuing involvement in the petroleum sector.

Where investors have withdrawn from continued involvement in petroleum exploration and/or production in a state (whether through the surrender of existing concessions, or through a lack of appetite to participate in new licensing rounds) as part of the realization of their own energy transition objectives, there could be an expectation on the state's part that a producing NOC will step in to take up the slack as an investor to maintain current and anticipated levels of petroleum production for the benefit of the state (assuming that the NOC has the necessary levels of staffing, competence, and financial resources to do so).

Such a step would increase the size of the NOC's estate and it could incline the NOC towards maintaining a long-term outlook for sustained petroleum production, despite the expectations of the energy transition. Engaging in carbon sequestration, reducing gas flaring, managing methane emissions, and other technological interventions that reduce carbon emissions or increase energy efficiency might be the limit of the NOC's ambitions, but these steps could be carried out against a backdrop of sustained and increasing responsibility for petroleum exploration and/or production, which could be seen by the NOC as the primary purpose of its continued existence.

Going forward, the NOC could come to depend on no diminution in petroleum demand as part of its business expectations, and consequently, would effectively be betting against the energy transition if this would entail growth in non-petroleum-related activities at the expense of continued petroleum production.[12]

NOCs are also not immune from the possibility of external influences which could be applied to implement energy transition measures. Where an NOC is the subject of a minority listing on a public stock exchange then shareholders and asset managers could make known their expectations. Accessing international bond and debt markets to raise finance could expose the NOC to similar expectations from bondholders and lenders. The inclination of an NOC to avoid becoming involved in such finance-generating activities, so as not to be encumbered by the expectations of others in respect of energy transition matters, could impair its options for the financing of its ongoing development needs in the most cost-effective manner.

Credit risks could also increase for an NOC which fails to develop a credible energy transition plan where the NOC is the subject of an independent credit rating, if the substance of credit rating includes the management of energy transition risks by the rated entity (which could be a possibility as the assessment of energy transition plans increasingly becomes a feature within credit rating methodologies).[13]

[12] Some commentators have suggested that, in this scenario, NOCs are effectively gambling with their countries' wealth by continuing to finance what could become an obsolescent business with public money—David Manley, Andrea Furnaro, and Patrick RP Heller, *Riskier Bets, Smaller Pockets: How National Oil Companies Are Spending Public Money Amid The Energy Transition* (Natural Resource Governance Institute, November 2023) <www.resourcegovernance.org/publications/riskier-bets-smaller-pockets-national-oil-companies-public-money-energy-transition> accessed 3 April 2025.

[13] Credit ratings agencies have begun to offer assessments of the energy transition plans of rated entities <www.ratings.moodys.io/products/nza> accessed 3 April 2025.

A producing NOC, as an investor party, could also be exposed to whatever energy transition initiatives the state decides to implement in respect of its investors. As a response to that exposure, the instinct of an NOC could be not to participate in a concession as an investor party, so that the NOC has no attributable petroleum production, which it could be required to subject to the state's energy transition initiatives. Such an approach overlooks: (1) that an NOC, in its capacity as an investor party, earns a share of the petroleum production revenues (which will accrue for the benefit of the state); (2) that an NOC could be obliged to enlarge its position as an investor party where external investor parties have chosen to surrender concession interests as part of their energy transition initiatives (see above); and (3) that an NOC's election not to participate in a concession as an investor party does not relieve the state from still having to address the energy transition's imperatives.

A producing NOC which is prepared to develop and implement a credible plan for transitioning away from petroleum exploration and/or production could become the beneficiary of certain transition finance initiatives[14] which are intended to promote decarbonization. These initiatives could oblige an NOC to stop increasing its acreage portfolio and engaging in new project developments, and could also oblige an NOC to reduce its levels of petroleum exploration and/or production, where the hope of the NOC is that the benefits provided by the transition finance initiatives will be sufficient to offset the associated loss of revenue.

[14] Financing could come from development finance institutions, blended with private sector investments, and could take the form of capital investments, concession payments, and grants <www.iea.org/commentaries/the-role-of-development-finance-institutions-in-energy-transitions> accessed 3 April 2025. At the COP29 summit in Baku in 2024, grant funding promised for methane abatement in connection with the Global Methane Pledge (see note 4, Chapter 3) topped US$2 billion.

Index

For the benefit of digital users, indexed terms that span two pages (e.g., 52–53) may, on occasion, appear on only one of those pages.

Introductory Note

References such as '178–9' indicate (not necessarily continuous) discussion of a topic across a range of pages. Wherever possible in the case of topics with many references, these have either been divided into subtopics or only the most significant discussions of the topic are listed. Because the entire work is about 'petroleum concessions' and the 'energy transition', the use of these terms (and certain others which occur constantly throughout the book) as an entry point has been restricted. Information will be found under the corresponding detailed topics.